Continuous Delivery with Docker and Jenkins

Delivering software at scale

Rafał Leszko

BIRMINGHAM - MUMBAI

Continuous Delivery with Docker and Jenkins

First published: August 2017

Production reference: 1230817

Published by Packt Publishing Ltd.
Livery Place
35 Livery Street
Birmingham
B3 2PB, UK.
ISBN 978-1-78712-523-0

www.packtpub.com

Credits

Author
Rafał Leszko

Reviewers
Michael Pailloncy
Mitesh Soni
Zhiwei Chen

Commissioning Editor
Pratik Shah

Acquisition Editor
Prachi Bisht

Content Development Editor
Deepti Thore

Technical Editor
Sneha Hanchate

Copy Editor
Ulka Manjrekar
Laxmi Subramanian

Project Coordinator
Shweta H Birwatkar

Proofreader
Safis Editing

Indexer
Pratik Shirodkar

Graphics
Tania Dutta

Production Coordinator
Arvindkumar Gupta

About the Author

Rafał Leszko is a passionate software developer, trainer, and conference speaker living in Krakow, Poland. He has spent his career writing code, designing architecture, and tech leading in a number of companies and organizations such as Google, CERN, and AGH University. Always open to new challenges, he has given talks and conducted workshops at more than a few international conferences such as Devoxx and Voxxed Days.

I would like to thank my wife, Maria, for her support. She was the very first reviewer of this book, always cheering me up, and taking care of our baby to give me time and space for writing. I also give deep thanks and gratitude to the Zooplus company, where I could first experiment with the Continuous Delivery approach and especially, to its former employee Robert Stern for showing me the world of Docker. I would also like to make a special mention of Patroklos Papapetrou for his trust and help in organizing Continuous Delivery workshops in Greece. Last but not the least, thanks to my mom, dad, and brother for being so supportive.

About the Reviewer

Michael Pailloncy is a developer tending toward the 'Ops' side, constantly trying to keep things simple and as much automated as possible. Michael is passionate about the DevOps culture and has a strong experience in Continuous Integration, Continuous Delivery, automation, big software factory management and loves to share the experiences with others.

Mitesh Soni is an avid learner with 10 years of experience in the IT industry. He is an SCJP, SCWCD, VCP, IBM Urbancode, and IBM Bluemix certified professional. He loves DevOps and cloud computing and also has an interest in programming in Java. He finds design patterns fascinating and believes that "a picture is worth a thousand words."

He occasionally contributes to etutorialsworld.com. He loves to play with kids, fiddle with his camera, and take photographs at Indroda Park. He is addicted to taking pictures without knowing many technical details. He lives in the capital of Mahatma Gandhi's home state.

 Mitesh has authored following books with Packt:

DevOps Bootcamp
Implementing DevOps with Microsoft Azure
DevOps for Web Development
Jenkins Essentials
Learning Chef

www.PacktPub.com

For support files and downloads related to your book, please visit www.PacktPub.com.

Did you know that Packt offers eBook versions of every book published, with PDF and ePub files available? You can upgrade to the eBook version at www.PacktPub.com and as a print book customer, you are entitled to a discount on the eBook copy. Get in touch with us at service@packtpub.com for more details.

At www.PacktPub.com, you can also read a collection of free technical articles, sign up for a range of free newsletters and receive exclusive discounts and offers on Packt books and eBooks.

https:/ / www. packtpub. com/ mapt

Get the most in-demand software skills with Mapt. Mapt gives you full access to all Packt books and video courses, as well as industry-leading tools to help you plan your personal development and advance your career.

Why subscribe?

- Fully searchable across every book published by Packt
- Copy and paste, print, and bookmark content
- On demand and accessible via a web browser

Customer Feedback

Thanks for purchasing this Packt book. At Packt, quality is at the heart of our editorial process. To help us improve, please leave us an honest review on this book's Amazon page at `https://www.amazon.com/dp/1787125238`.

If you'd like to join our team of regular reviewers, you can e-mail us at `customerreviews@packtpub.com`. We award our regular reviewers with free eBooks and videos in exchange for their valuable feedback. Help us be relentless in improving our products!

To my wonderful wife Maria, for all of her love, wisdom, and smile.

Table of Contents

Preface

I've observed software delivery processes for years. I wrote this book because I know how many people still struggle with releases and get frustrated after spending days and nights on getting their products into production. This all happens even though a lot of automation tools and processes have been developed throughout the years. After I saw for the first time how simple and effective the Continuous Delivery process was, I would never come back to the tedious traditional manual delivery cycle. This book is a result of my experience and a number of Continuous Delivery workshops I conducted. I share the modern approach using Jenkins, Docker, and Ansible; however, this book is more than just the tools. It presents the idea and the reasoning behind Continuous Delivery, and what's most important, my main message to everyone I meet: Continuous Delivery process is simple, use it!

What this book covers

Chapter 1, *Introducing Continuous Delivery*, presents how companies traditionally deliver their software and explains the idea to improve it using the Continuous Delivery approach. This chapter also discusses the prerequisites for introducing the process and presents the system that will be built throughout the book.

Chapter 2, *Introducing Docker*, explains the idea of containerization and the fundamentals of the Docker tool. This chapter also shows how to use Docker commands, package an application as a Docker image, publish Docker container's ports, and use Docker volumes.

Chapter 3, *Configuring Jenkins*, presents how to install, configure, and scale Jenkins. This chapter also shows how to use Docker to simplify Jenkins configuration and to enable dynamic slave provisioning.

Chapter 4, *Continuous Integration Pipeline*, explains the idea of pipelining and introduces the Jenkinsfile syntax. This chapters also shows how to configure a complete Continuous Integration pipeline.

Chapter 5, *Automated Acceptance Testing*, presents the idea and implementation of acceptance testing. This chapters also explains the meaning of artifact repositories, the orchestration using Docker Compose, and frameworks for writing BDD-oriented acceptance tests.

Chapter 6, *Configuration Management with Ansible,* introduces the concept of configuration management and its implementation using Ansible. The chapter also shows how to use Ansible together with Docker and Docker Compose.

Chapter 7, *Continuous Delivery Pipeline,* combines all the knowledge from the previous chapters in order to build the complete Continuous Delivery process. The chapter also discusses various environments and the aspects of nonfunctional testing.

Chapter 8, *Clustering with Docker Swarm,* explains the concept of server clustering and the implementation using Docker Swarm. The chapter also compares alternative clustering tools (Kubernetes and Apache Mesos) and explains how to use clustering for dynamic Jenkins agents.

Chapter 9, *Advanced Continuous Delivery,* presents a mixture of different aspects related to the Continuous Delivery process: database management, parallel pipeline steps, rollback strategies, legacy systems, and zero-downtime deployments. The chapter also includes best practices for the Continuous Delivery process.

What you need for this book

Docker requires the 64-bit Linux operating system. All examples in this book have been developed using Ubuntu 16.04, but any other Linux system with the kernel version 3.10 or above is sufficient.

Who this book is for

This book is for developers and DevOps who would like to improve their delivery process. No prior knowledge is required to understand this book.

Conventions

In this book, you will find a number of styles of text that distinguish between different kinds of information. Here are some examples of these styles, and an explanation of their meaning.

Code words in text, database table names, folder names, filenames, file extensions, pathnames, dummy URLs, user input, and Twitter handles are shown as follows: `docker info`

A block of code is set as follows:

```
pipeline {
    agent any
    stages {
        stage("Hello") {
            steps {
                echo 'Hello World'
            }
        }
    }
}
```

When we wish to draw your attention to a particular part of a code block, the relevant lines or items are set in bold:

```
FROM ubuntu:16.04
RUN apt-get update && \
    apt-get install -y python
```

Any command-line input or output is written as follows:

```
$ docker images
REPOSITORY                TAG      IMAGE ID      CREATED             SIZE
ubuntu_with_python        latest   d6e85f39f5b7  About a minute ago  202.6 MB
ubuntu_with_git_and_jdk   latest   8464dc10abbb  3 minutes ago       610.9 MB
```

New terms and important words are shown in bold. Words that you see on the screen, in menus or dialog boxes for example, appear in the text like this: "Click on **New Item**".

Warnings or important notes appear in a box like this.

If your Docker daemon is run inside the corporate network, you have to configure the HTTP proxy. The detailed description can be found at https://docs.docker.com/engine/admin/systemd/.

Tips and tricks appear like this.

The installation guides for all supported operating systems and cloud platforms can be found on the official Docker page, https://docs.docker.com/engine/installation/.

Reader feedback

Feedback from our readers is always welcome. Let us know what you think about this book—what you liked or may have disliked. Reader feedback is important for us to develop titles that you really get the most out of.

To send us general feedback, simply send an e-mail to feedback@packtpub.com, and mention the book title via the subject of your message.

If there is a topic that you have expertise in and you are interested in either writing or contributing to a book, see our author guide on www.packtpub.com/authors.

Customer support

Now that you are the proud owner of a Packt book, we have a number of things to help you to get the most from your purchase.

Downloading the example code

You can download the example code files for all Packt books you have purchased from your account at http://www.packtpub.com. If you purchased this book elsewhere, you can visit http://www.packtpub.com/support and register to have the files e-mailed directly to you.

You can download the code files by following these steps:

1. Log in or register to our website using your e-mail address and password.
2. Hover the mouse pointer on the **SUPPORT** tab at the top.
3. Click on **Code Downloads & Errata**.
4. Enter the name of the book in the **Search** box.
5. Select the book for which you're looking to download the code files.
6. Choose from the drop-down menu where you purchased this book from.
7. Click on **Code Download**.

Once the file is downloaded, please make sure that you unzip or extract the folder using the latest version of:

- WinRAR / 7-Zip for Windows
- Zipeg / iZip / UnRarX for Mac
- 7-Zip / PeaZip for Linux

The code bundle for the book is also hosted on GitHub at `https://github.com/PacktPublishing/Continuous-Delivery-with-Docker-and-Jenkin s`. We also have other code bundles from our rich catalog of books and videos available at `https://github.com/PacktPublishing/`. Check them out!

Downloading the color images of this book

We also provide you with a PDF file that has color images of the screenshots/diagrams used in this book. The color images will help you better understand the changes in the output. You can download this file from `https://www.packtpub.com/sites/default/files/downloads/ContinuousDeliveryw ithDockerandJenkins_ColorImages.pdf`.

Errata

Although we have taken every care to ensure the accuracy of our content, mistakes do happen. If you find a mistake in one of our books—maybe a mistake in the text or the code—we would be grateful if you would report this to us. By doing so, you can save other readers from frustration and help us improve subsequent versions of this book. If you find any errata, please report them by visiting `http://www.packtpub.com/submit-errata`, selecting your book, clicking on the errata `submission form` link, and entering the details of your errata. Once your errata are verified, your submission will be accepted and the errata will be uploaded on our website, or added to any list of existing errata, under the Errata section of that title. Any existing errata can be viewed by selecting your title from `http://www.packtpub.com/support`.

Piracy

Piracy of copyright material on the Internet is an ongoing problem across all media. At Packt, we take the protection of our copyright and licenses very seriously. If you come across any illegal copies of our works, in any form, on the Internet, please provide us with the location address or website name immediately so that we can pursue a remedy.

Please contact us at copyright@packtpub.com with a link to the suspected pirated material.

We appreciate your help in protecting our authors, and our ability to bring you valuable content.

Questions

You can contact us at questions@packtpub.com if you are having a problem with any aspect of the book, and we will do our best to address it.

1
Introducing Continuous Delivery

The common problem faced by most developers is how to release the implemented code quickly and safely. The delivery process used traditionally is, however, a source of pitfalls and usually leads to the disappointment of both developers and clients. This chapter presents the idea of the Continuous Delivery approach and provides the context for the rest of the book.

This chapter covers the following points:

- Introducing the traditional delivery process and its drawbacks
- Describing the idea of Continuous Delivery and the benefits it brings
- Comparing how different companies deliver their software
- Explaining the automated deployment pipeline and its phases
- Classifying different types of tests and their place in the process
- Pointing out the prerequisites to the successful Continuous Delivery process
- Presenting tools that will be used throughout the book
- Showing the complete system that will be built throughout the book

What is Continuous Delivery?

The most accurate definition of the Continuous Delivery is stated by Jez Humble and reads as follows: "Continuous Delivery is the ability to get changes of all types—including new features, configuration changes, bug fixes, and experiments—into production, or into the hands of users, safely and quickly in a sustainable way." That definition covers the key points.

To understand it better, let's imagine a scenario. You are responsible for the product, let's say, the email client application. Users come to you with a new requirement—they want to sort emails by size. You decide that the development will take around one week. When can the user expect to use the feature? Usually, after the development is done, you hand over the completed feature first to the QA team and then to the operations team, which takes additional time ranging from days to months. Therefore, even though the development took only one week, the user receives it in a couple of months! The Continuous Delivery approach addresses that issue by automating manual tasks so that the user could receive a new feature as soon as it's implemented.

To present better what to automate and how, let's start by describing the delivery process that is currently used for most software systems.

The traditional delivery process

The traditional delivery process, as the name suggests, has been in place for many years now and is implemented in most IT companies. Let's define how it works and comment on its shortcomings.

Introducing the traditional delivery process

Any delivery process begins with the requirements defined by a customer and ends up with the release on the production. The differences are in between. Traditionally, it looks as presented in the following release cycle diagram:

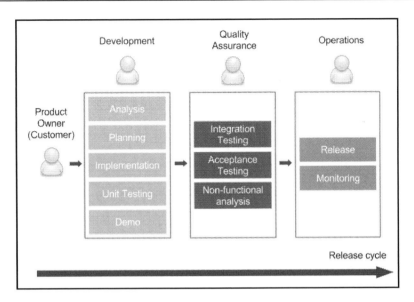

The release cycle starts with the requirements provided by the **Product Owner**, who represents the **Customer** (stakeholders). Then there are three phases, during which the work is passed between different teams:

- **Development**: Here, the developers (sometimes together with business analysts) work on the product. They often use Agile techniques (Scrum or Kanban) to increase the development velocity and to improve the communication with the client. Demo sessions are organized to obtain a customer's quick feedback. All good development techniques (like test-driven development or extreme programming practices) are welcome. After the implementation is completed, the code is passed to the QA team.

- **Quality Assurance**: This phase is usually called **User Acceptance Testing (UAT)** and it requires a code freeze on the trunk codebase, so that no new development would break the tests. The QA team performs a suite of **Integration Testing,** **Acceptance Testing,** and **Non-functional Testing** (performance, recovery, security, and so on). Any bug that is detected goes back to the development team, so developers usually also have their hands full of work. After the UAT phase is completed, the QA team approves the features that are planned for the next release.

- **Operations**: The last phase, usually the shortest one, means passing the code to the **Operations** team, so that they can perform the release and monitor the production. If anything goes wrong, they contact developers to help with the production system.

The length of the release cycle depends on the system and the organization, but it usually ranges from a week to a few months. The longest I've heard about was one year. The longest I worked with was quarterly-based and each part took as follows: development-1.5 months, UAT-1 month and 3 weeks, release (and strict production monitoring)-1 week.

The traditional delivery process is widely used in the IT industry and it's probably not the first time you've read about such an approach. Nevertheless, it has a number of drawbacks. Let's look at them explicity to understand why we need to strive for something better.

Shortcomings of the traditional delivery process

The most significant shortcomings of the traditional delivery process include the following:

- **Slow delivery**: Here, the customer receives the product long after the requirements were specified. It results in the unsatisfactory time to market and delays of the customer's feedback.
- **Long feedback cycle**: The feedback cycle is not only related to customers, but also to developers. Imagine that you accidentally created a bug and you learn about it during the UAT phase. How long does it take to fix something you worked on two months ago? Even minor bugs can consume weeks.
- **Lack of automation**: Rare releases don't encourage the automation, which leads to unpredictable releases.
- **Risky hotfixes**: Hotfixes can't usually wait for the full UAT phase, so they tend to be tested differently (the UAT phase is shortened) or not tested at all.
- **Stress**: Unpredictable releases are stressful for the operations team. What's more, the release cycle is usually tightly scheduled which imposes an additional stress on developers and testers.
- **Poor communication**: Work passed from one team to another represents the waterfall approach, in which people start to care only about their part, rather than the complete product. In case anything goes wrong, that usually leads to the blaming game instead of cooperation.
- **Shared responsibility**: No team takes the responsibility for the product from A to Z. For developers: "done" means that requirements are implemented. For testers: "done" means that the code is tested. For operations: "done" means that the code is released.

- **Lower job satisfaction**: Each phase is interesting for a different team, but other teams need to support the process. For example, the development phase is interesting for developers but, during two other phases, they still need to fix bugs and support the release, which usually is not interesting for them at all.

These drawbacks represent just a tip of the iceberg of the challenges related to the traditional delivery process. You may already feel that there must be a better way to develop the software and this better way is, obviously, the Continuous Delivery approach.

Benefits of Continuous Delivery

"How long would it take your organization to deploy a change that involves just one single line of code? Do you do this on a repeatable, reliable basis?" These are the famous questions from Mary and Tom Poppendieck (authors of *Implementing Lean Software Development*), which have been quoted many times by Jez Humble and other authors. Actually, the answer to these questions is the only valid measurement of the health of your delivery process.

To be able to deliver continuously, and not to spend a fortune on the army of operations teams working 24/7, we need automation. That is why, in short, Continuous Delivery is all about changing each phase of the traditional delivery process into a sequence of scripts, called the automated deployment pipeline or the Continuous Delivery pipeline. Then, if no manual steps are required, we can run the process after every code change and, therefore, deliver the product continuously to the users.

Continuous Delivery lets us get rid of the tedious release cycle and, therefore, brings the following benefits:

- **Fast delivery**: Time to market is significantly reduced as customers can use the product as soon as the development is completed. Remember, the software delivers no revenue until it is in the hands of its users.
- **Fast feedback cycle**: Imagine you created a bug in the code, which goes into the production the same day. How much time does it take to fix something you worked on the same day? Probably not much. This, together with the quick rollback strategy, is the best way to keep the production stable.
- **Low-risk releases**: If you release on a daily basis, then the process becomes repeatable and therefore much safer. As the saying goes, "If it hurts, do it more often."
- **Flexible release options**: In case you need to release immediately, everything is already prepared, so there is no additional time/cost associated with the release decision.

Needless to say, we could achieve all the benefits simply by eliminating all delivery phases and proceeding with the development directly on the production. It would, however, cause the quality to decline. Actually, the whole difficulty of introducing Continuous Delivery is the concern that the quality would decrease together with eliminating manual steps. In this book, we will show how to approach it in a safe manner and explain why, contrary to common beliefs, the products delivered continuously have fewer bugs and are better adjusted to the customer's needs.

Success stories

My favorite story on Continuous Delivery was told by Rolf Russell at one of his talks. It goes as follows. In 2005, Yahoo acquired Flickr and it was a clash of two cultures in the developer's world. Flickr, by that time, was a company with the start-up approach in mind. Yahoo, on the contrary, was a huge corporation with strict rules and the safety-first attitude. Their release processes differed a lot. While Yahoo used the traditional delivery process, Flickr released many times a day. Every change implemented by developers went on the production the same day. They even had a footer at the bottom of their page showing the time of the last release and the avatars of the developers who did the changes.

Yahoo deployed rarely and each release brought a lot of changes well tested and prepared. Flickr worked in very small chunks, each feature was divided into small incremental parts and each part was deployed quickly to the production. The difference is presented in the following diagram:

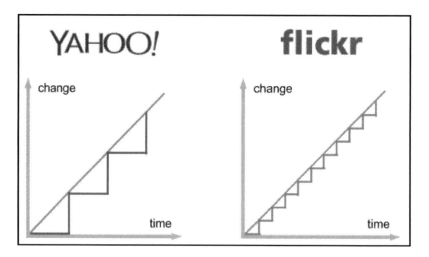

You can imagine what happened when the developers from two companies met. Yahoo obviously treated Flickr's colleagues as junior irresponsible developers, "a bunch of software cowboys who don't know what they are doing." So, the first thing they wanted to change was to add a QA team and the UAT phase into Flickr's delivery process. Before they applied the change, however, Flickr's developers had only one wish. They asked to evaluate the most reliable products in the whole Yahoo company. What a surprise when it happened that of all the software in Yahoo, Flickr had the lowest downtime. The Yahoo team didn't understand it at first, but let Flickr stay with their current process anyway. After all, they were engineers, so the evaluation result was conclusive. Only after some time, they realized that the Continuous Delivery process can be beneficial for all products in Yahoo and they started to gradually introduce it everywhere.

The most important question of the story remains-how was it possible that Flickr was the most reliable system? Actually, the reason for that fact was what we already mentioned in the previous sections. A release is less risky if:

- The delta of code changes is small
- The process is repeatable

That is why, even though the release itself is a difficult activity, it is much safer when done frequently.

The story of Yahoo and Flickr is only an example of many successful companies for which the Continuous Delivery process proved to be right. Some of them even proudly share details from their systems, as follows:

- **Amazon**: In 2011, they announced reaching 11.6 seconds (on average) between deployments
- **Facebook**: In 2013, they announced deployment of code changes twice a day
- **HubSpot**: In 2013, they announced deployment 300 times a day
- **Atlassian**: In 2016, they published a survey stating that 65% of their customers practice continuous delivery

You can read more about the research on the Continuous Delivery process and individual case studies at `https://continuousdelivery.com/evidence-case-studies/`.

Keep in mind that the statistics get better every day. However, even without any numbers, just imagine a world in which every line of code you implement goes safely into the production. Clients can react quickly and adjust their requirements, developers are happy because they don't have to solve that many bugs, managers are satisfied because they always know what is the current state of work. After all, remember, the only true measure of progress is the released software.

The automated deployment pipeline

We already know what the Continuous Delivery process is and why we use it. In this section, we describe how to implement it.

Let's start by emphasizing that each phase in the traditional delivery process is important. Otherwise, it would never have been created in the first place. No one wants to deliver software without testing it first! The role of the UAT phase is to detect bugs and to ensure that what developers created is what the customer wanted. The same applies to the operations team—the software must be configured, deployed to the production, and monitored. That's out of the question. So, how do we automate the process so that we preserve all the phases? That is the role of the automated deployment pipeline, which consists of three stages as presented in the following diagram:

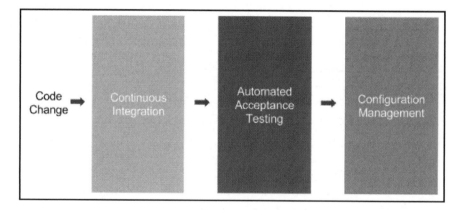

The automated deployment pipeline is a sequence of scripts that is executed after every code change committed to the repository. If the process is successful, it ends up with the deployment to the production environment.

Each step corresponds to a phase in the traditional delivery process as follows:

- **Continuous Integration**: This checks to make sure that the code written by different developers integrates together
- **Automated Acceptance Testing**: This replaces the manual QA phase and checks if the features implemented by developers meet the client's requirements
- **Configuration Management**: This replaces the manual operations phase-configures the environment and deploys the software

Let's take a deeper look at each phase to understand what is its responsibility and what steps it includes.

Continuous Integration

The Continuous Integration phase provides the first feedback to developers. It checks out the code from the repository, compiles it, runs unit tests, and verifies the code quality. If any step fails, the pipeline execution is stopped and the first thing the developers should do is fix the Continuous Integration build. The essential aspect of the phase is time; it must be executed in a timely manner. For example, if this phase took an hour to complete then the developers would commit the code faster, which would result in the constantly failing pipeline.

The Continuous Integration pipeline is usually the starting point. Setting it up is simple because everything is done within the development team and no agreement with the QA and operations teams is necessary.

Automated acceptance testing

The automated acceptance testing phase is a suite of tests written together with the client (and QAs) that is supposed to replace the manual UAT stage. It acts as a quality gate to decide whether a product is ready for the release or not. If any of the acceptance tests fail, then the pipeline execution is stopped and no further steps are run. It prevents movement to the Configuration Management phase and therefore the release.

The whole idea of automating the acceptance phase is to build the quality into the product instead of verifying it later. In other words, when a developer completes the implementation, the software is delivered already together with acceptance tests which verify that the software is what the client wanted. That is a large shift in thinking about testing software. There is no longer a single person (or team) who approves the release, but everything depends on passing the acceptance test suite. That is why creating this phase is usually the most difficult part of the Continuous Delivery process. It requires a close cooperation with the client and creating tests at the beginning (not at the end) of the process.

> Introducing automated acceptance tests is especially challenging in the case of legacy systems. We describe more on that topic in `Chapter 9`, *Advanced Continuous Delivery*.

There is usually a lot of confusion about the types of tests and their place in the Continuous Delivery process. It's also often unclear how to automate each type, what should be the coverage, and what should be the role of the QA team in the whole development process. Let's clarify it using the Agile testing matrix and the testing pyramid.

The Agile testing matrix

Brian Marick, in a series of his blog posts, made a classification of software tests in a form of the so-called agile testing matrix. It places tests in two dimensions: business or technology facing and support programmers or critique the product. Let's have a look at that classification:

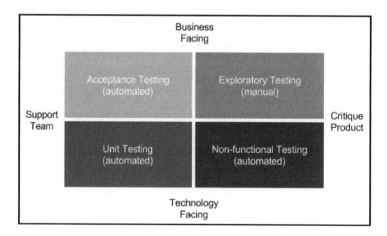

Let's comment briefly on each type of test:

- **Acceptance Testing (automated)**: These are tests that represent functional requirements seen from the business perspective. They are written in the form of stories or examples by clients and developers to agree on how the software should work.
- **Unit Testing (automated)**: These are tests that help developers to provide the high-quality software and minimize the number of bugs.
- **Exploratory Testing (manual)**: This is the manual black-box testing, which tries to break or improve the system.
- **Non-functional Testing (automated)**: These are tests that represent system properties related to the performance, scalability, security, and so on.

This classification answers one of the most important questions about the Continuous Delivery process: what is the role of a QA in the process?

Manual QAs perform the exploratory testing, so they play with the system, try to break it, ask questions, think about improvements. Automation QAs help with nonfunctional and acceptance testing, for example, they write code to support load testing. In general, QAs don't have their special place in the delivery process, but rather a role in the development team.

 In the automated Continuous Delivery process, there is no longer a place for manual QAs who perform repetitive tasks.

You may look at the classification and wonder why you see no integration tests there. Where are they up to Brian Marick and where to put them in the Continuous Delivery pipeline?

To explain it well, we first need to mention that the meaning of an integration test differs depending on the context. For (micro) service architecture, they usually mean exactly the same as the acceptance testing, as services are small and need nothing more than unit and acceptance tests. If you build a modular application, then by integration tests we usually mean component tests that bind multiple modules (but not the whole application) and test them together. In that case, integration tests place themselves somewhere between acceptance and unit tests. They are written in a similar way as acceptance tests, but are usually more technical and require mocking not only external services, but also internal modules. Integration tests, similar to unit tests, represent the "code" point of view, while acceptance tests represent the "user" point of view. Concerning the Continuous Delivery pipeline, integration tests are simply implemented as a separate phase in the process.

The testing pyramid

The previous section explained what each test type represents in the process, but mentioned nothing about how many tests we should develop. So, what should be the code coverage in case of unit testing? What about acceptance testing?

To answer these questions, Mike Cohn, in his book *Succeeding with Agile: Software Development Using Scrum*, created a so-called testing pyramid. Let's look at the diagram to understand it well.

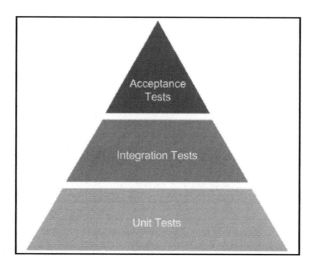

When we move up the pyramid, the tests become slower and more expensive to create. They often require touching user interface and hiring a separate test automation team. That is why acceptance tests should not target 100% coverage. On the contrary, they should be feature-oriented and verify only selected test scenarios. Otherwise, we would spend a fortune on the test development and maintenance, and our Continuous Delivery pipeline build would take ages to execute.

The case is different at the bottom of the pyramid. Unit tests are cheap and fast, so we should strive for 100% code coverage. They are written by developers and providing them should be a standard procedure for any mature team.

I hope that the agile testing matrix and the testing pyramid clarified the role and the importance of acceptance testing.

Let's move to the last phase of the Continuous Delivery process, configuration management.

Configuration management

The configuration management phase is responsible for tracking and controlling changes in the software and its environment. It concerns taking care of preparing and installing the necessary tools, scaling the number of service instances and their distribution, infrastructure inventory, and all tasks related to the application deployment.

Configuration management is a solution to the problems posed by manually deploying and configuring applications on the production. Such common practice results in an issue whereby we no longer knows where each service is running and with what properties. Configuration management tools (such as Ansible, Chef, or Puppet) enable storing configuration files in the version control system and tracking every change that was made on the production servers.

An additional effort to replace manual tasks of the operations team is to take care of application monitoring. That is usually done by streaming logs and metrics of the running systems to a common dashboard, which is monitored by developers (or the DevOps team, as explained in the next section).

Prerequisites to Continuous Delivery

The rest of the book is dedicated to technical details on how to implement a successful Continuous Delivery pipeline. The success of the process, however, depends not only on the tools we present throughout the book. In this section, we take a holistic look at the whole process and define the Continuous Delivery requirements in three areas:

- Your organization's structure and its impact on the development process
- Your products and their technical details
- Your development team and the practices you use

Organizational prerequisites

The way your organization works has a high impact on the success of introducing the Continuous Delivery process. It's a bit similar to introducing Scrum. Many organizations would like to use the Agile process, but they don't change their culture. You can't use Scrum in your development team unless the organization's structure is adjusted to that. For example, you need a product owner, stakeholders, and management that understands that no requirement changes are possible during the sprint. Otherwise, even with good will, you won't make it. The same applies to the Continuous Delivery process; it requires an adjustment of how the organization is structured. Let's have a look at three aspects: the DevOps culture, a client in the process, and business decisions.

DevOps culture

A long time ago, when software was written by individuals or microteams, there was no clear separation between the development, quality assurance, and operations. A person developed the code, tested it, and then put it into the production. If anything went wrong, the same person investigated the issue, fixed it, and redeployed to the production. The way the development is organized now changed gradually, when systems became larger and development teams grew. Then, engineers started to become specialized in one area. That made perfect sense, because specialization caused a boost in the productivity. However, the side effect was the communication overhead. It is especially visible if developers, QAs, and operations are under separate departments in the organization, sit in different buildings, or are outsourced to different countries. Such organization structure is no good for the Continuous Delivery process. We need something better, we need to adapt the so-called DevOps culture.

DevOps culture means, in a sense, coming back to the roots. A single person or a team is responsible for all three areas, as presented in the following diagram:

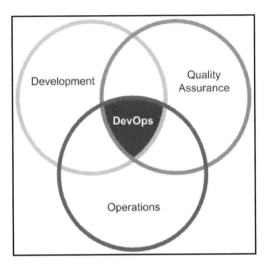

The reason why it's possible to move to the DevOps model without losing on the productivity is the automation. Most of the tasks related to the quality assurance and operations are moved to the automated delivery pipeline and can be therefore managed by the development team.

 A DevOps team doesn't necessarily need to consist only of developers. A very common scenario in many organization's under transformation is to create teams with four developers, one QA, and one person from operations. They need, however, to work closely together (sit in one area, have stand-ups together, work on the same product).

The culture of small DevOps teams affects the software architecture. Functional requirements have to be well separated into (micro) services or modules, so that each team can take care of an independent part.

 The impact of the organization's structure on the software architecture was already observed in 1967 and formulated as Conway's Law: "Any organization that designs a system (defined broadly) will produce a design whose structure is a copy of the organization's communication structure."

Client in the process

The role of a client (or a product owner) slightly changes during the Continuous Delivery adoption. Traditionally, clients are involved in defining requirements, answering questions from developers, attending demos, and taking part in the UAT phase to agree if what was built is what they had in mind.

In Continuous Delivery, there is no UAT, and a client is essential in the process of writing acceptance tests. For some clients, who already wrote their requirements in a testable manner, it is not a big shift. For the others, it means a change in a way of thinking to make requirements more technical-oriented.

In the Agile environment, some teams don't even accept user stories (requirements) without acceptance tests attached. Such techniques, even though they may sound too strict, often lead to better development productivity.

Business decisions

In most companies, the business has an impact on the release schedule. After all, the decision what features are delivered, and when, is related to different departments of the company (for example, marketing) and can be strategic for the enterprise. That is why the release scheduling has to be reapproached and discussed between the business and the development teams.

Obviously, there are techniques such as feature toggles or manual pipeline steps, which help with releasing features at the specified time. We will describe them later in the book. To be precise, the term Continuous Delivery is not the same as Continuous Deployment. The former means that each commit to the repository is automatically released to the production. Continuous Delivery is less strict and means that each commit ends up with a release candidate, so it allows the last step (release to the production) to be manual.

In the rest of the book, we will use the terms Continuous Delivery and Continuous Deployment interchangeably.

Technical and development prerequisites

From the technical side, there are a few requirements to keep in mind. We will discuss them throughout the book, so let's only mention them here without going into detail:

- **Automated build, test, package, and deploy operations**: All operations need to be possible to automate. If we deal with the system that is non-automatable, for example, due to security reasons or its complexity, then it's impossible to create a fully automated delivery pipeline.
- **Quick pipeline execution**: The pipeline must be executed in a timely manner, preferably in 5-15 minutes. If our pipeline execution takes hours or days, then it won't be possible to run it after every commit to the repository.
- **Quick failure recovery**: A possibility of the quick rollback or system recovery is a must. Otherwise, we risk the production health due to frequent releases.
- **Zero-downtime deployment**: The deployment cannot have any downtime since we release many times a day.
- **Trunk-based development**: Developers must check in regularly into one master branch. Otherwise, if everyone develops in their own branches, the integration is rare and therefore the releases are rare, which is exactly the opposite of what we want to achieve.

We will write more on these prerequisites and how to address them throughout the book. Keeping that in mind, let's move to the last section of this chapter and introduce what system we plan to build in this book and what tools we will use for that purpose.

Building the Continuous Delivery process

We introduced the idea, benefits, and prerequisites with regards to the Continuous Delivery process. In this section, we describe the tools that will be used throughout the book and their place in the complete system.

 If you're interested more in the idea of the Continuous Delivery process, then have a look at an excellent book by Jez Humble and David Farley, *Continuous Delivery: Reliable Software Releases through Build, Test, and Deployment Automation.*

Introducing tools

First of all, the specific tool is always less important than understanding its role in the process. In other words, any tool can be replaced with another one which plays the same role. For example, Jenkins can be replaced with Atlassian Bamboo and Chief can be used instead of Ansible. That is why each chapter begins with the general description of why such a tool is necessary and what its role is in the whole process. Then, the exact tool is described with comparison to its substitutes. That form gives you the flexibility to choose the right one for your environment.

Another approach could be to describe the Continuous Delivery process on the level of ideas; however, I strongly believe that giving an exact example with the code extract, something that readers can run by themselves, results in a much better understanding of the concept.

 There are two ways to read this book. The first is to read and understand the concepts of the Continuous Delivery process. The second is to create your own environment and execute all scripts while reading to understand the details.

Let's have a quick look at the tools we will use throughout the book. In this section, however, it is only a brief introduction of each technology and much more detail is presented as this book goes on.

Docker ecosystem

Docker, as the clear leader of the containerization movement, has dominated the software industry in the recent years. It allows the packaging of an application in the environment-agnostic image and therefore treats servers as a farm of resources, rather than machines that must be configured for each application. Docker was a clear choice for this book because it perfectly fits the (micro) service world and the Continuous Delivery process.

Together with Docker comes additional technologies, which are as follows:

- **Docker Hub**: This is a registry for Docker images
- **Docker Compose**: This is a tool to define multicontainer Docker applications
- **Docker Swarm**: This is a clustering and scheduling tool

Jenkins

Jenkins is by far the most popular automation server on the market. It helps to create Continuous Integration and Continuous Delivery pipelines and, in general, any other automated sequence of scripts. Highly plugin-oriented, it has a great community which constantly extends it with new features. What's more, it allows to write the pipeline as code and supports distributed build environments.

Ansible

Ansible is an automation tool that helps with software provisioning, configuration management, and application deployment. It is trending faster than any other configuration management engine and can soon overtake its two main competitors: Chef and Puppet. It uses agentless architecture and integrates smoothly with Docker.

GitHub

GitHub is definitely the number one of all hosted version control systems. It provides a very stable system, a great web-based UI, and a free service for public repositories. Having said that, any source control management service or tool will work with Continuous Delivery, no matter if it's in the cloud or self-hosted and if it's based on Git, SVN, Mercurial, or any other tool.

Java/Spring Boot/Gradle

Java has been the most popular programming language for years. That is why it is being used for most code examples in this book. Together with Java, most companies develop with the Spring framework, so we used it to create a simple web service needed to explain some concepts. Gradle is used as a build tool. It's still less popular than Maven, however, trending much faster. As always, any programming language, framework, or build tool can be exchanged and the Continuous Delivery process would stay the same, so don't worry if your technology stack is different.

The other tools

Cucumber was chosen arbitrarily as the acceptance testing framework. Other similar solutions are Fitnesse and JBehave. For the database migration we use Flyway, but any other tool would do, for example, Liquibase.

Creating a complete Continuous Delivery system

You can look at how this book is organized from two perspectives.

The first one is based on the steps of the automated deployment pipeline. Each chapter takes you closer to the complete Continuous Delivery process. If you look at the names of the chapters, some of them are even named like the pipeline phases:

- Continuous Integration pipeline
- Automated acceptance testing
- Configuration management with Ansible

The rest of the chapters give the introduction, summary, or additional information complementary to the process.

There is also a second perspective to the content of this book. Each chapter describes one piece of the environment, which in turn is well prepared for the Continuous Delivery process. In other words, the book presents, step by step, technology by technology, how to build a complete system. To help you get the feeling of what we plan to build throughout the book, let's now have a look at how the system will evolve in each chapter.

Don't worry if you don't understand the concepts and the terminology at this point. We explain everything from scratch in the corresponding chapters.

Introducing Docker

In Chapter 2, *Introducing Docker*, we start from the center of our system and build a working application packaged as a Docker image. The output of this chapter is presented in the following diagram:

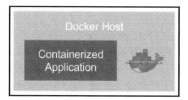

A dockerized application (web service) is run as a container on a **Docker Host** and is reachable as it would run directly on the host machine. That is possible thanks to port forwarding (port publishing in the Docker's terminology).

Configuring Jenkins

In Chapter 3, *Configuring Jenkins*, we prepare the Jenkins environment. Thanks to the support of multiple agent (slave) nodes, it is able to handle the heavy concurrent load. The result is presented in the following diagram:

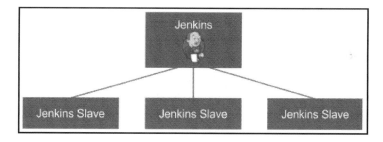

The **Jenkins** master accepts a build request, but the execution is started at one of the **Jenkins Slave** (agent) machines. Such an approach provides horizontal scaling of the Jenkins environment.

Continuous Integration Pipeline

In Chapter 4, *Continuous Integration Pipeline*, we show how to create the first phase of the Continuous Delivery pipeline, the commit stage. The output of this chapter is the system presented in the following diagram:

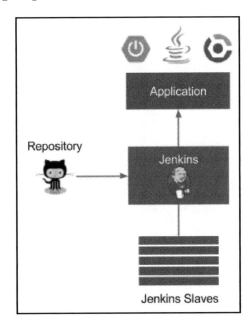

The application is a simple web service written in Java with the Spring Boot framework. Gradle is used as a build tool and GitHub as the source code repository. Every commit to GitHub automatically triggers the Jenkins build, which uses Gradle to compile Java code, run unit tests, and perform additional checks (code coverage, static code analysis, and so on). After the Jenkins build is completed, a notification is sent to the developers.

After this chapter, you will be able to create a complete Continuous Integration pipeline.

Automated acceptance testing

In `Chapter 5`, *Automated Acceptance Testing*, we finally merge the two technologies from the book title: *Docker* and *Jenkins*. It results in the system presented in the following diagram:

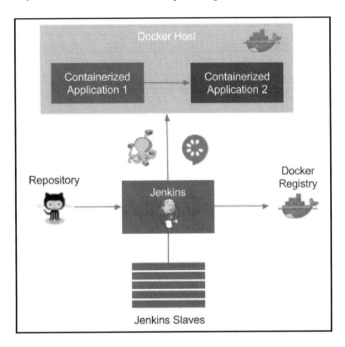

The additional elements in the diagram are related to the automated acceptance testing stage:

- **Docker Registry**: After the Continuous Integration phase, the application is packaged first into a JAR file and then as a Docker image. That image is then pushed to the **Docker Registry**, which acts as a storage for dockerized applications.
- **Docker Host**: Before performing the acceptance test suite, the application has to be started. Jenkins triggers a **Docker Host** machine to pull the dockerized application from the **Docker Registry** and starts it.
- **Docker Compose**: If the complete application consists of more than one Docker container (for example, two web services: Application 1 using Application 2), then **Docker Compose** helps to run them together.
- **Cucumber**: After the application is started on the **Docker Host**, Jenkins runs a suite of acceptance tests written in the **Cucumber** framework.

Configuration management with Ansible/Continuous Delivery pipeline

In the next two chapters, that is, Chapter 6, *Configuration Management with Ansible* and Chapter 7, *Continuous Delivery Pipeline*, we complete the Continuous Delivery pipeline. The output is the environment presented in the following diagram:

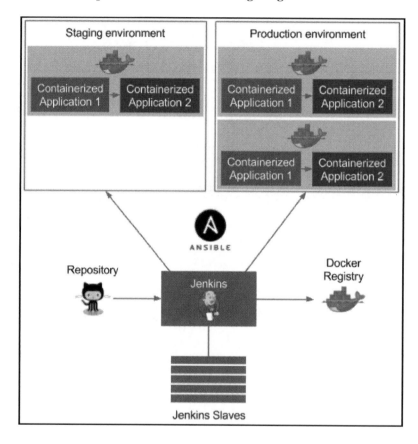

Ansible takes care of the environments and enables the deployment of the same applications on multiple machines. As a result, we deploy the application to the staging environment, run the acceptance testing suite, and finally release the application to the production environment, usually in many instances (on multiple Docker Host machines).

Clustering with Docker Swarm/Advanced Continuous Delivery

In Chapter 8, *Clustering with Docker Swarm*, we replace single hosts in each of the environments with clusters of machines. Chapter 9, *Advanced Continuous Delivery*, additionally adds databases to the Continuous Delivery process. The final environment created in this book is presented in the following diagram:

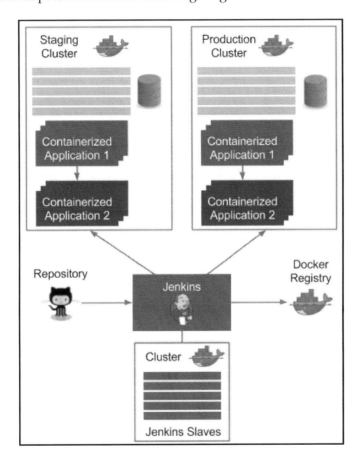

Staging and production environments are equipped with Docker Swarm clusters and therefore multiple instances of the application are run on the cluster. We don't have to think anymore on which exact machine our applications are deployed. All we care about is the number of their instances. The same applies to Jenkins slaves, they are also run on a cluster. The last improvement is the automatic management of the database schemas using Flyway migrations integrated into the delivery process.

I hope you are already excited by what we plan to build throughout this book. We will approach it step by step, explaining every detail and all the possible options in order to help you understand the procedures and tools. After reading this book, you will be able to introduce or improve the Continuous Delivery process in your projects.

Summary

In this chapter, we have introduced the Continuous Delivery process starting from the idea, discussing the prerequisites, to end up with tools that are used in the rest of the book. The key takeaway from this chapter is as follows:

- The delivery process used currently in most companies has significant shortcomings and can be improved using modern tools for automation
- The Continuous Delivery approach provides a number of benefits, of which the most significant ones are: fast delivery, fast feedback cycle, and low-risk releases
- The Continuous Delivery pipeline consists of three stages: Continuous Integration, automated acceptance testing, and configuration management
- Introducing Continuous Delivery usually requires a change in the organization's culture and structure
- The most important tools in the context of Continuous Delivery are Docker, Jenkins, and Ansible

In the next chapter, we introduce Docker and present how to build a dockerized application.

2
Introducing Docker

We will discuss how the modern Continuous Delivery process should look by introducing Docker, the technology that changed the IT industry and the way the servers are used.

This chapter covers the following points:

- Introducing the idea of virtualization and containerization
- Installing Docker for different local and server environments
- Explaining the architecture of the Docker toolkit
- Building Docker images with Dockerfile and by committing changes
- Running applications as Docker containers
- Configuring Docker networks and port forwarding
- Introducing Docker volumes as a shared storage

What is Docker?

Docker is an open source project designed to help with application deployment using software containers. This quote is from the official Docker page:

> *"Docker containers wrap a piece of software in a complete filesystem that contains everything needed to run: code, runtime, system tools, system libraries - anything that can be installed on a server. This guarantees that the software will always run the same, regardless of its environment."*

Docker, therefore, in a similar way as virtualization, allows packaging an application into an image that can be run everywhere.

Containerization versus virtualization

Without Docker, isolation and other benefits can be achieved with the use of hardware virtualization, often called virtual machines. The most popular solutions are VirtualBox, VMware, and Parallels. A virtual machine emulates a computer architecture and provides the functionality of a physical computer. We can achieve complete isolation of applications if each of them is delivered and run as a separate virtual machine image. The following figure presents the concept of virtualization:

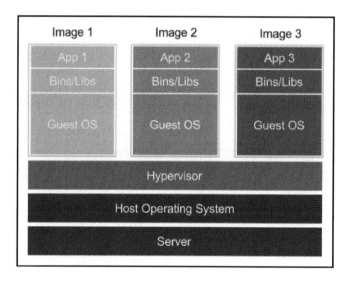

Each application is launched as a separate image with all dependencies and a guest operating system. Images are run by the hypervisor, which emulates the physical computer architecture. This method of deployment is widely supported by many tools (such as Vagrant) and dedicated to development and testing environments. Virtualization, however, has three significant drawbacks:

- **Low performance**: The virtual machine emulates the whole computer architecture to run the guest operating system, so there is a significant overhead associated with each operation.
- **High resource consumption**: Emulation requires a lot of resources and has to be done separately for each application. This is why, on a standard desktop machine, only a few applications can be run simultaneously.
- **Large image size**: Each application is delivered with a full operating system, so the deployment on a server implies sending and storing a large amount of data.

The concept of containerization presents a different solution:

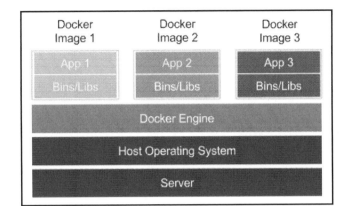

Each application is delivered together with its dependencies, but, without the operating system. Applications interface directly with the host operating system, so there is no additional layer of the guest operating system. It results in better performance and no waste of resources. Moreover, shipped Docker images are significantly smaller.

Notice that in the case of containerization, the isolation happens at the level of the host operating system's processes. It doesn't mean, however, that the containers share their dependencies. Each of them has their own libraries in the right version, and if any of them is updated, it has no impact on the others. To achieve this, Docker Engine creates a set of Linux namespaces and control groups for the container. This is why the Docker security is based on the Linux kernel process isolation. This solution, although mature enough, could be considered slightly less secure than the complete operating system-based isolation offered by virtual machines.

The need for Docker

Docker containerization solves a number of problems seen in traditional software delivery. Let's take a closer look.

Environment

Installing and running software is complex. You need to decide about the operating system, resources, libraries, services, permissions, other software, and everything your application depends on. Then, you need to know how to install it. What's more, there may be some conflicting dependencies. What do you do then? What if your software needs an upgrade of a library but the other does not? In some companies, such issues are solved by having **classes of applications**, and each class is served by a dedicated server, for example, a server for web services with Java 7, another one for batch jobs with Java 8, and so on. This solution, however, is not balanced in terms of resources and requires an army of IT operations teams to take care of all production and test servers.

Another problem with the environment complexity is that it often requires a specialist to run an application. A less technical person may have a hard time setting up MySQL, ODBC, or any other slightly more sophisticated tool. This is particularly true for applications not delivered as an operating system-specific binary but which require source code compilation or any other environment-specific configuration.

Isolation

Keep the workspace tidy. One application can change the behavior of the other one. Imagine what can happen. Applications share one filesystem, so if application A writes something to the wrong directory, application B reads the incorrect data. They share resources, so if there is a memory leak in application A, it can freeze not only itself but also application B. They share network interfaces, so if applications A and B both use port 8080, one of them will crash. Isolation concerns the security aspects too. Running a buggy application or malicious software can cause damage to other applications. This is why it is a much safer approach to keep each application inside a separate sandbox, which limits the scope of damage impact to the application itself.

Organizing applications

Servers often end up looking messy with a ton of running applications nobody knows anything about. How will you check what applications are running on the server and what dependencies each of them is using? They could depend on libraries, other applications, or tools. Without the exhaustive documentation, all we can do is look at the running processes and start guessing. Docker keeps things organized by having each application as a separate container that can be listed, searched, and monitored.

Portability

Write once, run anywhere, said the slogan while advertising the earliest versions of Java. Indeed, Java addresses the portability issue quite well; however, I can still think of a few cases where it fails, for example, the incompatible native dependencies or the older version of the Java runtime. Moreover, not all software is written in Java.

Docker moves the concept of portability one level higher; if the Docker version is compatible, then the shipped software works correctly regardless of the programming language, operating system, or environment configuration. Docker, then, can be expressed by the slogan *Ship the entire environment instead of just code.*

Kittens and cattle

The difference between traditional software deployment and Docker-based deployment is often expressed with an analogy of kittens and cattle. Everybody likes kittens. Kittens are unique. Each has its own name and needs special treatment. Kittens are treated with emotion. We cry when they die. On the contrary, cattle exist only to satisfy our needs. Even the form cattle is singular since it's just a pack of animals treated together. No naming, no uniqueness. Surely, they are unique (the same as each server is unique), but it is irrelevant. This is why the most straightforward explanation of the idea behind Docker is *Treat your servers like cattle, not pets.*

Alternative containerization technologies

Docker is not the only containerization system available on the market. Actually, the first versions of Docker were based on the open source **LXC** (**Linux Containers**) system, which is an alternative platform for containers. Other known solutions are FreeBSD Jails, OpenVZ, and Solaris Containers. Docker, however, overtook all other systems because of its simplicity, good marketing, and startup approach. It works under most operating systems, allows you to do something useful in less than 15 minutes, has a lot of simple-to-use features, good tutorials, a great community, and probably the best logo in the IT industry.

Docker installation

Docker's installation process is quick and simple. Currently, it's supported on most Linux operating systems and a wide range of them have dedicated binaries provided. Mac and Windows are also well supported with native applications. However, it's important to understand that Docker is internally based on the Linux kernel and its specifics, and this is why, in the case of Mac and Windows, it uses virtual machines (xhyve for Mac and Hyper-V for Windows) to run the Docker Engine environment.

Prerequisites for Docker

Docker requirements are specific for each operating system.

Mac:

- 2010 or newer model, with Intel's hardware support for **memory management unit** (**MMU**) virtualization
- macOS 10.10.3 Yosemite or newer
- At least 4GB of RAM
- No VirtualBox prior to version 4.3.30 installed

Windows:

- 64-bit Windows 10 Pro
- The Hyper-V package enabled

Linux:

- 64-bit architecture
- Linux kernel 3.10 or later

If your machine does not meet the requirements, then the solution is to use VirtualBox with the Ubuntu operating system installed. This workaround, even though it sounds complicated, is not necessarily the worst method, especially taking into consideration that the Docker Engine environment is virtualized anyway in the case of Mac and Windows. Furthermore, Ubuntu is one of the best-supported systems for using Docker.

 All examples in this book have been tested on the Ubuntu 16.04 operating system.

Installing on a local machine

Dockers installation process is straightforward and very well described on its official pages.

Docker for Ubuntu

`https://docs.docker.com/engine/installation/linux/ubuntulinux/` contains a guide on how to install Docker on an Ubuntu machine.

In the case of Ubuntu 16.04, I've executed the following commands:

```
$ sudo apt-get update
$ sudo apt-key adv --keyserver hkp://p80.pool.sks-keyservers.net:80 --recv-
keys 9DC858229FC7DD38854AE2D88D81803C0EBFCD88
$ sudo apt-add-repository 'deb [arch=amd64]
https://download.docker.com/linux/ubuntu xenial main stable'
$ sudo apt-get update
$ sudo apt-get install -y docker-ce
```

After all operations are completed, Docker should be installed. However, at the moment, the only user allowed to use Docker commands is `root`. This means that the `sudo` keyword must precede every Docker command.

We can enable other users to use Docker by adding them to the `docker` group:

```
$ sudo usermod -aG docker <username>
```

After a successful logout, everything is set up. With the latest command, however, we need to take some precautions not to give the Docker permissions to an unwanted user, and therefore create a vulnerability in the Docker Engine. This is particularly important in the case of installation on the server machine.

Docker for Linux

`https://docs.docker.com/engine/installation/linux/` contains installation guides for most Linux distributions.

Docker for Mac

`https://docs.docker.com/docker-for-mac/` contains a step-by-step guide on how to install Docker on a Mac machine. It is delivered together with a collection of Docker components:

- Virtual machine with Docker Engine
- Docker Machine (a tool used to create Docker hosts on the virtual machine)
- Docker Compose
- Docker client and server
- Kitematic: a GUI application

The Docker Machine tool helps in installing and managing Docker Engine on Mac, Windows, on company networks, in data centers, and on cloud providers such as AWS or Digital Ocean.

Docker for Windows

`https://docs.docker.com/docker-for-windows/` contains a step-by-step guide on how to install Docker on a Windows machine. It is delivered together with a collection of Docker components similar to Mac.

The installation guides for all supported operating systems and cloud platforms can be found on the official Docker page, `https://docs.docker.com/engine/installation/`.

Testing Docker installation

No matter which installation you've chosen (Mac, Windows, Ubuntu, Linux, or other), Docker should be set up and ready. The best way to test it is to run the `docker info` command. The output message should be similar to the following one:

```
$ docker info
Containers: 0
   Running: 0
    Paused: 0
   Stopped: 0
    Images: 0
 . . .
```

Installing on a server

In order to use Docker over the network, it is possible to either take advantage of cloud platform providers or to manually install Docker on a dedicated server.

In the first case, the Docker configuration differs from one platform to another, but it is always very well described in dedicated tutorials. Most cloud platforms enable creating Docker hosts via user-friendly web interfaces or describe exact commands to execute on their servers.

The second case (installing Docker manually) requires, however, a few words of comment.

Dedicated server

Installing Docker manually on a server does not differ much from the local installation.

Two additional steps are required that include setting the Docker daemon to listen on the network socket and setting security certificates.

Let's start from the first step. By default, due to security reasons, Docker runs via a non-networked Unix socket that only allows local communication. It's necessary to add listening on the chosen network interface socket so that the external clients can connect. `https://docs.docker.com/engine/admin/` describes in detail all the configuration steps needed for each Linux distribution.

In the case of Ubuntu, the Docker daemon is configured by the systemd, so in order to change the configuration of how it's started, we need to modify one line in the `/lib/systemd/system/docker.service` file:

```
ExecStart=/usr/bin/dockerd -H <server_ip>:2375
```

By changing this line, we enabled the access to the Docker daemon via the specified IP address. All the details on the systemd configuration can be found at `https://docs.docker.com/engine/admin/systemd/`.

The second step of server configuration concerns the Docker security certificates. This enables only clients authenticated by a certificate to access the server. The comprehensive description of the Docker certificates configuration can be found at `https://docs.docker.com/engine/security/https/`. This step isn't strictly required; however, unless your Docker daemon server is inside the firewalled network, it is essential.

If your Docker daemon is run inside the corporate network, you have to configure the HTTP proxy. The detailed description can be found at `https://docs.docker.com/engine/admin/systemd/`.

Running Docker hello world>

The Docker environment is set up and ready, so we can start the first example.

Enter the following command in your console:

```
$ docker run hello-world
Unable to find image 'hello-world:latest' locally
latest: Pulling from library/hello-world
78445dd45222: Pull complete
Digest:
sha256:c5515758d4c5e1e838e9cd307f6c6a0d620b5e07e6f927b07d05f6d12a1ac8d7
Status: Downloaded newer image for hello-world:latest

Hello from Docker!
This message shows that your installation appears to be working correctly.
...
```

Congratulations, you've just run your first Docker container. I hope you already feel how simple Docker is. Let's examine step-by-step what happened under the hood:

1. You ran the Docker client with the `run` command.
2. The Docker client contacted the Docker daemon asking to create a container from the image called `hello-world`.
3. The Docker daemon checked if it contained the `hello-world` image locally and, since it didn't, requested the `hello-world` image from the remote Docker Hub registry.
4. The Docker Hub registry contained the `hello-world` image, so it was pulled into the Docker daemon.
5. The Docker daemon created a new container from the `hello-world` image that started the executable producing the output.
6. The Docker daemon streamed this output to the Docker client.
7. The Docker client sent it to your terminal.

The projected flow can be presented in the following diagram:

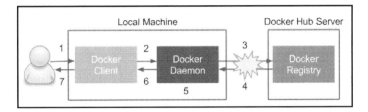

Let's look at each Docker component that was illustrated in this section.

Docker components

The official Docker page says this:

> *"Docker Engine is a client-server application that creates and manages Docker objects, such as images and containers."*

Let's sort out what this means.

Docker client and server

Let's look at a diagram that presents the Docker Engine architecture:

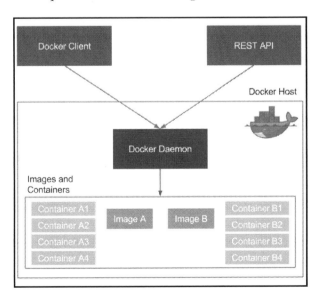

Docker Engine consists of three components:

- **Docker Daemon** (server) running in the background
- **Docker Client** running as a command tool
- **REST API**

Installing Docker Engine means installing all the components so that the Docker daemon runs on our computer all the time as a service. In the case of the `hello-world` example, we used the Docker client to interact with the Docker daemon; however, we could do exactly the same using REST API. Also, in the case of the hello-world example, we connected to the local Docker daemon; however, we could use the same client to interact with the Docker daemon running on a remote machine.

> To run the Docker container on a remote machine, you can use the –H option: `docker –H <server_ip>:2375 run hello-world`

Docker images and containers

An image is a stateless building block in the Docker world. You can imagine an image as a collection of all files necessary to run your application together with the recipe on how to run it. The image is stateless, so you can send it over the network, store it in the registry, name it, version it, and save it as a file. Images are layered, which means that you can build an image on top of another image.

A container is a running instance of an image. We can create many containers from the same image if we want to have many instances of the same application. Since containers are stateful, we can interact with them and make changes to their states.

Let's look at the example of a container and the image layers structure:

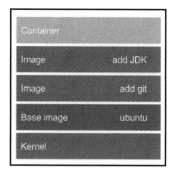

At the bottom, there is always the base image. In most cases, it represents an operating system, and we build our images on top of the existing base images. It's technically possible to create own base images however, this is rarely needed.

In our example, the `ubuntu` base image provides all the capabilities of the Ubuntu operating system. The `add git` image adds the Git toolkit. Then, there is an image adding the JDK environment. Finally, on the top, there is a container created from the `add JDK` image. Such container is able, for example, to download a Java project from the GitHub repository and compile it to a JAR file. As a result, we can use this container to compile and run Java projects without installing any tools on our operating system.

It is important to notice that layering is a very smart mechanism to save bandwidth and storage. Imagine that we have an application that is also based on `ubuntu`:

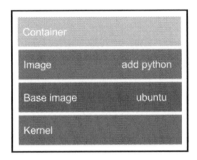

This time we will use the Python interpreter. While installing the `add python` image, the Docker daemon will note that the `ubuntu` image is already installed, and what it needs to do is only to add the `python` layer, which is very small. So, the `ubuntu` image is a dependency that is reused. The same if we would like to deploy our image in the network. When we deploy the Git and JDK application, we need to send the whole `ubuntu` image. However, while subsequently deploying the `python` application, we need to send just the small `add python` layer.

Docker applications

A lot of applications are provided in the form of Docker images that can be downloaded from the internet. If we knew the image name, then it would be enough to run it in the same way we did with the hello world example. How can we find the desired application image on the Docker Hub?

Let's take MongoDB as an example. If we like to find it on the Docker Hub, we have two options:

- Search on the Docker Hub Explore page (`https://hub.docker.com/explore/`)
- Use the `docker search` command

In the second case, we can perform the following operation:

```
$ docker search mongo
NAME DESCRIPTION STARS OFFICIAL AUTOMATED
mongo MongoDB document databases provide high av... 2821 [OK]
mongo-express Web-based MongoDB admin interface, written... 106 [OK]
mvertes/alpine-mongo light MongoDB container 39 [OK]
mongoclient/mongoclient Official docker image for Mongoclient, fea... 19
[OK]
...
```

There are many interesting options. How do we choose the best image? Usually, the most appealing one is the one without any prefix, since it means that it's an official Docker Hub image and should be therefore stable and maintained. The images with prefixes are unofficial, usually maintained as open source projects. In our case, the best choice seems to be mongo, so in order to run the MongoDB server, we can run the following command:

```
$ docker run mongo
Unable to find image 'mongo:latest' locally
latest: Pulling from library/mongo
5040bd298390: Pull complete
ef697e8d464e: Pull complete
67d7bf010c40: Pull complete
bb0b4f23ca2d: Pull complete
8efff42d23e5: Pull complete
11dec5aa0089: Pull complete
e76feb0ad656: Pull complete
5e1dcc6263a9: Pull complete
2855a823db09: Pull complete
Digest:
sha256:aff0c497cff4f116583b99b21775a8844a17bcf5c69f7f3f6028013bf0d6c00c
Status: Downloaded newer image for mongo:latest
2017-01-28T14:33:59.383+0000 I CONTROL [initandlisten] MongoDB starting :
pid=1 port=27017 dbpath=/data/db 64-bit host=0f05d9df0dc2
...
```

That's all, MongoDB has started. Running applications as Docker containers is that simple because we don't need to think of any dependencies; they are all delivered together with the image.

On the Docker Hub service, you can find a lot of applications; they store more than 100,000 different images.

Building images

Docker can be treated as a useful tool to run applications; however, the real power lies in building own Docker images that wrap the programs together with the environment. In this section, we will see how to do this using two different methods, the Docker `commit` command and the Dockerfile automated build.

Docker commit

Let's start with an example and prepare an image with the Git and JDK toolkits. We will use Ubuntu 16.04 as a base image. There is no need to create it; most base images are available in the Docker Hub registry:

1. Run a container from the `ubuntu:16.04` and connect it to its command line:

   ```
   $ docker run -i -t ubuntu:16.04 /bin/bash
   ```

   We've pulled the `ubuntu:16.04` image and run it as a container and then called the `/bin/bash` command in an interactive way (`-i` flag). You should see the terminal of the container. Since containers are stateful and writable, we can do anything we want in its terminal.

2. Install the Git toolkit:

   ```
   root@dee2cb192c6c:/# apt-get update
   root@dee2cb192c6c:/# apt-get install -y git
   ```

3. Check if the Git toolkit is installed:

   ```
   root@dee2cb192c6c:/# which git
   /usr/bin/git
   ```

4. Exit the container:

   ```
   root@dee2cb192c6c:/# exit
   ```

5. Check what has changed in the container comparing it to the `ubuntu` image:

```
$ docker diff dee2cb192c6c
```

The command should print a list of all files changed in the container.

6. Commit the container to the image:

```
$ docker commit dee2cb192c6c ubuntu_with_git
```

We've just created our first Docker image. Let's list all the images of our Docker host to see if the image is present:

```
$ docker images
REPOSITORY          TAG      IMAGE ID       CREATED             SIZE
ubuntu_with_git     latest   f3d674114fe2   About a minute ago  259.7 MB
ubuntu              16.04    f49eec89601e   7 days ago          129.5 MB
mongo               latest   0dffc7177b06   10 days ago         402 MB
hello-world         latest   48b5124b2768   2 weeks ago         1.84 kB
```

As expected, we see `hello-world`, `mongo` (installed before), `ubuntu` (base image pulled from Docker Hub), and freshly built `ubuntu_with_git`. By the way, we can observe the size of each image that corresponds to what we've installed on the image.

Now, if we create a container from the image, it will have the Git tool installed:

```
$ docker run -i -t ubuntu_with_git /bin/bash
root@3b0d1ff457d4:/# which git
/usr/bin/git
root@3b0d1ff457d4:/# exit
```

Using the exact same method, we can build `ubuntu_with_git_and_jdk` on top of the `ubuntu_with_git` image:

```
$ docker run -i -t ubuntu_with_git /bin/bash
root@6ee6401ed8b8:/# apt-get install -y openjdk-8-jdk
root@6ee6401ed8b8:/# exit
$ docker commit 6ee6401ed8b8 ubuntu_with_git_and_jdk
```

Dockerfile

Creating each Docker image manually with the commit command could be laborious, especially in the case of build automation and the Continuous Delivery process. Luckily, there is a built-in language to specify all the instructions that should be executed to build the Docker image.

Let's start with an example similar to the one with Git and JDK. This time, we will prepare the `ubuntu_with_python` image.

1. Create a new directory and a file called `Dockerfile` with the following content:

   ```
   FROM ubuntu:16.04
   RUN apt-get update && \
       apt-get install -y python
   ```

2. Run the command to create the `ubuntu_with_python` image:

   ```
   $ docker build -t ubuntu_with_python .
   ```

3. Check that the image was created:

   ```
   $ docker images
   REPOSITORY                 TAG      IMAGE ID       CREATED
   SIZE
   ubuntu_with_python         latest   d6e85f39f5b7   About a minute ago
   202.6 MB
   ubuntu_with_git_and_jdk latest    8464dc10abbb   3 minutes ago
   610.9 MB
   ubuntu_with_git            latest   f3d674114fe2   9 minutes ago
   259.7 MB
   ubuntu                     16.04    f49eec89601e   7 days ago
   129.5 MB
   mongo                      latest   0dffc7177b06   10 days ago
   402 MB
   hello-world                latest   48b5124b2768   2 weeks ago
   1.84 kB
   ```

We can now create a container from the image and check that the Python interpreter exists in exactly the same way we did after executing the `docker commit` command. Note that the `ubuntu` image is listed only once even though it's the base image for both `ubuntu_with_git` and `ubuntu_with_python`.

In this example, we used the first two Dockerfile instructions:

- FROM defines the image on top of which the new image will be built
- RUN specifies the commands to run inside the container

All Dockerfile instructions can be found on the official Docker page at `https://docs.docker.com/engine/reference/builder/`. The most widely-used instructions are as follows:

- `MAINTAINER` defines the metainformation about the author
- `COPY` copies a file or a directory into the filesystem of the image
- `ENTRYPOINT` defines which application should be run in the executable container

> A complete guide of all Dockerfile instructions can be found on the official Docker page at `https://docs.docker.com/engine/reference/builder/`.

Complete Docker application

We already have all the information necessary to build a fully working application as a Docker image. As an example, we will prepare, step by step, a simple Python hello world program. The same steps exist always, no matter what environment or programming language we use.

Write the application

Create a new directory and inside this directory, a `hello.py` file with the following content:

```
print "Hello World from Python!"
```

Close the file. This is the source code of our application.

Prepare the environment

Our environment will be expressed in the Dockerfile. We need the instructions to define:

- what base image should be used
- (optionally) who the maintainer is
- how to install the Python interpreter
- how to include `hello.py` in the image
- how to start the application

In the same directory, create the Dockerfile:

```
FROM ubuntu:16.04
MAINTAINER Rafal Leszko
RUN apt-get update && \
    apt-get install -y python
COPY hello.py .
ENTRYPOINT ["python", "hello.py"]
```

Build the image

Now, we can build the image exactly the same way we did before:

```
$ docker build -t hello_world_python .
```

Run the application

We run the application by running the container:

```
$ docker run hello_world_python
```

You should see the friendly **Hello World from Python!** message. The most interesting thing in this example is that we are able to run the application written in Python without having the Python interpreter installed in our host system. This is possible because the application packed as an image has all the environment needed inside.

> An image with the Python interpreter already exists in the Docker Hub service, so in the real-life scenario, it would be enough to use it.

Environment variables

We've run our first home-made Docker application. However, what if the execution of the application should depend on some conditions?

For example, in the case of the production server, we would like to print Hello to the logs, not to the console, or we may want to have different dependent services during the testing phase and the production phase. One solution would be to prepare a separate Dockerfile for each case; however, there is a better way, environment variables.

Let's change our hello world application to print `Hello World from <name_passed_as_environment_variable>` !. In order to do this, we need to proceed with the following steps:

1. Change the Python script to use the environment variable:

   ```
   import os
   print "Hello World from %s !" % os.environ['NAME']
   ```

2. Build the image:

   ```
   $ docker build -t hello_world_python_name .
   ```

3. Run the container passing environment variable:

   ```
   $ docker run -e NAME=Rafal hello_world_python_name
   Hello World from Rafal !
   ```

4. Alternatively, we can define the environment variable value in Dockerfile, for example:

   ```
   ENV NAME Rafal
   ```

5. Then, we can run the container without specifying the -e option.

   ```
   $ docker build -t hello_world_python_name_default .
   $ docker run hello_world_python_name_default
   Hello World from Rafal !
   ```

Environment variables are especially useful when we need to have different versions of the Docker container depending on its purpose, for example, to have separate profiles for production and testing servers.

 If the environment variable is defined both in Dockerfile and as a flag, then the command flag takes precedence.

Docker container states

Every application we've run so far was supposed to do some work and stop. For example, we've printed `Hello from Docker!` and exited. There are, however, applications that should run continuously such as services. To run a container in the background, we can use the `-d` (`--detach`) option. Let's try it with the `ubuntu` image:

```
$ docker run -d -t ubuntu:16.04
```

This command started the Ubuntu container but did not attach the console to it. We can see that it's running using the following command:

```
$ docker ps
CONTAINER ID IMAGE          COMMAND      STATUS PORTS NAMES
95f29bfbaadc ubuntu:16.04 "/bin/bash" Up 5 seconds kickass_stonebraker
```

This command prints all containers that are in the running state. What about our old, already-exited containers? We can find them by printing all containers:

```
$ docker ps -a
CONTAINER ID IMAGE              COMMAND           STATUS PORTS   NAMES
95f29bfbaadc ubuntu:16.04 "/bin/bash"       Up 33 seconds kickass_stonebraker
34080d914613 hello_world_python_name_default "python hello.py" Exited
lonely_newton
7ba49e8ee677 hello_world_python_name "python hello.py" Exited mad_turing
dd5eb1ed81c3 hello_world_python "python hello.py" Exited thirsty_bardeen
6ee6401ed8b8 ubuntu_with_git "/bin/bash" Exited      grave_nobel
3b0d1ff457d4 ubuntu_with_git "/bin/bash" Exited      desperate_williams
dee2cb192c6c ubuntu:16.04 "/bin/bash"    Exited      small_dubinsky
0f05d9df0dc2 mongo          "/entrypoint.sh mongo" Exited trusting_easley
47ba1c0ba90e hello-world  "/hello"        Exited      tender_bell
```

Note that all the old containers are in the exited state. There are two more states we haven't observed yet: paused and restarting.

All of the states and the transitions between them are presented in the following diagram:

Pausing Docker containers is very rare, and technically, it's realized by freezing the processes using the SIGSTOP signal. Restarting is a temporary state when the container is run with the `--restart` option to define the restarting strategy (the Docker daemon is able to automatically restart the container in case of failure).

The diagram also shows the Docker commands used to change the Docker container state from one to another.

For example, we can stop the running Ubuntu container:

```
$ docker stop 95f29bfbaadc

$ docker ps
CONTAINER ID IMAGE COMMAND CREATED STATUS PORTS NAMES
```

> We always used the `docker run` command to create and start the container; however, it's possible to just create the container without starting it.

Docker networking

Most applications these days do not run in isolation but need to communicate with other systems over the network. If we want to run a website, web service, database, or a cache server inside a Docker container, then we need to understand at least the basics of Docker networking.

Running services

Let's start with a simple example, and run a Tomcat server directly from Docker Hub:

```
$ docker run -d tomcat
```

Tomcat is a web application server whose user interface can be accessed by the port 8080. Therefore, if we installed Tomcat on our machine, we could browse it at http://localhost:8080.

In our case, however, Tomcat is running inside the Docker container. We started it the same way we did with the first Hello World example. We can see it's running:

```
$ docker ps
CONTAINER ID IMAGE    COMMAND            STATUS              PORTS    NAMES
d51ad8634fac tomcat   "catalina.sh run"  Up About a minute  8080/tcp
jovial_kare
```

Since it's run as a daemon (with the −d option), we don't see the logs in the console right away. We can, however, access it by executing the following code:

```
$ docker logs d51ad8634fac
```

If there are no errors, we should see a lot of logs that concludes Tomcat has been started and is accessible via port 8080. We can try going to http://localhost:8080, but we won't be able to connect. The reason for this is that Tomcat has been started inside the container and we're trying to reach it from the outside. In other words, we can reach it only if we connect with the command to the console in the container and check it there. How to make the running Tomcat accessible from outside?

We need to start the container specifying the port mapping with the −p (−−publish) flag:

```
-p, --publish <host_port>:<container_port>
```

So, let's first stop the running container and start a new one:

```
$ docker stop d51ad8634fac
$ docker run -d -p 8080:8080 tomcat
```

After waiting a few seconds, Tomcat must have started and we should be able to open its page, `http://localhost:8080`.

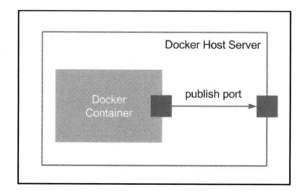

Such a simple port mapping command is sufficient in most common Docker use cases. We are able to deploy (micro) services as Docker containers and expose their ports to enable communication. However, let's dive a little deeper into what happened under the hood.

Docker allows publishing to the specified host network interface with `-p <ip>:<host_port>:<container_port>`.

Container networks

We have connected to the application running inside the container. In fact, the connection is two-way, because if you remember our previous examples, we executed the `apt-get install` commands from inside and the packages were downloaded from the internet. How is this possible?

If you check the network interfaces on your machine, you can see that one of the interfaces is called `docker0`:

```
$ ifconfig docker0
docker0 Link encap:Ethernet HWaddr 02:42:db:d0:47:db
      inet addr:172.17.0.1 Bcast:0.0.0.0 Mask:255.255.0.0
...
```

The docker0 interface is created by the Docker daemon in order to connect with the Docker container. Now, we can see what interfaces are created inside the Docker container with the docker inspect command:

```
$ docker inspect 03d1e6dc4d9e
```

It prints all the information about the container configuration in the JSON format. Among others, we can find the part related to the network settings:

```
"NetworkSettings": {
    "Bridge": "",
    "Ports": {
        "8080/tcp": [
            {
                "HostIp": "0.0.0.0",
                "HostPort": "8080"
            }
        ]
    },
    "Gateway": "172.17.0.1",
    "IPAddress": "172.17.0.2",
    "IPPrefixLen": 16,
}
```

In order to filter the docker inspect response, we can use the --format option, for example, docker inspect --format '{{ .NetworkSettings.IPAddress }}' <container_id>.

We can observe that the Docker container has the IP address 172.17.0.2 and it communicates with the Docker host with the IP address 172.17.0.1. This means that in our previous example, we could access the Tomcat server even without the port forwarding, using the address http://172.17.0.2:8080. Nevertheless, in most cases, we run the Docker container on a server machine and want to expose it outside, so we need to use the -p option.

Note that by default, the containers are protected by the host's firewall system and don't open any routes from external systems. We can change this default behavior by playing with the `--network` flag and setting it as follows:

- `bridge` (default): network via the default Docker bridge
- `none`: no network
- `container`: network joined with the other (specified) container
- `host`: host network (no firewall)

The different networks can be listed and managed by the `docker network` command:

```
$ docker network ls
NETWORK ID     NAME     DRIVER SCOPE
b3326cb44121 bridge bridge local
84136027df04 host    host    local
80c26af0351c none    null    local
```

If we specify `none` as the network, then we will not be able to connect to the container, and vice versa; the container has no network access to the external world. The `host` option makes the container network interfaces identical to the host. They share the same IP addresses, so everything started on the container is visible outside. The most often used option is the default one (`bridge`) because it lets us define explicitly which ports should be published. It is both secure and accessible.

Exposing container ports

We mentioned a few times that the container exposes the port. In fact, if we dug deeper into the Tomcat image on GitHub (`https://github.com/docker-library/tomcat`), we can notice the following line in the Dockerfile:

```
EXPOSE 8080
```

This Dockerfile instruction expresses that the port 8080 should be exposed from the container. However, as we have already seen, this doesn't mean that the port is automatically published. The EXPOSE instruction only informs the users which ports they should publish.

Automatic port assignment

Let's try to run the second Tomcat container without stopping the first one:

```
$ docker run -d -p 8080:8080 tomcat
0835c95538aeca79e0305b5f19a5f96cb00c5d1c50bed87584cfca8ec790f241
docker: Error response from daemon: driver failed programming external
connectivity on endpoint distracted_heyrovsky
(1b1cee9896ed99b9b804e4c944a3d9544adf72f1ef3f9c9f37bc985e9c30f452): Bind
for 0.0.0.0:8080 failed: port is already allocated.
```

This error may be common. In such cases, we have to either take care of the uniqueness of the ports on our own or let Docker assign the ports automatically using one of the following versions of the `publish` command:

- `-p <container_port>`: publish the container port to the unused host port
- `-P` (`--publish-all`): publish all ports exposed by the container to the unused host ports:

  ```
  $ docker run -d -P tomcat
  078e9d12a1c8724f8aa27510a6390473c1789aa49e7f8b14ddfaaa328c8f737b

  $ docker port 078e9d12a1c8
  8080/tcp -> 0.0.0.0:32772
  ```

We can see that the second Tomcat has been published to port 32772, so it can be browsed at http://localhost:32772.

Using Docker volumes

Imagine that you would like to run the database as a container. You can start such a container and enter the data. Where is it stored? What happens when you stop the container or remove it? You can start the new one, but the database will be empty again. Unless it's your testing environment, you don't expect such a scenario.

Docker volume is the Docker host's directory mounted inside the container. It allows the container to write to the host's filesystem as it was writing to its own. The mechanism is presented in the following diagram:

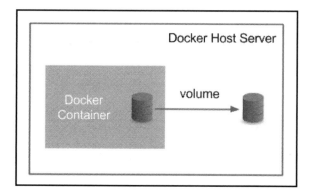

Docker volume enables the persistence and sharing of the container's data. Volumes also clearly separate the processing from the data.

Let's start with an example and specify the volume with the `-v` `<host_path>:<container_path>` option and connect to the container:

```
$ docker run -i -t -v ~/docker_ubuntu:/host_directory ubuntu:16.04
/bin/bash
```

Now, we can create an empty file in `host_directory` in the container:

```
root@01bf73826624:/# touch host_directory/file.txt
```

Let's check if the file was created in the Docker host's filesystem:

```
root@01bf73826624:/# exit
exit

$ ls ~/docker_ubuntu/
file.txt
```

We can see that the filesystem was shared and the data was therefore persisted permanently. We can now stop the container and run a new one to see that our file will still be there:

```
$ docker stop 01bf73826624

$ docker run -i -t -v ~/docker_ubuntu:/host_directory ubuntu:16.04
/bin/bash
root@a9e0df194f1f:/# ls host_directory/
```

```
file.txt

root@a9e0df194f1f:/# exit
```

Instead of specifying the volume with the −v flag, it's possible to specify the volume as an instruction in the Dockerfile, for example:

```
VOLUME /host_directory
```

In this case, if we run the docker container without the −v flag, then the container's /host_directory will be mapped into the host's default directory for volumes, /var/lib/docker/vfs/. This is a good solution if you deliver an application as an image and you know it needs the permanent storage for some reason (for example, storing application logs).

If the volume is defined both in Dockerfile and as a flag, then the command flag takes precedence.

Docker volumes can be much more complicated, especially in the case of databases. More complex use cases of the Docker volume are, however, out of the scope of this book.

A very common approach to data management with Docker is to introduce an additional layer in the form of data volume containers. A data volume container is a Docker container whose only purpose is to declare the volume. Then, other containers can use it (with the −−volumes-from <container> option) instead of declaring the volume directly. Read more at https://docs.docker.com/engine/tutorials/dockervolumes/#creating-and-mounting-a-data-volume-container.

Using names in Docker

So far, when we operated on the containers, we always used autogenerated names. This approach has some advantages, such as the names being unique (no naming conflicts) and automatic (no need to do anything). In many cases, however, it's better to give a real user-friendly name for the container or the image.

Naming containers

There are two good reasons to name the container: convenience and the possibility of automation:

- Convenience, because it's simpler to make any operations on the container addressing it by name than checking the hashes or the autogenerated name
- Automation, because sometimes we would like to depend on the specific naming of the container

For example, we would like to have containers that depend on each other and to have one linked to another. Therefore, we need to know their names.

To name a container, we use the `--name` parameter:

```
$ docker run -d --name tomcat tomcat
```

We can check (by `docker ps`) that the container has a meaningful name. Also, as a result, any operation can be performed using the container's name, for example:

```
$ docker logs tomcat
```

Please note that when the container is named, it does not lose its identity. We can still address the container by its autogenerated hash ID like we did before.

> The container always has both ID and name. It can be addressed by any of them and both of them are unique.

Tagging images

Images can be tagged. We've already done this while creating our own images, for example, in the case of building the `hello-world_python` image:

```
$ docker build -t hello-world_python .
```

The `-t` flag describes the tag of the image. If we didn't use it, then the image would be built without any tags and, as a result, we would have to address it by its ID (hash) in order to run the container.

The image can have multiple tags, and they should follow the naming convention:

```
<registry_address>/<image_name>:<version>
```

The tag consists of the following parts:

- `registry_address`: IP and port of the registry or the alias name
- `image_name`: name of the image that is built, for example, `ubuntu`
- `version`: a version of the image in any form, for example, 16.04, 20170310

We will cover Docker registries in `Chapter 5`, *Automated Acceptance Testing*. If the image is kept on the official Docker Hub registry, then we can skip the registry address. This is why we've run the `tomcat` image without any prefix. The last version is always tagged as the latest and it can also be skipped, so we've run the `tomcat` image without any suffix.

Images usually have multiple tags, for example, all four tags are the same image: `ubuntu:16.04`, `ubuntu:xenial-20170119`, `ubuntu:xenial`, and `ubuntu:latest`.

Docker cleanup

Throughout this chapter, we have created a number of containers and images. This is, however, only a small part of what you will see in real-life scenarios. Even when the containers are not running at the moment, they need to be stored on the Docker host. This can quickly result in exceeding the storage space and stopping the machine. How can we approach this concern?

Cleaning up containers

First, let's look at the containers that are stored on our machine. To print all the containers (no matter of their state), we can use the `docker ps -a` command:

```
$ docker ps -a
CONTAINER ID IMAGE        COMMAND            STATUS     PORTS     NAMES
95c2d6c4424e tomcat       "catalina.sh run"  Up 5 minutes 8080/tcp tomcat
a9e0df194f1f ubuntu:16.04 "/bin/bash"        Exited               jolly_archimedes
01bf73826624 ubuntu:16.04 "/bin/bash"        Exited               suspicious_feynman
078e9d12a1c8 tomcat       "catalina.sh run"  Up 14 minutes 0.0.0.0:32772->8080/tcp
nauseous_fermi
0835c95538ae tomcat       "catalina.sh run"  Created              distracted_heyrovsky
03d1e6dc4d9e tomcat       "catalina.sh run"  Up 50 minutes 0.0.0.0:8080->8080/tcp
drunk_ritchie
d51ad8634fac tomcat       "catalina.sh run"  Exited               jovial_kare
95f29bfbaadc ubuntu:16.04 "/bin/bash"        Exited               kickass_stonebraker
```

```
34080d914613 hello_world_python_name_default "python hello.py" Exited
lonely_newton
7ba49e8ee677 hello_world_python_name "python hello.py" Exited mad_turing
dd5eb1ed81c3 hello_world_python "python hello.py" Exited thirsty_bardeen
6ee6401ed8b8 ubuntu_with_git "/bin/bash" Exited        grave_nobel
3b0d1ff457d4 ubuntu_with_git "/bin/bash" Exited        desperate_williams
dee2cb192c6c ubuntu:16.04 "/bin/bash" Exited           small_dubinsky
0f05d9df0dc2 mongo  "/entrypoint.sh mongo" Exited      trusting_easley
47ba1c0ba90e hello-world "/hello"       Exited         tender_bell
```

In order to delete a stopped container, we can use the `docker rm` command (if the container is running, we need to stop it first):

```
$ docker rm 47ba1c0ba90e
```

If we want to remove all stopped containers, we can use the following command:

```
$ docker rm $(docker ps --no-trunc -aq)
```

The `-aq` option specifies to pass only IDs (no additional data) for all containers. Additionally, `--no-trunc` asks Docker not to truncate the output.

We can also adopt a different approach and ask the container to remove itself, when it's stopped using the `--rm` flag, for example:

```
$ docker run --rm hello-world
```

In most real-life scenarios, we don't use the stopped containers, and they are left only for the debugging purpose.

Cleaning up images

Images are just as important as containers. They can occupy a lot of space, especially in the case of the Continuous Delivery process, when each build ends up in a new Docker image. This can quickly result in the **no space left on device** error. To check all the images in the Docker container, we can use the `docker images` command:

```
$ docker images
REPOSITORY TAG                           IMAGE ID      CREATED      SIZE
hello_world_python_name_default latest 9a056ca92841 2 hours ago 202.6 MB
hello_world_python_name latest          72c8c50ffa89 2 hours ago 202.6 MB
hello_world_python latest               3e1fa5c29b44 2 hours ago 202.6 MB
ubuntu_with_python latest               d6e85f39f5b7 2 hours ago 202.6 MB
ubuntu_with_git_and_jdk latest          8464dc10abbb 2 hours ago 610.9 MB
ubuntu_with_git latest                  f3d674114fe2 3 hours ago 259.7 MB
tomcat latest                           c822d296d232 2 days ago  355.3 MB
```

```
ubuntu 16.04                 f49eec89601e 7 days ago  129.5 MB
mongo latest                 0dffc7177b06 11 days ago 402 MB
hello-world latest           48b5124b2768 2 weeks ago 1.84 kB
```

To remove an image, we can call the following command:

```
$ docker rmi 48b5124b2768
```

In the case of images, the automatic cleanup process is slightly more complex. Images don't have states, so we cannot ask them to remove themselves when not used. The common strategy would be to set up the Cron cleanup job, which removes all old and unused images. We could do this using the following command:

```
$ docker rmi $(docker images -q)
```

In order to prevent removing the images with tags (for example, to not remove all the latest images), it's very common to use the dangling parameter:

```
$ docker rmi $(docker images -f "dangling=true" -q)
```

 If we have containers that use volumes, then, in addition to images and containers, it's worth to think about cleaning up volumes. The easiest way to do this is to use the docker volume ls -qf dangling=true | xargs -r docker volume rm command.

Docker commands overview

All Docker commands can be found by executing the following help command:

```
$ docker help
```

To see all the options of any particular Docker command, we can use docker help <command>, for example:

```
$ docker help run
```

There is also a very good explanation of all Docker commands on the official Docker page https://docs.docker.com/engine/reference/commandline/docker/. It's really worth reading or at least skimming through.

In this chapter, we've covered the most useful commands and their options. As a quick reminder, let's walk through them:

Command	Explanation
`docker build`	Build an image from a Dockerfile
`docker commit`	Create an image from the container
`docker diff`	Show changes in the container
`docker images`	List images
`docker info`	Display Docker information
`docker inspect`	Show the configuration of the Docker image/container
`docker logs`	Show logs of the container
`docker network`	Manage networks
`docker port`	Show all exposed ports by the container
`docker ps`	List containers
`docker rm`	Remove container
`docker rmi`	Remove image
`docker run`	Run a container from the image
`docker search`	Search for the Docker image in Docker Hub
`docker start/stop/pause/unpause`	Manage the container's state

Exercises

We've covered a lot of material in this chapter. To make well-remembered, we recommend two exercises.

1. Run CouchDB as a Docker container and publish its port:

> You can use the docker search command to find the CouchDB image.

   - Run the container
   - Publish the CouchDB port
   - Open the browser and check that CouchDB is available

2. Create a Docker image with the REST service replying Hello World! to localhost:8080/hello. Use any language and framework you prefer:

> The easiest way to create a REST service is to use Python with the Flask framework, http://flask.pocoo.org/. Note that a lot of web frameworks start the application on the localhost interface only by default. In order to publish a port, it's necessary to start it on all interfaces (app.run(host='0.0.0.0') in the case of a Flask framework).

   - Create a web service application
   - Create a Dockerfile to install dependencies and libraries
   - Build the image
   - Run the container publishing the port
   - Check if it's running correctly using the browser

Summary

In this chapter, we have covered the Docker basics that are enough to build images and run applications as containers. The key takeaway, from the chapter are the following points:

- The containerization technology addresses the issues of isolation and environment dependencies using the Linux kernel features. This is based on the process separation mechanism, therefore no real performance drop is observed.
- Docker can be installed on most of the systems but is supported natively only on Linux.
- Docker allows running applications from the images available on the internet and to build own images.
- An image is an application packed together with all dependencies.
- Docker provides two methods for building the images: Dockerfile or committing the container. In most cases, the first option is used.
- Docker containers can communicate over the network by publishing the ports they expose.
- Docker containers can share the persistent storage using volumes.
- For the purpose of convenience, Docker containers should be named, and Docker images should be tagged. In the Docker world, there is a specific convention of how to tag images.
- Docker images and containers should be cleaned from time to time in order to save the server space and avoid the *no space left on device* error.

In the next chapter, we will cover Jenkins configuration and the way Jenkins can be used together with Docker.

3

Configuring Jenkins

We have seen how to configure and use Docker. In this chapter, we will present Jenkins, which can be used separately or together with Docker. We will show that the combination of these two tools outcomes in the surprisingly good results: automated configuration and flexible scalability.

This chapter covers the following topics:

- Introducing Jenkins and its advantages
- Installing and starting Jenkins
- Creating the first pipeline
- Scaling Jenkins with agents
- Configuring Docker-based agents
- Building custom master and slave Docker images
- Configuring strategies for the security and backup

What is Jenkins?

Jenkins is an open source automation server written in Java. With the very active community-based support and a huge number of plugins, it is the most popular tool to implement the Continuous Integration and Continuous Delivery processes. Formerly known as Hudson, it was renamed after Oracle bought Hudson and decided to develop it as the proprietary software. Jenkins remained under the MIT license and is highly valued for its simplicity, flexibility, and versatility.

Jenkins outstands other Continuous Integration tools and is the most widely used software of its kind. That is all possible because of its features and capabilities.

Let's walk through the most interesting parts of the Jenkins' characteristics.

- **Language agnostic**: Jenkins has a lot of plugins, which support most of the programming languages and frameworks. Moreover, since it can use any shell command and any software installed, it is suitable for every automation process that can be imagined.
- **Extensible by plugins**: Jenkins has a great community and a lot of plugins available (1000 plus). It also allows you to write your own plugins in order to customize Jenkins for your needs.
- **Portable**: Jenkins is written in Java, so it can be run on any operating system. For convenience, it is also delivered in a lot of versions: web application archive (WAR), Docker image, Windows binary, Mac binary, and Linux binaries.
- **Supports most SCM**: Jenkins integrates with virtually every source code management or build tool that exists. Again, because of its wide community and plugins, there is no other continuous integration tool that supports so many external systems.
- **Distributed**: Jenkins has a built-in mechanism for the master/slave mode, which distributes its executions across multiple nodes located on multiple machines. It can also use heterogeneous environment, for example, different nodes can have different operating system installed.
- **Simplicity**: The installation and configuration process is simple. There is no need to configure any additional software, nor the database. It can be configured completely via GUI, XML, or Groovy scripts.
- **Code-oriented**: Jenkins pipelines are defined as code. Also, the Jenkins itself can be configured using XML files or Groovy scripts. That allows keeping the configuration in the source code repository and helps in the automation of the Jenkins configuration.

Jenkins installation

The Jenkins installation process is quick and simple. There are different methods to do it, but since we're already familiar with the Docker tool and the benefits it gives, we will start from the Docker-based solution. This is also the easiest, the most predictable, and the smartest way to go. However, let's mention the installation requirements first.

Requirements for installation

The minimal system requirements are relatively low:

- Java 8
- 256MB free memory
- 1 GB+ free disk space

However, it's essential to understand that the requirements strictly depend on what you plan to do with Jenkins. If Jenkins is used to serve the whole team as the Continuous Integration server, then even in case of a small team, it's advised to have 1 GB plus free memory and 50 GB plus free disk space. Needless to say, Jenkins also performs some computations and transfers a lot of data across the network, so CPU and bandwidth are crucial.

> To get a feeling what could be the requirements in case of a big company, the Netflix example is presented in the *Jenkins architecture* section.

Installing on Docker

Let's see the step-by-step procedure to install Jenkins using Docker.

The Jenkins image is available in the official Docker Hub registry, so in order to install it we should execute the following command:

```
$ docker run -p <host_port>:8080 -v <host_volume>:/var/jenkins_home
jenkins:2.60.1
```

We need to specify the first `host_port` parameter—the port under which Jenkins is visible outside of the container. The second parameter, `host_volume`, specifies the directory where the Jenkins home is mapped. It needs to be specified as volume, and therefore persisted permanently, because it contains the configuration, pipeline builds, and logs.

As an example, let's see what the installation steps would look like in case of the Docker host on Linux/Ubuntu.

1. **Prepare the volume directory**: We need a separate directory with the admin ownership to keep the Jenkins home. Let's prepare one with the following commands:

```
$ mkdir $HOME/jenkins_home
$ chown 1000 $HOME/jenkins_home
```

2. **Run the Jenkins container**: Let's run the container as a daemon and give it a proper name:

```
$ docker run -d -p 49001:8080
-v $HOME/jenkins_home:/var/jenkins_home --name
jenkins jenkins:2.60.1
```

3. **Check if Jenkins is running**: After a moment, we can check whether Jenkins has started correctly by printing the logs:

```
$ docker logs jenkins
Running from: /usr/share/jenkins/jenkins.war
webroot: EnvVars.masterEnvVars.get("JENKINS_HOME")
Feb 04, 2017 9:01:32 AM Main deleteWinstoneTempContents
WARNING: Failed to delete the temporary Winstone file
/tmp/winstone/jenkins.war
Feb 04, 2017 9:01:32 AM org.eclipse.jetty.util.log.JavaUtilLog info
INFO: Logging initialized @888ms
Feb 04, 2017 9:01:32 AM winstone.Logger logInternal
...
```

In the production environment, you may also want to set up the reverse proxy in order to hide the Jenkins infrastructure behind the proxy server. The short description how to do it using the Nginx server can be found at https://wiki.jenkins-ci.org/display/JENKINS/ Installing+Jenkins+with+Docker.

After performing these few steps, Jenkins is ready to use. The Docker-based installation has two major advantages:

- **Failure recovery**: If Jenkins crashes, then it's enough to run a new container with the same volume specified.
- **Custom images**: You can configure Jenkins as per your needs and store it as the Jenkins image. Then it can be shared within your organization or team, and there is no need to repeat the same configuration steps all the time, many times.

Everywhere in this book, we use Jenkins in version 2.60.1.

Installing without Docker

For the reasons mentioned earlier, the Docker installation is recommended. However, if it's not an option or there are other reasons to proceed otherwise, then the installation process is just as simple. As an example, in case of Ubuntu, it's enough to run:

```
$ wget -q -O - https://pkg.jenkins.io/debian/jenkins.io.key | sudo apt-key
add -
$ sudo sh -c 'echo deb http://pkg.jenkins.io/debian-stable binary/ >
/etc/apt/sources.list.d/jenkins.list'
$ sudo apt-get update
$ sudo apt-get install jenkins
```

 All installation guides (Ubuntu, Mac, Windows, and others) can be found on the official Jenkins page https://jenkins.io/doc/book/getting-started/installing/.

Initial configuration

No matter which installation you choose, the first start of Jenkins requires a few configuration steps. Let's walk through them step by step:

1. Open Jenkins in the browser: http://localhost:49001 (for binary installations, the default port is 8080).

2. Jenkins should ask for the administrator password. It can be found in the Jenkins logs:

```
$ docker logs jenkins
...
Jenkins initial setup is required. An admin user has been created
and a password generated.
Please use the following password to proceed to installation:

c50508effc6843a1a7b06f6491ed0ca6

...
```

3. After accepting the initial password, Jenkins asks whether to install the suggested plugins, which are adjusted to the most common use cases. Your answer depends, of course, on your needs. However, as the first Jenkins installation, it's reasonable to let Jenkins install all the recommended plugins.

4. After the plugin installation, Jenkins asks to set up username, password, and other basic information. If you skip it, the token from step 2 will be used as the admin password.

The installation is complete and you should see the Jenkins dashboard:

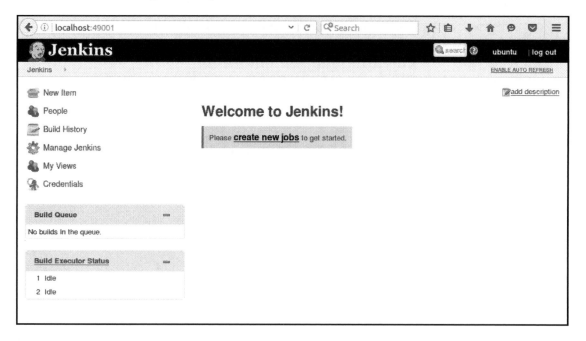

We are ready to use Jenkins and create the first pipeline.

Jenkins hello world

Everything in the entire IT world starts from the Hello World example.

Let's follow this rule and see the steps to create the first Jenkins pipeline:

1. Click on **New Item**.
2. Enter `hello world` as the item name, choose **Pipeline**, and click on **OK**.
3. There are a lot of options. We will skip them for now and go directly to the **Pipeline** section.
4. There, in the **Script** textbox, we can enter the pipeline script:

```
pipeline {
    agent any
    stages {
        stage("Hello") {
            steps {
                echo 'Hello World'
            }
        }
    }
}
```

5. Click on **Save**.
6. Click on **Build Now**.

We should see **#1** under the **Build History**. If we click on it, and then on **Console Output**, we will see the log from the Pipeline build.

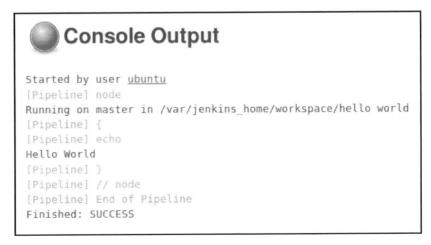

We have just seen the first example and its successful output means that Jenkins is installed correctly. Now, let's move to slightly more advanced Jenkins configuration.

 We will describe more on the pipeline syntax in `Chapter 4`, *Continuous Integration Pipeline*.

Jenkins architecture

The hello world job executed in almost no time at all. However, the pipelines are usually more complex and spend time on tasks such as downloading files from the internet, compiling the source code, or running tests. One build can take from minutes to hours.

In common scenarios, there are also many concurrent pipelines. Usually, the whole team, or even the whole organization, uses the same Jenkins instance. How to ensure that the builds will run quickly and smoothly?

Master and slaves

Jenkins becomes overloaded sooner than it seems. Even in case of a small (micro) service, the build can take a few minutes. That means that one team committing frequently can easily kill the Jenkins instance.

For that reason, unless the project is really small, Jenkins should not execute builds at all, but delegate them to the slave (agent) instances. To be precise, the Jenkins we're currently running is called the Jenkins master and it can delegate to the Jenkins agents.

Let's look at the diagram presenting the master-slave interaction:

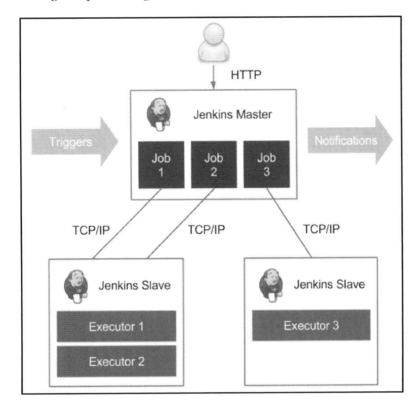

In a distributed builds environment, the Jenkins master is responsible for:

- Receiving build triggers (for example, after a commit to GitHub)
- Sending notifications (for example, email or HipChat message sent after the build failure)
- Handling HTTP requests (interaction with clients)
- Managing the build environment (orchestrating the job executions on slaves)

The build agent is a machine that take care of everything that happens after the build is started.

Since the responsibilities of the master and the slaves are different, they have different environmental requirements:

- **Master**: This is usually (unless the project is really small) a dedicated machine with RAM ranging from 200 MB for small projects to 70GB plus for huge single-master projects.
- **Slave**: There are no general requirements (other than the fact that it should be capable of executing a single build, for example, if the project is a huge monolith that requires 100 GB of RAM, then the slave machine needs to satisfy these needs).

Agents should also be as generic as possible. For instance, if we have different projects: one in Java, one in Python, and one in Ruby, then it would be perfect if each agent could build any of these projects. In such a case, the agents can be interchanged, which helps to optimize the usage of resources.

 If agents cannot be generic enough to match all projects, then it's possible to label (tag) agents and projects, so that the given build would be executed on a given type of agent.

Scalability

We can use Jenkins slaves to balance the load and scale up the Jenkins infrastructure. Such a process is called the horizontal scaling. The other possibility would be to use only one master node and increase resources of its machine. That process is called the vertical scaling. Let's look closer at these two concepts.

Vertical scaling

Vertical scaling means that, when the master's load grows, then more resources are applied to the master's machine. So, when new projects appear in our organization, we buy more RAM, add CPU cores, and extend the HDD drives. This may sound like a no-go solution; however, it's often used, even by well-known organizations. Having a single Jenkins master set on the ultra-efficient hardware has one very strong advantage: maintenance. Any upgrades, scripts, security settings, roles assignment, or plugin installations have to be done in one place only.

Horizontal scaling

Horizontal scaling means that, when an organization grows, then more master instances are launched. This requires a smart allocation of instances to teams and, in the extreme case, each team can have its own Jenkins master. In that case, it might even happen that no slaves are needed.

The drawbacks are that it may be difficult to automate cross-project integrations and that a part of the team's development time is spent on the Jenkins maintenance. However, the horizontal scaling has some significant advantages:

- Master machines don't need to be special in terms of hardware
- Different teams can have different Jenkins settings (for example, different set of plugins)
- Teams usually feel better and work with Jenkins more efficiently if the instance is their own
- If one master instance is down, it does not impact the whole organization
- The infrastructure can be segregated into standard and mission-critical
- Some maintenance aspects can be simplified, for example, the team of five could reuse the same Jenkins password, so we may skip the roles and security settings (surely that is possible only if the corporate network is well firewalled)

Test and production instances

Apart from the scaling approach, there is one more issue: how to test the Jenkins upgrades, new plugins, or pipeline definitions? Jenkins is critical to the whole company. It guarantees the quality of the software and (in case of Continuous Delivery) deploys to the production servers. That is why it needs to be highly available, so it is definitely not for the purpose of testing. It means there should always be two instances of the same Jenkins infrastructure: test and production.

 Test environment should always be as similar as possible to the production, so it also requires the similar number of agents attached.

Sample architecture

We already know that there should be slaves, (possibly multiple) master(s), and that everything should be duplicated into the test and production environments. However, what would the complete picture look like?

Luckily, there are a lot of companies that published how they used Jenkins and what kind of architectures they created. It would be difficult to measure if more of them preferred vertical or horizontal scaling, but it ranged from having only one master instance to having one master for each team.

Let's look at the example of Netflix to have a complete picture of the Jenkins infrastructure (they shared it as the **planned infrastructure** at Jenkins User Conference San Francisco 2012):

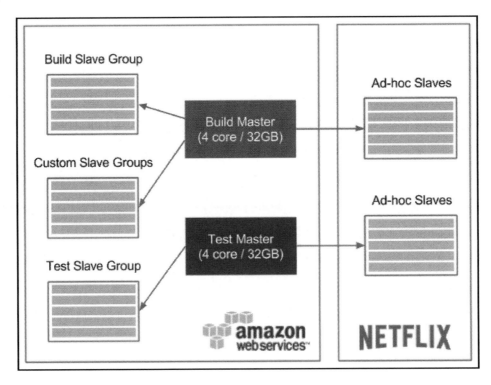

They have test and production master instances, each of them owning a poll of slaves and additional ad hoc slaves. Altogether, it serves around 2000 builds per day. Note also that a part of their infrastructure is hosted on AWS and a part is on their own servers.

We should already have at least a rough idea of what the Jenkins infrastructure can look like depending on the type of the organization.

Let's now focus on the practical aspects of setting the agents.

Configuring agents

We've seen what the agents are and when they can be used. However, how to set up an agent and let it communicate with the master? Let's start with the second part of the question and describe the communication protocols between the master and the agent.

Communication protocols

In order for the master and the agent to communicate, the bi-directional connection has to be established.

There are different options how it can be initiated:

- **SSH**: Master connects to slave using the standard SSH protocol. Jenkins has an SSH-client built-in, so the only requirement is the SSHD server configured on slaves. This is the most convenient and stable method because it uses standard Unix mechanisms.
- **Java Web Start**: Java application is started on each agent machine and the TCP connection is established between the Jenkins slave application and the master Java application. This method is often used if the agents are inside the firewalled network and the master cannot initiate the connection.
- **Windows service**: The master registers an agent on the remote machine as a Windows service. This method is discouraged since the setup is tricky and there are limitations on the graphical interfaces usage.

If we know the communication protocols, let's see how we can use them to set the agents.

Setting agents

At the low level, agents communicate with the Jenkins master always using one of the protocols described above. However, at the higher level, we can attach slaves to the master in various ways. The differences concern two aspects:

- **static versus dynamic**: The simplest option is to add slaves permanently in the Jenkins master. The drawback of such solution is that we always need to manually change something if we need more (or less) slave nodes. A better option is to dynamically provision slaves as they are needed.
- **specific versus general-purpose**: Agents can be specific (for example, different agents for the projects based on Java 7 and different agents for Java 8) or general-purpose (an agent acts as a Docker host and a pipeline is built inside a Docker container).

These differences resulted in four common strategies how agents are configured:

- Permanent agents
- Permanent Docker agents
- Jenkins Swarm agents
- Dynamically provisioned Docker agents

Let's examine each of the solutions.

Permanent agents

We start from the simplest option which is to permanently add specific agent nodes. It can be done entirely via the Jenkins web interface.

Configuring permanent agents

In the Jenkins master, when we open **Manage Jenkins** and then **Manage Nodes**, we can view all the attached agents. Then, by clicking on **New Node**, giving it a name, and confirming with the **OK** button, we should finally see the agent's setup page:

Let's walk through the parameters we need to fill:

- **Name**: This is the unique name of the agent
- **Description**: This is any human-readable description of the agent
- **# of executors**: This is the number of concurrent builds that can be run on the slave
- **Remote root directory**: This is the dedicated directory on the slave machine that the agent can use to run build jobs (for example, /var/jenkins); the most important data is transferred back to the master, so the directory is not critical
- **Labels**: This includes the tags to match only the specific builds (tagged the same), for example, only projects based on Java 8
- **Usage**: This is the option to decide whether the agent should be used only for matched labels (for example, only for Acceptance Testing builds) or for any builds

- **Launch method**: This includes the following:

    - **Launch agent via Java Web Start**: Here, the connection will be established by the agent; it is possible to download the JAR file and the instructions on how to run it on the slave machine

    - **Launch agent via execution of command on the master**: This is the custom command run on the master to start the slave; in most cases it will send the Java Web Start JAR application and start it on the slave (for example, `ssh <slave_hostname> java -jar ~/bin/slave.jar`)
    - **Launch slave agents via SSH**: Here, the master will connect to the slave using the SSH protocol
    - **Let Jenkins control this Windows slave as a Windows service**: Here, the master will start a remote management facility built into Windows
- **Availability**: This is the option to decide whether the agent should be up all the time or the master should turn it offline under certain conditions

When the agents are set up correctly, it's possible to switch the master node offline, so that no builds would be executed on it and it would serve only as the Jenkins UI and the builds' coordinator.

Understanding permanent agents

As already mentioned, the drawback of such a solution is that we need to maintain multiple slave types (labels) for different project types. Such a situation is presented in the following diagram:

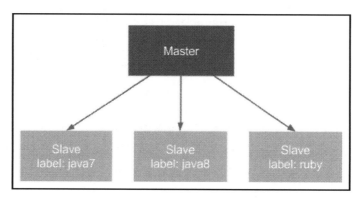

In our example, if we have three types of projects (**java7**, **java8**, and **ruby**), then we need to maintain three separately labeled (sets of) slaves. That is the same issue we had while maintaining multiple production server types, as described in Chapter 2, *Introducing Docker*. We addressed the issue by having the Docker Engine installed on the production servers. Let's try to do the same with Jenkins slaves.

Permanent Docker agents

The idea behind this solution is to permanently add general-purpose slaves. Each slave is identically configured (Docker Engine installed) and each build is defined together with the Docker image inside which the build is run.

Configuring permanent Docker agents

The configuration is static, so it's done exactly the same way as we did for the permanent agents. The only difference is that we need to install Docker on each machine that will be used as a slave. Then, we usually don't need labels because all slaves can be the same. After the slaves are configured, we define the Docker image in each pipeline script.

```
pipeline {
    agent {
        docker {
            image 'openjdk:8-jdk-alpine'
        }
    }
    ...
}
```

When the build is started, the Jenkins slave starts a container from the Docker image openjdk:8-jdk-alpine and then executes all pipeline steps inside that container. This way, we always know the execution environment and don't have to configure each slave separately depending on the particular project type.

Understanding permanent Docker agents

Looking at the same scenario we took for the permanent agents, the diagram looks like this:

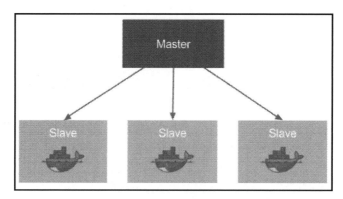

Each slave is exactly the same and if we would like to build a project that depends on Java 8, then we define the appropriate Docker image in the pipeline script (instead of specifying the slave label).

Jenkins Swarm agents

So far, we always had to permanently define each of the agents in the Jenkins master. Such a solution, even though good enough in many cases, can be a burden if we need to frequently scale the number of slave machines. Jenkins Swarm allows you to dynamically add slaves without the need to configure them in the Jenkins master.

Configuring Jenkins Swarm agents

The first step to use Jenkins Swarm is to install the **Self-Organizing Swarm Plug-in Modules** plugin in Jenkins. We can do it via the Jenkins web UI under **Manage Jenkins** and **Manage Plugins**. After this step, the Jenkins master is prepared for Jenkins slaves to be dynamically attached.

The second step is to run the Jenkins Swarm slave application on every machine that would act as a Jenkins slave. We can do it using the `swarm-client.jar` application.

> The `swarm-client.jar` application can be downloaded from the Jenkins Swarm plugin page: `https://wiki.jenkins-ci.org/display/JENKINS/Swarm+Plugin`. On that page, you can also find all the possible options of its execution.

In order to attach the Jenkins Swarm slave node, it's enough to run the following command:

```
$ java -jar swarm-client.jar -master <jenkins_master_url> -username
<jenkins_master_user> -password <jenkins_master_password> -name jenkins-
swarm-slave-1
```

 By the time of writing this book, there was an open bug that `client-slave.jar` didn't work via the secured HTTPS protocol, so it was necessary to add the `-disableSslVerification` option to the command execution.

After the successful execution, we should notice that a new slave appeared on the Jenkins master as presented on the screenshot:

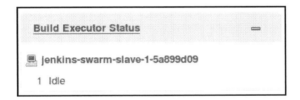

Now, when we run a build, it will be started on this agent.

 The other possibility to add the Jenkins Swarm agent is to use the Docker image built from the `swarm-client.jar` tool. There are a few of them available on the Docker Hub. We can use the `csanchez/jenkins-swarm-slave` image.

Understanding Jenkins Swarm agents

Jenkins Swarm allows to dynamically add agents, but it says nothing about whether to use specific or Docker-based slaves, so we can use it for both. At first glance, Jenkins Swarm may not seem very useful. After all, we moved setting agents from master to slave, but still have to do it manually. However, as we will see later in Chapter 8, *Clustering with Docker Swarm*, Jenkins Swarm enables dynamic scaling of slaves on a cluster of servers.

Dynamically provisioned Docker agents

Another option is to set up Jenkins to dynamically create a new agent each time a build is started. Such a solution is obviously the most flexible one since the number of slaves dynamically adjust to the number of builds. Let's have a look at how to configure Jenkins this way.

Configuring dynamically provisioned Docker agents

We need to first install the **Docker plugin**. As always with Jenkins plugins, we can do in **Manage Jenkins** and **Manage Plugins**. After the plugin is installed, we can start the following configuration steps:

1. Open the **Manage Jenkins** page.
2. Click on the **Configure System** link.
3. At the bottom of the page, there is the **Cloud** section.
4. Click on **Add a new cloud** and choose **Docker**.
5. Fill the Docker agent details.

6. Most parameters do not need to be changed; however, we need to set two of them as follows:

   - **Docker URL**: The address of the Docker host machine where agents will be run
   - **Credentials**: The credentials in case the Docker host requires authentication

If you plan to use the same Docker host where the master is running, then the Docker daemon needs to listen on the `docker0` network interface. You can do it in a similar way as described in the *Installing on a server* section ofts of) slaves. That is the same issue we had while maintaining multiple production server types, as described in `Chapter 2`, *Introducing Docker*, by changing one line in the `/lib/systemd/system/docker.service` file to `ExecStart=/usr/bin/dockerd -H 0.0.0.0:2375 -H fd://`

7. Click on **Add Docker Template** and select **Docker Template**.
8. Fill the details about the Docker slave image:

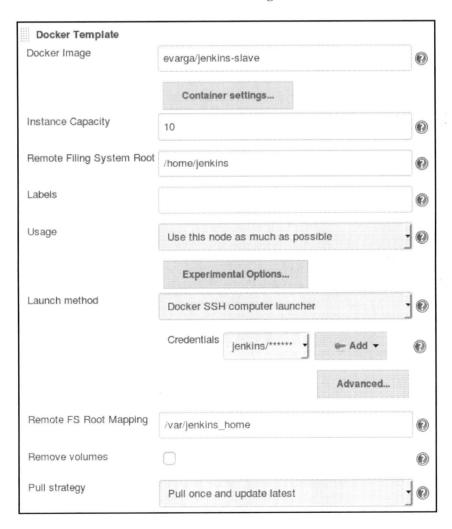

We can use the following parameters:

- **Docker Image**: The most popular slave image from the Jenkins community is `evarga/jenkins-slave`
- **Credentials**: The credentials to the `evarga/jenkins-slave` image are:
    - username: `jenkins`
    - password: `jenkins`
- **Instance capacity**: This defines the maximum number of agents running at the same time; for the beginning, it can be set to 10

 Instead of `evarga/jenkins-slave`, it's possible to build and use your own slave images. This is necessary when there are specific environment requirements, for example, the Python interpreter installed. In all examples for this book we used `leszko/jenkins-docker-slave`.

After saving, everything is set up. We could run the pipeline to observe that the execution really takes place on the Docker agent, but first let's dig a little deeper to understand how the Docker agents work.

Understanding dynamically provisioned Docker agents

Dynamically provisioned Docker agents can be treated as a layer over the standard agent mechanism. It changes neither the communication protocol nor how the agent is created. So, what does Jenkins do with the Docker agent configuration we provided?

The following diagram presents the Docker master-slave architecture we've configured:

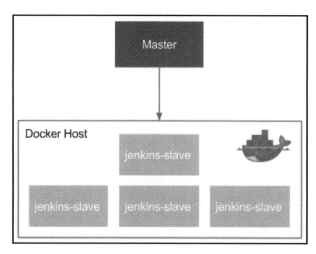

Let's describe step by step how the Docker agent mechanism is used:

1. When the Jenkins job is started, the master runs a new container from the `jenkins-slave` image on the slave Docker host.
2. The jenkins-slave container is, actually, the ubuntu image with the SSHD server installed.
3. The Jenkins master automatically adds the created agent to the agent list (same as what we did manually in the *Setting agents* section).
4. The agent is accessed using the SSH communication protocol to perform the build.
5. After the build, the master stops and removes the slave container.

Running Jenkins master as a Docker container is independent from running Jenkins agents as Docker containers. It's reasonable to do both, but any of them will work separately.

The solution is somehow similar to the permanent Docker agents solution, because in result, we run the build inside a Docker container. The difference is, however, in the slave node configuration. Here, the whole slave is dockerized, not only the build environment. Therefore, it has two great advantages as follows:

- **Automatic agent lifecycle**: The process of creating, adding, and removing the agent is automated.
- **Scalability**: Actually, the slave Docker host could be not a single machine, but a cluster composed of multiple machines (we'll cover clustering using Docker Swarm in Chapter 8, *Clustering with Docker Swarm*). In that case, adding more resources is as simple as adding a new machine to the cluster and does not require any changes in Jenkins.

Jenkins build usually needs to download a lot of project dependencies (for example, Gradle/Maven dependencies), which may take a lot of time. If Docker slaves are automatically provisioned for each build, then it may be worth to set up a Docker volume for them to enable caching between the builds.

Testing agents

No matter which agent configuration you chose, we should now check if it works correctly.

Let's go back to the hello world pipeline. Usually, the builds last longer than the hello-world example, so we can simulate it by adding sleeping to the pipeline script:

```
pipeline {
    agent any
    stages {
        stage("Hello") {
            steps {
                sleep 300 // 5 minutes
                echo 'Hello World'
            }
        }
    }
}
```

After clicking on **Build Now** and going to the Jenkins main page, we should see that the build is executed on an agent. Now, if we click on build many times, then different agents should be executing different builds (as shown in the following screenshot):

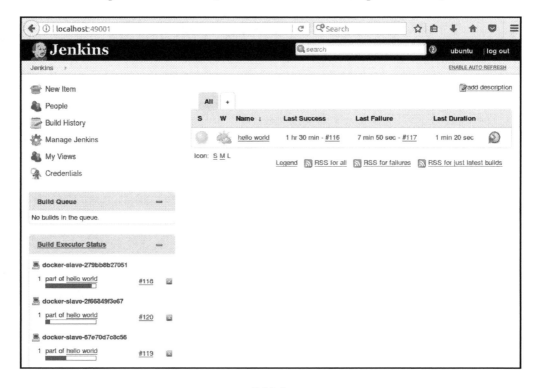

To prevent job executions on master, remember about turning the master node offline or setting # **of executors** to 0 in the **Manage Nodes** configuration.

Having seen that the agents are executing our builds, we've confirmed that they are configured correctly. Now, let's see how and for what reason we could create our own Jenkins images.

Custom Jenkins images

So far, we have used the Jenkins images pulled from the internet. We used `jenkins` for the master container and `evarga/jenkins-slave` for the slave container. However, we may want to build our own images to satisfy the specific build environment requirements. In this section, we cover how to do it.

Building Jenkins slave

Let's start from the slave image, because it's more often customized. The build execution is performed on the agent, so it's the agent that needs to have the environment adjusted to the project we would like to build. For example, it may require the Python interpreter if our project is written in Python. The same is applied to any library, tool, testing framework, or anything that is needed by the project.

You can check what is already installed inside the `evarga/jenkins-slave` image by looking at its Dockerfile at `https://github.com/evarga/docker-images`.

There are three steps to build and use the custom image:

1. Create a Dockerfile.
2. Build the image.
3. Change the agent configuration on master.

As an example, let's create a slave that serves the Python project. We can build it on top of the `evarga/jenkins-slave` image for the sake of simplicity. Let's do it using the following three steps:

1. **Dockerfile**: Let's create a new directory inside the Dockerfile with the following content:

   ```
   FROM evarga/jenkins-slave
   RUN apt-get update && \
       apt-get install -y python
   ```

   The base Docker image `evarga/jenkins-slave` is suitable for the dynamically provisioned Docker agents solution. In case of permanent Docker agents, it's enough to use `alpine`, `ubuntu`, or any other image, since it's not the slave that is dockerized, but only the build execution environment.

2. **Build the image**: We can build the image by executing the following command:

   ```
   $ docker build -t jenkins-slave-python .
   ```

3. **Configure the master**: The last step, of course, is to set `jenkins-slave-python` instead of `evarga/jenkins-slave` in the Jenkins master's configuration (as described in the *Setting Docker agent* section).

   The slave Dockerfile should be kept in the source code repository and the image build can be performed automatically by Jenkins. There is nothing wrong with building the new Jenkins slave image using the old Jenkins slave.

What if we need Jenkins to build two different kinds of projects, for example, one based on Python and another based on Ruby? In that case, we could prepare an agent, which is generic enough to support both: Python and Ruby. However, in case of Docker, it's recommended to create the second slave image (`jenkins-slave-ruby` by analogy). Then, in the Jenkins configuration we need to create two Docker templates and label them accordingly.

Building Jenkins master

We already have a custom slave image. Why would we also want to build our own master image? One of the reasons might be that we don't want to use slaves at all, and, since the execution would be done on master, its environment has to be adjusted to the project's needs. That is, however, a very rare case. More often, we will want to configure the master itself.

Imagine the following scenario, your organization scales Jenkins horizontally and each team has its own instance. There is, however, some common configuration, for example: a set of base plugins, backup strategies, or the company logo. Then, repeating the same configuration for each of the teams is a waste of time. So, we can prepare the shared master image and let the teams use it.

Jenkins is configured using XML files and it provides the Groovy-based DSL language to manipulate over them. That is why we can add the Groovy script to the Dockerfile in order to manipulate the Jenkins configuration. What is more, there are special scripts to help with the Jenkins configuration if it requires something more than XML changes, for instance, plugin installation.

 All possibilities of the Dockerfile instructions are well described on the GitHub page `https://github.com/jenkinsci/docker`.

As an example, let's create a master image with the docker-plugin already installed and a number of executors set to 5. In order to do it, we need to:

1. Create the Groovy script to manipulate on `config.xml` and set the number of executors to 5.
2. Create the Dockerfile to install docker-plugin and execute the Groovy script.
3. Build the image.

Let's use the three steps mentioned and build the Jenkins master image.

1. **Groovy script**: Let's create a new directory inside the `executors.groovy` file with the following content:

   ```
   import jenkins.model.*
   Jenkins.instance.setNumExecutors(5)
   ```

The complete Jenkins API can be found on the official page `http://javadoc.jenkins.io/`.

2. **Dockerfile**: In the same directory, let's create the Dockerfile:

```
FROM jenkins
COPY executors.groovy
     /usr/share/jenkins/ref/init.groovy.d/executors.groovy
RUN /usr/local/bin/install-plugins.sh docker-plugin
```

3. **Build the image**: We can finally build the image:

```
$ docker build -t jenkins-master .
```

After the image is created, each team in the organization can use it to launch their own Jenkins instance.

Having our own master and slave images lets us provide the configuration and the build environment for the teams in our organization. In the next section, we'll see what else is worth being configured in Jenkins.

Configuration and management

We have already covered the most crucial part of the Jenkins configuration: agents provisioning. Since Jenkins is highly configurable, you can expect much more possibilities to adjust it to your needs. The good news is that the configuration is intuitive and accessible via the web interface, so it does not require any detailed description. Everything can be changed under the **Manage Jenkins** subpage. In this section, we will focus only on a few aspects that are most likely to be changed: plugins, security, and backup.

Plugins

Jenkins is highly plugin-oriented, which means that a lot of features are delivered by the use of plugins. They can extend Jenkins almost in the unlimited way, which, taking into consideration the large community, is one of the reasons why Jenkins is such a successful tool. With Jenkins' openness, comes the risk and it's better to download plugins only from the reliable source or check their source code.

There are literally tons of plugins to choose from. Some of them were already installed automatically during the initial configuration. Another one (Docker plugin) was installed while setting the Docker agents. There are plugins for cloud integration, source control tools, code coverage, and much more. You can also write your own plugin, but it's better to check first if the one you need is not already written.

 There is an official Jenkins page to browse plugins from `https://plugins. jenkins.io/`.

Security

The way you should approach the Jenkins security depends on the Jenkins architecture you have chosen within your organization. If you have a Jenkins master for every small team, then you may not need it at all (under the assumption that the corporate network is firewalled). However, if you have a single Jenkins master instance for the whole organization, then you'd better be sure you secured it well.

Jenkins comes with its own user database-we have already created a user during the initial configuration process. You can create, delete, and modify users by opening the **Manage Users** setting page. The built-in database can be a solution in case of small organizations; however, for the large group of users, you will probably want to use LDAP instead. You can choose it on the **Configure Global Security** page. There, you can also assign roles, groups, and users. By default, the **Logged-in users can do anything** option is set, but in a large-scale organization you should probably think of more detailed granularity.

Backup

As the old saying goes: *There are two types of people: those who backup, and those who will backup*. Believe it or not, the backup is something you probably want to configure. What files to back up and from which machines? Luckily, agents automatically send all the relevant data back to the master, so we don't need to bother about them. If you run Jenkins in the container, then the container itself is also not interesting, since it does not hold any persistent state. The only place we are interested in is the Jenkins home directory.

We can either install a Jenkins plugin (which will help us to set periodic backups) or simply set a cron job to archive the directory into a safe place. To reduce the size, we can exclude the subfolders which are not interesting (that will depend on your needs; however, almost certainly, you don't need to copy: "war", "cache", "tools", and "workspace").

There are quite a few plugins, which can help with the backup process; the most common one is called **Backup Plugin**.

Blue Ocean UI

The first version of Hudson (former Jenkins) was released in 2005. It's been on the market for more than 10 years now. However, its look and feel hasn't changed much. We've already used it for a while and it's hard to deny that it looks outdated. Blue Ocean is the plugin, which redefines the user experience of Jenkins. If Jenkins is aesthetically displeasing to you, then it's definitely worth giving a try.

You can read more on the Blue Ocean page at `https://jenkins.io/ projects/blueocean/`.

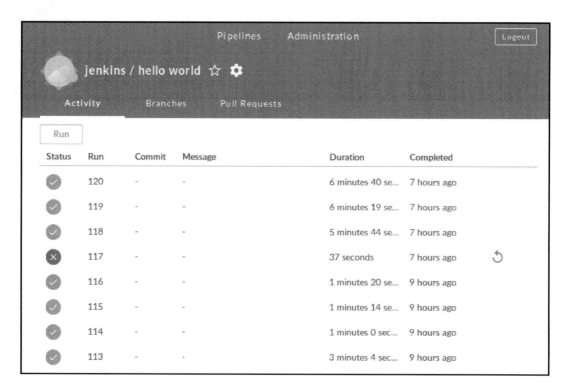

Exercises

We have learned a lot about Jenkins configuration throughout this chapter. To consolidate the knowledge, we recommend two exercises on preparing the Jenkins images and testing the Jenkins environment.

1. Create Jenkins master and slave Docker images and use them to run the Jenkins infrastructure capable of building the Ruby projects:
    *   Create the master Dockerfile, which automatically installs the Docker plugin.
    *   Build the master image and run the Jenkins instance
    *   Create the slave Dockerfile (suitable for the dynamic slave provisioning), which installs the Ruby interpreter
    *   Build the slave image
    *   Change the configuration in the Jenkins instance to use the slave image

2. Create a pipeline, which runs a Ruby script printing `Hello World from Ruby`:
    *   Create a new pipeline
    *   Use the following shell command to create the `hello.rb` script on the fly:
        ```
        sh "echo "puts 'Hello World from Ruby'" > hello.rb"
        ```
    *   Add the command to run `hello.rb` using the Ruby interpreter
    *   Run the build and observe the console output

Summary

In this chapter, we have covered the Jenkins environment and its configuration. The knowledge gained is sufficient to set up the complete Docker-based Jenkins infrastructure. The key takeaway from the chapter is as follows:

*   Jenkins is a general-purpose automation tool that can be used with any language or framework.
*   Jenkins is highly extensible by plugins, which can be written or found on the internet.
*   Jenkins is written in Java, so it can be installed on any operating system. It's also officially delivered as a Docker image.

- Jenkins can be scaled using the master-slave architecture. The master instances can be scaled horizontally or vertically depending on the organization's needs.
- Jenkins' agents can be implemented with the use of Docker, which helps in automatic configuration and dynamic slaves allocation.
- Custom Docker images can be created for both: Jenkins master and Jenkins slave.
- Jenkins is highly configurable and the aspects that should always be considered are: security and backups.

In the next chapter, we will focus on the part that we've already touched with the "hello world" example, pipelines. We will describe the idea and the method to build a complete Continuous Integration pipeline.

4
Continuous Integration Pipeline

We already know how to configure Jenkins. In this chapter, you will see how to use it effectively, focusing on the feature that lays at the heart of Jenkins, pipelines. By building a complete Continuous Integration process from scratch, we will describe all aspects of modern team-oriented code development.

This chapter covers the following points:

- Explaining the idea of pipelining
- Introducing the Jenkins pipeline syntax
- Creating a Continuous Integration pipeline
- Explaining the idea of Jenkinsfile
- Creating code quality checks
- Adding pipeline triggers and notifications
- Explaining development workflows and branching strategies
- Introducing Jenkins Multibranch

Introducing pipelines

A pipeline is a sequence of automated operations that usually represents a part of software delivery and the quality assurance process. It can be simply seen as a chain of scripts providing the following additional benefits:

- **Operation grouping**: Operations are grouped together into stages (also known as **gates** or **quality gates**) that introduce a structure into the process and clearly defines the rule: if one stage fails, no further stages are executed
- **Visibility**: All aspects of the process are visualized, which help in quick failure analysis and promotes team collaboration
- **Feedback**: Team members learn about any problems as soon as they occur, so they can react quickly

> The concept of pipelining is similar for most Continuous Integration tools, however, the naming can differ. In this book, we stick to the Jenkins terminology.

Pipeline structure

A Jenkins pipeline consists of two kinds of elements: stages and steps. The following figure shows how they are used:

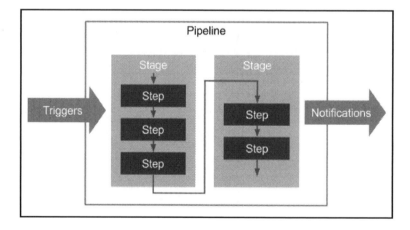

The following are the basic pipeline elements:

- **Step**: A single operation (tells Jenkins what to do, for example, checkout code from repository, execute a script)
- **Stage**: A logical separation of steps (groups conceptually distinct sequences of steps, for example, **Build, Test,** and **Deploy**) used to visualize the Jenkins pipeline progress

 Technically, it's possible to create parallel steps; however, it's better to treat it as an exception when really needed for optimization purposes.

Multi-stage Hello World

As an example, let's extend the `Hello World` pipeline to contain two stages:

```
pipeline {
    agent any
    stages {
        stage('First Stage') {
            steps {
                echo 'Step 1. Hello World'
            }
        }
        stage('Second Stage') {
            steps {
                echo 'Step 2. Second time Hello'
                echo 'Step 3. Third time Hello'
            }
        }
    }
}
```

The pipeline has no special requirements in terms of environment (any slave agent), and it executes three steps inside two stages. When we click on **Build Now**, we should see the visual representation:

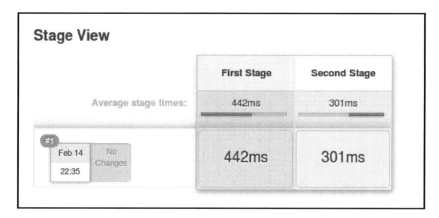

The pipeline succeeded, and we can see the step execution details by clicking on the console. If any of the steps failed, the processing would stop and no further steps would run. Actually, the entire reason for a pipeline is to prevent all further steps from execution and visualize the point of failure.

Pipeline syntax

We have discussed the pipeline elements and already used a few of the pipeline steps, for example, `echo`. What other operations can we use inside the pipeline definition?

 In this book, we use the declarative syntax that is recommended for all new projects. The different options are Groovy-based DSL and (prior to Jenkins 2) XML (created via the web interface).

The declarative syntax was designed to make it as simple as possible to understand the pipeline, even by the people who do not write code on a daily basis. This is why the syntax is limited only to the most important keywords.

Let's prepare an experiment and, before we describe all the details, read the following pipeline definition and try to guess what it does:

```
pipeline {
    agent any
    triggers { cron('* * * * *') }
    options { timeout(time: 5) }
    parameters {
        booleanParam(name: 'DEBUG_BUILD', defaultValue: true,
        description: 'Is it the debug build?')
    }
    stages {
        stage('Example') {
            environment { NAME = 'Rafal' }
            when { expression { return params.DEBUG_BUILD } }
            steps {
                echo "Hello from $NAME"
                script {
                    def browsers = ['chrome', 'firefox']
                    for (int i = 0; i < browsers.size(); ++i) {
                        echo "Testing the ${browsers[i]} browser."
                    }
                }
            }
        }
    }
    post { always { echo 'I will always say Hello again!' } }
}
```

Hopefully, the pipeline didn't scare you. It is quite complex. Actually, it is so complex that it contains all possible Jenkins instructions. To answer the experiment puzzle, let's see what the pipeline does instruction by instruction:

1. Use any available agent.
2. Execute automatically every minute.
3. Stop if the execution takes more than 5 minutes.
4. Ask for the Boolean input parameter before starting.
5. Set `Rafal` as the environment variable NAME.
6. Only in the case of the `true` input parameter:
    - Print `Hello from Rafal`
    - Print `Testing the chrome browser`
    - Print `Testing the firefox browser`
7. Print `I will always say Hello again!` no matter if there are any errors during the execution.

Let's describe the most important Jenkins keywords. A declarative pipeline is always specified inside the `pipeline` block and contains sections, directives, and steps. We will walk through each of them.

 The complete pipeline syntax description can be found on the official Jenkins page at `https://jenkins.io/doc/book/pipeline/syntax/`.

Sections

Sections define the pipeline structure and usually contain one or more directives or steps. They are defined with the following keywords:

- **Stages**: This defines a series of one or more stage directives
- **Steps**: This defines a series of one or more step instructions
- **Post**: This defines a series of one or more step instructions that are run at the end of the pipeline build; marked with a condition (for example, always, success, or failure), usually used to send notifications after the pipeline build (we will cover this in detail in the *Triggers and notifications* section.)

Directives

Directives express the configuration of a pipeline or its parts:

- **Agent**: This specifies where the execution takes place and can define the `label` to match the equally labeled agents or `docker` to specify a container that is dynamically provisioned to provide an environment for the pipeline execution
- **Triggers**: This defines automated ways to trigger the pipeline and can use `cron` to set the time-based scheduling or `pollScm` to check the repository for changes (we will cover this in detail in the *Triggers and notifications* section)
- **Options**: This specifies pipeline-specific options, for example, `timeout` (maximum time of pipeline run) or `retry` (number of times the pipeline should be rerun after failure)
- **Environment**: This defines a set of key values used as environment variables during the build

- **Parameters**: This defines a list of user-input parameters
- **Stage**: This allows for logical grouping of steps
- **When**: This determines whether the stage should be executed depending on the given condition

Steps

Steps are the most fundamental part of the pipeline. They define the operations that are executed, so they actually tell Jenkins **what to do**.

- **sh**: This executes the shell command; actually, it's possible to define almost any operation using `sh`
- **custom**: Jenkins offers a lot of operations that can be used as steps (for example, `echo`); many of them are simply wrappers over the `sh` command used for convenience; plugins can also define their own operations
- **script**: This executes a block of the Groovy-based code that can be used for some non-trivial scenarios, where flow control is needed

> The complete specification of the available steps can be found at: `https://jenkins.io/doc/pipeline/steps/`.

Notice that the pipeline syntax is very generic and technically, can be used for almost any automation process. This is why the pipeline should be treated as a method of structurization and visualization. The most common use case is, however, implementing the Continuous Integration server that we will look at in the following section.

Commit pipeline

The most basic Continuous Integration process is called a commit pipeline. This classic phase, as its name says, starts with a commit (or push in Git) to the main repository and results in a report about the build success or failure. Since it runs after each change in the code, the build should take no more than 5 minutes and should consume a reasonable amount of resources. The commit phase is always the starting point of the Continuous Delivery process, and it provides the most important feedback cycle in the development process, constant information if the code is in a healthy state.

The commit phase works as follows. A developer checks in the code to the repository, the Continuous Integration server detects the change, and the build starts. The most fundamental commit pipeline contains three stages:

- **Checkout**: This stage downloads the source code from the repository
- **Compile**: This stage compiles the source code
- **Unit test**: This stage runs a suite of unit tests

Let's create a sample project and see how to implement the commit pipeline.

 This is an example of a pipeline for the project that uses technologies such as Git, Java, Gradle, and Spring Boot. Nevertheless, the same principles apply to any other technology.

Checkout

Checking out code from the repository is always the first operation in any pipeline. In order to see this, we need to have a repository. Then, we will be able to create a pipeline.

Creating a GitHub repository

Creating a repository on the GitHub server takes just a few steps:

1. Go to the `https://github.com/` page.
2. Create an account if you don't have one yet.
3. Click on **New repository**.
4. Give it a name, `calculator`.
5. Tick **Initialize this repository with a README**.
6. Click on **Create repository**.

Now, you should see the address of the repository, for example, `https://github.com/leszko/calculator.git`.

Creating a checkout stage

We can create a new pipeline called `calculator` and, as **Pipeline script**, put the code with a stage called **Checkout**:

```
pipeline {
    agent any
    stages {
        stage("Checkout") {
            steps {
                git url: 'https://github.com/leszko/calculator.git'
            }
        }
    }
}
```

The pipeline can be executed on any of the agents, and its only step does nothing more than downloading code from the repository. We can click on **Build Now** and see if it was executed successfully.

 Note that the Git toolkit needs to be installed on the node where the build is executed.

When we have the checkout, we're ready for the second stage.

Compile

In order to compile a project, we need to:

1. Create a project with the source code.
2. Push it to the repository.
3. Add the **Compile** stage to the pipeline.

Creating a Java Spring Boot project

Let's create a very simple Java project using the Spring Boot framework built by Gradle.

Spring Boot is a Java framework that simplifies building enterprise applications. Gradle is a build automation system that is based on the concepts of Apache Maven.

The simplest way to create a Spring Boot project is to perform the following steps:

1. Go to the `http://start.spring.io/` page.
2. Select **Gradle project** instead of **Maven project** (you can also leave Maven if you prefer it to Gradle).
3. Fill **Group** and **Artifact** (for example, `com.leszko` and `calculator`).
4. Add **Web** to **Dependencies**.
5. Click on **Generate Project**.
6. The generated skeleton project should be downloaded (the `calculator.zip` file).

The following screenshot presents the `http://start.spring.io/` page:

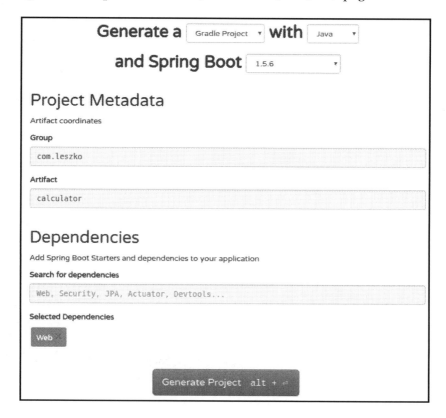

Pushing code to GitHub

We will use the Git tool to perform the `commit` and `push` operations:

 In order to run the `git` command, you need to have the Git toolkit installed (it can be downloaded from `https://git-scm.com/downloads`).

Let's first clone the repository to the filesystem:

```
$ git clone https://github.com/leszko/calculator.git
```

Extract the project downloaded from `http://start.spring.io/` into the directory created by Git.

 If you prefer, you can import the project into IntelliJ, Eclipse, or your favorite IDE tool.

As a result, the `calculator` directory should have the following files:

```
$ ls -a
.  ..  build.gradle .git .gitignore gradle gradlew gradlew.bat README.md src
```

 In order to perform the Gradle operations locally, you need to have Java JDK installed (in Ubuntu, you can do it by executing `sudo apt-get install -y default-jdk`).

We can compile the project locally using the following code:

```
$ ./gradlew compileJava
```

In the case of Maven, you can run `./mvnw compile`. Both Gradle and Maven compile the Java classes located in the `src` directory.

 You can find all possible Gradle instructions (for the Java project) at `https://docs.gradle.org/current/userguide/java_plugin.html`.

Now, we can `commit` and `push` to the GitHub repository:

```
$ git add .
$ git commit -m "Add Spring Boot skeleton"
$ git push -u origin master
```

 After running the `git push` command, you will be prompted to enter the GitHub credentials (username and password).

The code is already in the GitHub repository. If you want to check it, you can go to the GitHub page and see the files.

Creating a compile stage

We can add a `Compile` stage to the pipeline using the following code:

```
stage("Compile") {
    steps {
        sh "./gradlew compileJava"
    }
}
```

Note that we used exactly the same command locally and in the Jenkins pipeline, which is a very good sign because the local development process is consistent with the Continuous Integration environment. After running the build, you should see two green boxes. You can also check that the project was compiled correctly in the console log.

Unit test

It's time to add the last stage that is Unit test, which checks if our code does what we expect it to do. We have to:

- Add the source code for the calculator logic
- Write unit test for the code
- Add a stage to execute the unit test

Creating business logic

The first version of the calculator will be able to add two numbers. Let's add the business logic as a class in the `src/main/java/com/leszko/calculator/Calculator.java` file:

```
package com.leszko.calculator;
import org.springframework.stereotype.Service;

@Service
public class Calculator {
    int sum(int a, int b) {
        return a + b;
    }
}
```

To execute the business logic, we also need to add the web service controller in a separate file `src/main/java/com/leszko/calculator/CalculatorController.java`:

```
package com.leszko.calculator;
import org.springframework.beans.factory.annotation.Autowired;
import org.springframework.web.bind.annotation.RequestMapping;
import org.springframework.web.bind.annotation.RequestParam;
import org.springframework.web.bind.annotation.RestController;

@RestController
class CalculatorController {
    @Autowired
    private Calculator calculator;

    @RequestMapping("/sum")
    String sum(@RequestParam("a") Integer a,
               @RequestParam("b") Integer b) {
        return String.valueOf(calculator.sum(a, b));
    }
}
```

This class exposes the business logic as a web service. We can run the application and see how it works:

```
$ ./gradlew bootRun
```

It should start our web service and we can check that it works by navigating to the browser and opening the page `http://localhost:8080/sum?a=1&b=2`. This should sum two numbers (1 and 2) and show 3 in the browser.

Writing a unit test

We already have the working application. How can we ensure that the logic works as expected? We have tried it once, but in order to know constantly, we need a unit test. In our case, it will be trivial, maybe even unnecessary; however, in real projects, unit tests can save from bugs and system failures.

Let's create a unit test in the file
`src/test/java/com/leszko/calculator/CalculatorTest.java`:

```java
package com.leszko.calculator;
import org.junit.Test;
import static org.junit.Assert.assertEquals;

public class CalculatorTest {
    private Calculator calculator = new Calculator();

    @Test
    public void testSum() {
        assertEquals(5, calculator.sum(2, 3));
    }
}
```

We can run the test locally using the `./gradlew test` command. Then, let's `commit` the code and `push` it to the repository:

```
$ git add .
$ git commit -m "Add sum logic, controller and unit test"
$ git push
```

Creating a unit test stage

Now, we can add a `Unit test` stage to the pipeline:

```
stage("Unit test") {
    steps {
        sh "./gradlew test"
    }
}
```

In the case of Maven, we would have to use `./mvnw test`.

When we build the pipeline again, we should see three boxes, which means that we've completed the Continuous Integration pipeline:

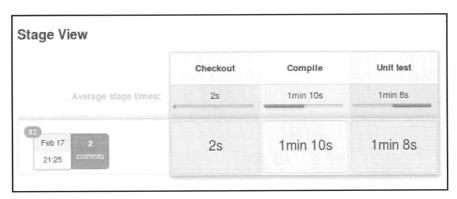

Jenkinsfile

All the time, so far, we created the pipeline code directly in Jenkins. This is, however, not the only option. We can also put the pipeline definition inside a file called `Jenkinsfile` and `commit` it to the repository together with the source code. This method is even more consistent because the way your pipeline looks is strictly related to the project itself.

For example, if you don't need the code compilation because your programming language is interpreted (and not compiled), then you won't have the `Compile` stage. The tools you use also differ depending on the environment. We used Gradle/Maven because we've built the Java project; however, in the case of a project written in Python, you could use PyBuilder. It leads to the idea that the pipelines should be created by the same people who write the code, developers. Also, the pipeline definition should be put together with the code, in the repository.

This approach brings immediate benefits, as follows:

- In case of Jenkins' failure, the pipeline definition is not lost (because it's stored in the code repository, not in Jenkins)
- The history of the pipeline changes is stored
- Pipeline changes go through the standard code development process (for example, they are subjected to code reviews)
- Access to the pipeline changes is restricted exactly in the same way as the access to the source code

Creating Jenkinsfile

We can create the `Jenkinsfile` and push it to our GitHub repository. Its content is almost the same as the commit pipeline we wrote. The only difference is that the checkout stage becomes redundant because Jenkins has to checkout the code (together with `Jenkinsfile`) first and then read the pipeline structure (from `Jenkinsfile`). This is why Jenkins needs to know the repository address before it reads `Jenkinsfile`.

Let's create a file called `Jenkinsfile` in the root directory of our project:

```
pipeline {
    agent any
    stages {
        stage("Compile") {
            steps {
                sh "./gradlew compileJava"
            }
        }
        stage("Unit test") {
            steps {
                sh "./gradlew test"
            }
        }
    }
}
```

We can now `commit` the added files and `push` to the GitHub repository:

```
$ git add .
$ git commit -m "Add sum Jenkinsfile"
$ git push
```

Running pipeline from Jenkinsfile

When `Jenkinsfile` is in the repository, then all we have to do is to open the pipeline configuration and in the `Pipeline` section:

- Change **Definition** from `Pipeline script` to `Pipeline script from SCM`
- Select **Git** in **SCM**
- Put `https://github.com/leszko/calculator.git` in **Repository URL**

After saving, the build will always run from the current version of Jenkinsfile into the repository.

We have successfully created the first complete commit pipeline. It can be treated as a minimum viable product, and actually, in many cases, it's sufficient as the Continuous Integration process. In the next sections, we will see what improvements can be done to make the commit pipeline even better.

Code quality stages

We can extend the classic three steps of Continuous Integration with additional steps. The most widely used are code coverage and static analysis. Let's look at each of them.

Code coverage

Think about the following scenario: you have a well-configured Continuous Integration process; however, nobody in your project writes unit tests. It passes all the builds, but it doesn't mean that the code is working as expected. What to do then? How to ensure that the code is tested?

The solution is to add the code coverage tool that runs all tests and verifies which parts of the code have been executed. Then, it creates a report showing not-tested sections. Moreover, we can make the build fail when there is too much untested code.

There are a lot of tools available to perform the test coverage analysis; for Java, the most popular are JaCoCo, Clover, and Cobertura.

Let's use JaCoCo and show how the coverage check works in practice. In order to do this, we need to perform the following steps:

1. Add JaCoCo to the Gradle configuration.
2. Add the code coverage stage to the pipeline.
3. Optionally, publish JaCoCo reports in Jenkins.

Adding JaCoCo to Gradle

In order to run JaCoCo from Gradle, we need to add the `jacoco` plugin to the `build.gradle` file by adding the following line in the plugin section:

```
apply plugin: "jacoco"
```

Next, if we would like to make the Gradle fail in case of too low code coverage, we can add the following configuration to the `build.gradle` file as well:

```
jacocoTestCoverageVerification {
    violationRules {
        rule {
            limit {
                minimum = 0.2
            }
        }
    }
}
```

This configuration sets the minimum code coverage to 20%. We can run it with the following command:

```
$ ./gradlew test jacocoTestCoverageVerification
```

The command checks if the code coverage is at least 20%. You can play with the minimum value to see the level at which the build fails. We can also generate a test coverage report using the following command:

```
$ ./gradlew test jacocoTestReport
```

You can also have a look at the full coverage report in the build/reports/jacoco/test/html/index.html file:

com.leszko.calculator

Element	Missed Instructions	Cov.	Missed Branches
ⓒ CalculatorController		25%	
ⓒ CalculatorApplication		38%	
ⓒ Calculator		100%	
Total	14 of 27	48%	0 of 0

Adding a code coverage stage

Adding a code coverage stage to the pipeline is as simple as the previous stages:

```
stage("Code coverage") {
    steps {
        sh "./gradlew jacocoTestReport"
        sh "./gradlew jacocoTestCoverageVerification"
    }
}
```

After adding this stage, if anyone commits code that is not well-covered with tests, the build will fail.

Publishing the code coverage report

When the coverage is low and the pipeline fails, it would be useful to look at the code coverage report and find what parts are not yet covered with tests. We could run Gradle locally and generate the coverage report; however, it is more convenient if Jenkins shows the report for us.

In order to publish the code coverage report in Jenkins, we need the following stage definition:

```
stage("Code coverage") {
    steps {
        sh "./gradlew jacocoTestReport"
        publishHTML (target: [
            reportDir: 'build/reports/jacoco/test/html',
            reportFiles: 'index.html',
            reportName: "JaCoCo Report"
        ])
        sh "./gradlew jacocoTestCoverageVerification"
    }
}
```

This stage copies the generated JaCoCo report to the Jenkins output. When we run the build again, we should see a link to the code coverage reports (in the menu on the left side, below "Build Now").

To perform the `publishHTML` step, you need to have the **HTML Publisher** plugin installed in Jenkins. You can read more about the plugin at `https://jenkins.io/doc/pipeline/steps/htmlpublisher/#publishhtml-publish-html-reports`.

We have created the code coverage stage, which shows the code that is not tested and therefore vulnerable to bugs. Let's see what else can be done in order to improve the code quality.

If you need code coverage that is more strict, you can check the concept of mutation testing and add the PIT framework stage to the pipeline. Read more at `http://pitest.org/`.

Static code analysis

Your code may work perfectly fine, however, what about the quality of the code itself? How do we ensure it is maintainable and written in a good style?

Static code analysis is an automatic process of checking the code without actually executing it. In most cases, it implies checking a number of rules on the source code. These rules may apply to a wide range of aspects; for example, all public classes need to have a Javadoc comment; the maximum length of a line is 120 characters, or if a class defines the `equals()` method, it has to define the `hashCode()` method as well.

The most popular tools to perform the static analysis on the Java code are Checkstyle, FindBugs, and PMD. Let's look at an example and add the static code analysis stage using Checkstyle. We will do this in three steps:

1. Add the Checkstyle configuration.
2. Add the Checkstyle stage.
3. Optionally, publish the Checkstyle report in Jenkins.

Adding the Checkstyle configuration

In order to add the Checkstyle configuration, we need to define the rules against which the code is checked. We can do this by specifying the `config/checkstyle/checkstyle.xml` file:

```xml
<?xml version="1.0"?>
<!DOCTYPE module PUBLIC
        "-//Puppy Crawl//DTD Check Configuration 1.2//EN"
        "http://www.puppycrawl.com/dtds/configuration_1_2.dtd">

<module name="Checker">
    <module name="TreeWalker">
        <module name="JavadocType">
            <property name="scope" value="public"/>
        </module>
    </module>
</module>
```

The configuration contains only one rule: Checking if public classes, interfaces, and enums are documented with Javadoc. If they are not, the build fails.

The complete Checkstyle description can be found at `http://checkstyle.sourceforge.net/config.html`.

We also need to add the `checkstyle` plugin to the `build.gradle` file:

```
apply plugin: 'checkstyle'
```

Then, we can run the `checkstyle` with the following code:

```
$ ./gradlew checkstyleMain
```

In the case of our project, it should result in a failure because none of our public classes (`Calculator.java`, `CalculatorApplication.java`, `CalculatorTest.java`, `CalculatorApplicationTests.java`) has a Javadoc comment. We need to fix it by adding the documentation, for example, in case of the `src/main/java/com/leszko/calculator/CalculatorApplication.java` file:

```
/**
 * Main Spring Application.
 */
@SpringBootApplication
public class CalculatorApplication {
    public static void main(String[] args) {
        SpringApplication.run(CalculatorApplication.class, args);
    }
}
```

Now, the build should be successful.

Adding a static code analysis stage

We can add a `Static code analysis` stage to the pipeline:

```
stage("Static code analysis") {
    steps {
        sh "./gradlew checkstyleMain"
    }
}
```

Now, if anyone commits a file with a public class without Javadoc, the build will fail.

Publishing static code analysis reports

Very similar to JaCoCo, we can add the Checkstyle report to Jenkins:

```
publishHTML (target: [
    reportDir: 'build/reports/checkstyle/',
    reportFiles: 'main.html',
    reportName: "Checkstyle Report"
])
```

It generates a link to the Checkstyle report.

We have added the static code analysis stage that can help in finding bugs and in standardizing the code style inside the team or organization.

SonarQube

SonarQube is the most widespread source code quality management tool. It supports multiple programming languages and can be treated as an alternative to the code coverage and static code analysis steps we looked at. Actually, it is a separate server that aggregates different code analysis frameworks, such as Checkstyle, FindBugs, and JaCoCo. It has its own dashboards and integrates well with Jenkins.

Instead of adding code quality steps to the pipeline, we can install SonarQube, add plugins there, and add a "sonar" stage to the pipeline. The advantage of this solution is that SonarQube provides a user-friendly web interface to configure rules and show code vulnerabilities.

 You can read more about SonarQube on its official page `https://www.sonarqube.org/`.

Triggers and notifications

So far, we have always built the pipeline manually by clicking on the **Build Now** button. It works but is not very convenient. All team members would have to remember that after committing to the repository, they need to open Jenkins and start the build. The same works with pipeline monitoring; so far, we manually opened Jenkins and checked the build status. In this section, we will see how to improve the process so that the pipeline would start automatically and, when completed, notify the team members about its status.

Triggers

An automatic action to start the build is called the pipeline trigger. In Jenkins, there are many options to choose from; however, they all boil down to three types:

- External
- Polling SCM (Source Control Management)
- Scheduled build

Let's take a look at each of them.

External

External triggers are natural to understand. They mean that Jenkins starts the build after it's called by the notifier, which can be the other pipeline build, the SCM system (for example, GitHub), or any remote script.

The following figure presents the communication:

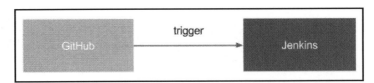

GitHub triggers Jenkins after a push to the repository and the build is started.

To configure the system this way, we need the following setup steps:

1. Install the GitHub plugin in Jenkins.
2. Generate a secret key for Jenkins.
3. Set the GitHub web hook and specify the Jenkins address and key.

In the case of the most popular SCM providers, dedicated Jenkins plugins are always provided.

There is also a more generic way to trigger Jenkins via the REST call to the endpoint `<jenkins_url>/job/<job_name>/build?token=<token>`. For security reasons, it requires setting `token` in Jenkins and then using it in the remote script.

> Jenkins must be accessible from the SCM server. In other words, if we use the public GitHub to trigger Jenkins, then our Jenkins server must be public as well. This also applies to the generic solution; the `<jenkins_url>` address must be accessible.

Polling SCM

Polling SCM trigger is a little less intuitive. The following figure presents the communication:

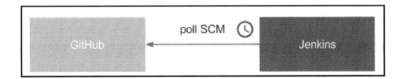

Jenkins periodically calls GitHub and checks if there was any push to the repository. Then, it starts the build. It may sound counter-intuitive, however, there are at least two good cases for using this method:

- Jenkins is inside the firewalled network (which GitHub does not have access to)
- Commits are frequent and the build takes a long time, so executing a build after every commit would cause an overload

The configuration of **poll SCM** is also somehow simpler because the way to connect from Jenkins to GitHub is already set up (Jenkins checks out the code from GitHub, so it needs to have access). In the case of our calculator project, we can set up an automatic trigger by adding the `triggers` declaration (just after `agent`) to the pipeline:

```
triggers {
    pollSCM('* * * * *')
}
```

After running the pipeline manually for the first time, the automatic trigger is set. Then, it checks GitHub every minute, and for new commits, it starts a build. To test that it works as expected, you can commit and push anything to the GitHub repository and see that the build starts.

We used the mysterious `* * * * *` as an argument to `pollSCM`. It specifies how often Jenkins should check for new source changes and is expressed in the cron-style string format.

> The cron string format is described (together with the cron tool) at `https://en.wikipedia.org/wiki/Cron`.

Scheduled build

Scheduled trigger means that Jenkins runs the build periodically, no matter if there was any commit to the repository or not.

As the following figure presents, there is no communication with any system needed:

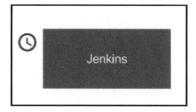

The implementation of **Scheduled build** is exactly the same as polling SCM. The only difference is that the keyword `cron` is used instead of `pollSCM`. This trigger method is rarely used for the commit pipeline but applies well to nightly builds (for example, complex integration testing executed at nights).

Notifications

Jenkins provides a lot of ways to announce its build status. What's more, as with everything in Jenkins, new notification types can be added using plugins.

Let's walk through the most popular types so that you can choose the one that fits your needs.

Email

The most classic way to notify about the Jenkins build status is to send emails. The advantage of this solution is that everybody has a mailbox; everybody knows how to use the mailbox; and everybody is used to receiving information by the mailbox. The drawback is that usually there are simply too many emails and the ones from Jenkins quickly become filtered out and never read.

The configuration of the email notification is very simple; it's enough to:

- Have the SMTP server configured
- Set its details in Jenkins (in **Manage Jenkins** | **Configure System**)
- Use `mail to` instruction in the pipeline

The pipeline configuration can be as follows:

```
post {
    always {
        mail to: 'team@company.com',
        subject: "Completed Pipeline: ${currentBuild.fullDisplayName}",
        body: "Your build completed, please check: ${env.BUILD_URL}"
    }
}
```

Note that all notifications are usually called in the `post` section of the pipeline, which is executed after all steps, no matter whether the build succeeded or failed. We used the `always` keyword; however, there are different options:

- **always:** Execute regardless of the completion status
- **changed:** Execute only if the pipeline changed its status
- **failure:** Execute only if the pipeline has the **failed** status
- **success:** Execute only if the pipeline has the **success** status
- **unstable:** Execute only if the pipeline has the **unstable** status (usually caused by test failures or code violations)

Group chat

If group chat (for example, Slack or HipChat) is the first method of communication in your team, then it's worth considering adding the automatic build notifications there. No matter which tool you use, the procedure to configure it is always the same:

1. Find and install plugin for your group chat tool (for example, the **Slack Notification** plugin).
2. Configure the plugin (server URL, channel, authorization token, and so on).
3. Add the sending instruction to the pipeline.

Let's see a sample pipeline configuration for Slack to send notifications after the build fails:

```
post {
    failure {
        slackSend channel: '#dragons-team',
        color: 'danger',
        message: "The pipeline ${currentBuild.fullDisplayName} failed."
    }
}
```

Team space

Together with the agile culture came the idea that it's better to have everything happening in the team space. Instead of writing emails, meet together; instead of online messaging, come and talk; instead of task-tracking tool, have a whiteboard. The same idea came to Continuous Delivery and Jenkins. Currently, it's very common to install big screens (also called **build radiators**) in the team space. Then, when you come to the office, the first thing you see is the current status of the pipeline. Build radiators are considered one of the most effective notification strategies. They ensure that everyone is aware of failing builds and, as a side-effect benefit, they boost team spirit and favor in-person communication.

Since developers are creative beings, they invented a lot of other ideas that play the same role as the radiators. Some teams hang large speakers that beep when the pipeline failed. Some others have toys that blink when the build is done. One of my favorites is Pipeline State UFO, which is provided as an open source project on GitHub. On its page, you can find the description of how to print and configure a UFO that hangs under the ceiling and signals the pipeline state. You can find more at https://github.com/Dynatrace/ufo.

Since Jenkins is extensible by plugins, its community wrote a lot of different ways to inform about the build statuses. Among them, you can find RSS feeds, SMS notifications, mobile applications, desktop notifiers, and much more.

Team development strategies

We have already described everything about how the Continuous Integration pipeline should look. However, when exactly should it be run? Of course, it is triggered after the commit to the repository but after the commit to which branch? Only to the trunk or to every branch? Or maybe it should run before, not after committing so that the repository would always be healthy? Or, how about the crazy idea to have no branches at all?

There is no single best answer to these questions. Actually, the way you use the Continuous Integration process depends on your team development workflow. So, before we go any further, let's describe what the possible workflows are.

Development workflows

A development workflow is the way your team puts the code into the repository. It depends, of course, on many factors such as the source control management tool, the project specifics, or the team size.

As a result, each team develops the code in a slightly different manner. We can, however, classify them into three types: trunk-based workflow, branching workflow, and forking workflow.

 All workflows are described in detail with examples at `https://www.atlassian.com/git/tutorials/comparing-workflows`.

Trunk-based workflow

Trunk-based workflow is the simplest possible strategy. Its overview is presented in the following figure:

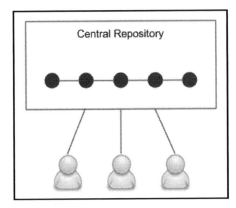

There is one central repository with a single entry for all changes to the project, which is called the trunk or master. Every member of the team clones the central repository to have their own local copies. The changes are committed directly to the central repository.

Branching workflow

Branching workflow, as its name suggests, means that the code is kept in many different branches. The idea is presented in the following figure:

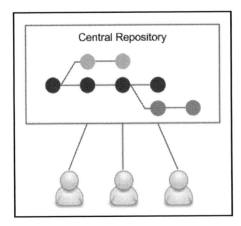

When developers start to work on a new feature, they create a dedicated branch from the trunk and commit all feature-related changes there. This makes it easy for multiple developers to work on a feature without breaking the main codebase. This is why, in the case of branching workflow, there is no problem in keeping the master healthy. When the feature is completed, a developer rebases the feature branch from master and creates a pull request that contains all feature-related code changes. It opens the code review discussions and makes space to check if the changes don't disturb the master. When the code is accepted by other developers and automatic system checks, then it is merged into the main codebase. Then, the build is run again on master but should almost never fail since it didn't fail on the branch.

Forking workflow

Forking workflow is very popular among the open source community. Its idea is presented in the following figure:

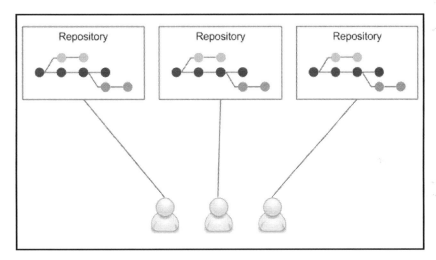

Each developer has his own server-side repository. They may or may not be the official repository, but technically, each repository is exactly the same.

Forking means literally creating a new repository from the other repository. Developers push to their own repositories and when they want to integrate the code, they create a pull request to the other repository.

The main advantage of the forking workflow is that the integration is not necessarily via a central repository. It also helps with the ownership because it allows accepting pull requests from others without giving them write access.

In the case of requirement-oriented commercial projects, the team usually works on one product and therefore has a central repository, so this model boils down to the branching workflow with the good ownership assignment, for example, only project leads can merge pull requests into the central repository.

Adopting Continuous Integration

We described different development workflows, but how do they influence the Continuous Integration configuration?

Branching strategies

Each development workflow implies a different Continuous Integration approach:

- **Trunk-based workflow**: implies constantly struggling against the broken pipeline. If everyone commits to the main codebase, then the pipeline often fails. In this case, the old Continuous Integration rule says, *"If the build is broken, then the development team stops whatever they are doing and fixes the problem immediately."*
- **Branching workflow**: solves the broken trunk issue but introduces another one: if everyone develops in their own branches, then where is the integration? A feature usually takes weeks or months to develop, and for all this time, the branch is not integrated into the main code, therefore it cannot be really called "continuous" integration; not to mention that there is a constant need for merging and resolving conflicts.
- **Forking workflow**: implies managing the Continuous Integration process by every repository owner, which isn't usually a problem. It shares, however, the same issues as the branching workflow.

There is no silver bullet, and different organizations choose different strategies. The solution that is the closest to perfection is using the technique of the branching workflow and the philosophy of the trunk-based workflow. In other words, we can create very small branches and integrate them frequently into master. This seems to take the best of both, however, requires either having tiny features or using feature toggles. Since the concept of feature toggles fits very well into Continuous Integration and Continuous Delivery, let's take a moment to explore it.

Feature toggles

Feature toggle is a technique that is an alternative to maintaining multiple source code branches such that the feature can be tested before it is completed and ready for release. It is used to disable the feature for users but enable it for developers while testing. Feature toggles are essentially variables used in conditional statements.

The simplest implementation of feature toggles are flags and the `if` statements. A development using feature toggles, as opposed to feature branching development, looks as follows:

1. A new feature has to be implemented.
2. Create a new flag or a configuration property `feature_toggle` (instead of the `feature` branch).
3. Every feature-related code is added inside the `if` statement (instead of committing to the `feature` branch), for example:

```
if (feature_toggle) {
    // do something
}
```

4. During the feature development:
   - Coding is done in master with `feature_toggle` = `true` (instead of coding in the feature branch)
   - Release is done from master with `feature_toggle` = `false`

5. When the feature development is completed, all `if` statements are removed and `feature_toggle` is removed from the configuration (instead of merging `feature` to master and removing the `feature` branch).

The benefit of feature toggle is that all development is done in the `trunk`, which enables the real Continuous Integration and mitigates problems with merging code.

Jenkins Multibranch

If you decide to use branches in any form, the long feature branches or the recommended short-lived branches, then it is convenient to know that the code is healthy before merging it into master. This approach results in always keeping the main codebase green and, luckily, there is an easy way to do it with Jenkins.

In order to use Multibranch in our calculator project, let's proceed with the following steps:

1. Open the main Jenkins page.
2. Click on **New Item**.
3. Enter `calculator-branches` as the item name, select **Multibranch Pipeline**, and click on **OK**.
4. In the **Branch Sources** section, click on **Add source**, and select **Git**.
5. Enter the repository address into **Project Repository**.

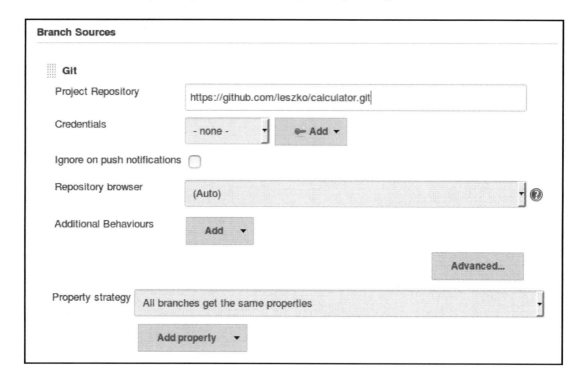

6. Tick **Periodically if not otherwise run** and set **1 minute** as **Interval**.
7. Click on **Save**.

Every minute, this configuration checks if there were any branches added (or removed) and creates (or deletes) the dedicated pipeline defined by Jenkinsfile.

We can create a new branch and see how it works. Let's create a new branch called `feature` and `push` it into the repository:

```
$ git checkout -b feature
$ git push origin feature
```

After a moment, you should see a new branch pipeline automatically created and run:

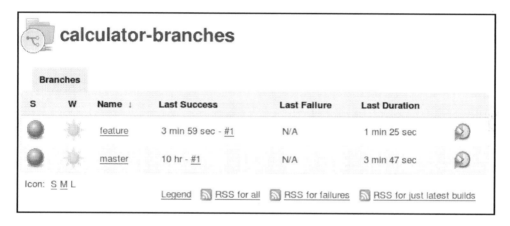

Now, before merging the feature branch to master, we can check if it's green. This approach should never break the master build.

 In the case of GitHub, there is an even better approach, using the `GitHub Organization Folder` plugin. It automatically creates pipelines with branches and pull requests for all projects.

A very similar approach is to build a pipeline per pull request instead of a pipeline per branch, which gives the same result; the main codebase is always healthy.

Non-technical requirements

Last but not least, Continuous Integration is not all about the technology. On the contrary, technology comes second. James Shore in his article *Continuous Integration on a Dollar a Day* described how to set up the Continuous Integration process without any additional software. All he used was a rubber chicken and a bell. The idea is to make the team work in one room and set up a separate computer with an empty chair. Put the rubber chicken and the bell in front of that computer. Now, when you plan to check in the code, take the rubber chicken, check in the code, go to the empty computer, checkout the fresh code, run all tests there, and if everything passes, put back the rubber chicken and ring the bell so that everyone knows that something has been added to the repository.

Continuous Integration on a Dollar a Day by *James Shore* can be found at: `http://www.jamesshore.com/Blog/Continuous-Integration-on-a-Dollar-a-Day.html`.

The idea is a little oversimplified, and automated tools are useful; however, the main message is that without each team member's engagement, even the best tools won't help. Jez Humble in his great book, *Continuous Delivery*, mentions the prerequisites for Continuous Integration that can be rephrased with the following points:

- **Check in regularly**: Quoting *Mike Roberts*, *"Continuously is more often than you think"*, the minimum is once a day.
- **Create comprehensive unit tests**: It's not only about the high test coverage, it's possible to have no assertions and still keep 100% coverage.
- **Keep the process quick**: Continuous Integration must take a short time, preferably under 5 minutes. 10 minutes is already a lot.
- **Monitor the builds**: It can be a shared responsibility or you can adapt the **build master** role that rotates weekly.

Exercises

You've learned a lot about how to configure the Continuous Integration process. Since *practice makes man perfect*, we recommend doing the following exercises:

1. Create a Python program that multiplies two numbers passed as the command-line parameters. Add unit tests and publish the project on GitHub:

    * Create two files `calculator.py` and `test_calculator.py`
    * You can use the `unittest` library at `https://docs.python.org/library/unittest.html`
    * Run the program and the unit test

2. Build the Continuous Integration pipeline for the Python calculator project:

    * Use Jenkinsfile for specifying the pipeline
    * Configure the trigger so that the pipeline runs automatically in case of any commit to the repository
    * The pipeline doesn't need the `Compile` step since Python is an interpretable language
    * Run the pipeline and observe the results
    * Try to commit the code that breaks each stage of the pipeline and observe how it is visualized in Jenkins

Summary

In this chapter, we covered all aspects of the Continuous Integration pipeline, which is always the first step for Continuous Delivery. The key takeaway from the chapter:

* Pipeline provides a general mechanism for organizing any automation processes; however, the most common use cases are Continuous Integration and Continuous Delivery
* Jenkins accepts different ways of defining pipelines but the recommended one is the declarative syntax
* Commit pipeline is the most basic Continuous Integration process and, as its name suggests, it should be run after every commit to the repository

- The pipeline definition should be stored in the repository as a Jenkinsfile
- Commit pipeline can be extended with the code quality stages
- No matter the project build tool, Jenkins commands should always be consistent with the local development commands
- Jenkins offers a wide range of triggers and notifications
- The development workflow should be carefully chosen inside the team or organization because it affects the Continuous Integration process and defines the way the code is developed

In the next chapter, we will focus on the next phase of the Continuous Delivery process, automated acceptance testing. It can be considered as the most important and, in many cases, the most difficult step to implement. We will explore the idea of acceptance testing and a sample implementation using Docker.

5
Automated Acceptance Testing

We already configured the commit phase of the Continuous Delivery process and now it's time to address the acceptance testing phase, which is usually the most challenging part. By gradually extending the pipeline, we will see different aspects of a well-done acceptance testing automation.

This chapter covers the following points:

- Introducing the acceptance testing process and its difficulties
- Explaining the idea of the artifact repository
- Creating the Docker registry on Docker Hub
- Installing and securing private Docker registry
- Implementing acceptance testing in the Jenkins pipeline
- Introducing and exploring Docker Compose
- Using Docker Compose in the acceptance testing process
- Writing acceptance tests with users

Introducing acceptance testing

Acceptance testing is a test performed to determine if the business requirements or contracts are met. It involves black-box testing against a complete system from a user perspective and its positive result should imply the acceptance of the software delivery. Sometimes, also called **UAT (user acceptance testing)**, end user testing, or beta testing, it is a phase of the development process when software meets the *real-world* audience.

Many projects rely on manual steps performed by QAs or users to verify the functional and nonfunctional requirements, but still, it's way more reasonable to run them as programmed repeatable operations.

Automated acceptance tests, however, can be considered difficult due to their specifics:

- **User-facing**: They need to be written together with a user, which requires an understanding between two worlds, technical and non-technical.
- **Dependencies integration**: The tested application should be run together with its dependencies in order to check whether the system as a whole works properly.
- **Environment identity**: Staging (testing) and production environments should be identical to ensure that when run in production, the application also behaves as expected.
- **Application identity**: Application should be built only once and the same binary should be transferred to production. That guarantees no changes in code between testing and releasing and eliminates the risk of different building environments.
- **Relevance and consequences**: If acceptance test passes, it should be clear that the application is ready for release from the user perspective.

We address all these difficulties in different sections of this chapter. Application identity can be achieved by building the Docker image only once and using Docker registry for its storage and versioning. Docker Compose helps with the dependencies integration providing a way to build a group of containerized applications working together. Creating tests in a user-facing manner is explained in the *Writing acceptance tests* section, and the environment identity is addressed by the Docker tool itself and can be also improved by other tools described in the next chapter. Concerning the relevance and consequences, the only good answer is to keep in mind that acceptance tests must always be of a high quality.

 Acceptance testing can have multiple meanings; in this book, we treat acceptance testing as a complete integration test from a user perspective, excluding nonfunctional testing, such as performance, load, and recovery.

Docker registry

Docker registry is a storage for Docker images. To be precise, it is a stateless server application that allows the images to be published (pushed) and later retrieved (pulled) when needed. We have already seen an example of the registry while running the official Docker images, such as `jenkins`. We pulled the images from Docker Hub, which is an official cloud-based Docker registry. Having a separate server to store, load, and search software packages is a more general concept called the software repository or, even more general, the artifact repository. Let's look closer at this idea.

Artifact repository

While the source control management stores the source code, the artifact repository is dedicated for storing software binary artifacts, for example, compiled libraries or components, later used to build a complete application. Why do we need to store binaries on a separate server using a separate tool?

- **File size**: Artifact files can be large, so the systems need to be optimized for their download and upload.
- **Versions**: Each uploaded artifact needs to have a version that makes it easy to browse and use. Not all versions, however, have to be stored forever; for example, if there was a bug detected, we may not be interested in the related artifact and remove it.
- **Revision mapping**: Each artifact should point to exactly one revision of the source control and, what's more, the binary creation process should be repeatable.
- **Packages**: Artifacts are stored in the compiled and compressed form so that these time-consuming steps need not be repeated.
- **Access control**: Users can be restricted differently to the source code and artifact binary access.
- **Clients**: Users of the artifact repository can be developers outside the team or organization, who want to use the library via its public API.
- **Use cases**: Artifact binaries are used to guarantee that exactly the same built version is deployed to every environment to ease the rollback procedure in case of failure.

The most popular artifact repositories are JFrog Artifactory and Sonatype Nexus.

The artifact repository plays a special role in the Continuous Delivery process because it guarantees that the same binary is used throughout all pipeline steps.

Let's look at the following figure presenting how it works:

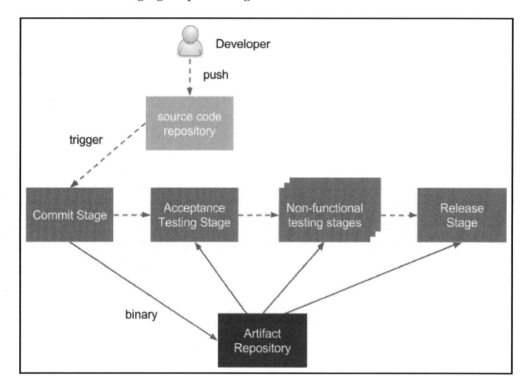

The **Developer** pushes a change to the **source code repository**, which triggers the pipeline build. As the last step of the **Commit Stage**, a binary is created and stored in the artifact repository. Afterward, during all other stages of the delivery process, the same binary is pulled and used.

 The built binary is often called the **release candidate** and the process of moving binary to the next stage is called **promotion**.

Depending on the programming language and technologies, the binary formats can differ.

For example, in the case of Java, usually, JAR files are stored and, in the case of Ruby, gem files. We work with Docker, so we will store Docker images as artifacts, and the tool to store Docker images is called Docker registry.

 Some teams maintain two repositories at the same time, artifact repository for JAR files and Docker registry for Docker images. While it may be useful during the first phase of the Docker introduction, there is no good reason to maintain both forever.

Installing Docker registry

First, we need to install a Docker registry. There are a number of options available, but two of them are more common than others, cloud-based Docker Hub registry and your own private Docker registry. Let's dig into them.

Docker Hub

Docker Hub is a cloud-based service that provides Docker registry and other features such as building images, testing them, and pulling code directly from the code repository. Docker Hub is cloud-hosted, so it does not really need any installation process. All you need to do is create a Docker Hub account:

1. Open `https://hub.docker.com/` in a browser.
2. Fill in the password, email address, and Docker ID.
3. After receiving an email and clicking the activation link, the account is created.

Docker Hub is definitely the simplest option to start with, and it allows storing both private and public images.

Private Docker registry

Docker Hub may not always be acceptable. It is not free for enterprises and, what's even more important, a lot of companies have policies not to store their software outside their own network. In this case, the only option is to install a private Docker registry.

The Docker registry installation process is quick and simple, however, making it secure and available in public requires setting up access restriction and the domain certificate. This is why we split this section into three parts:

- Installing the Docker registry application
- Adding domain certificate
- Adding access restriction

Installing the Docker registry application

Docker registry is available as a Docker image. To start this, we can run the following command:

```
$ docker run -d -p 5000:5000 --restart=always --name registry registry:2
```

By default, the registry data is stored as a docker volume in the default host filesystem's directory. To change it, you can add `-v <host_directory>:/var/lib/registry`. Another alternative is to use a volume container.

The command starts the registry and makes it accessible via port 5000. The `registry` container is started from the registry image (version 2). The `--restart=always` option causes the container to automatically restart whenever it's down.

Consider setting up a load balancer and starting a few Docker registry containers in case of a large number of users.

Adding a domain certificate

If the registry is run on the localhost, then everything works fine and no other installation steps are required. However, in most cases, we want to have a dedicated server for the registry, so that the images are widely available. In that case, Docker requires securing the registry with SSL/TLS. The process is very similar to the public web server configuration and, similarly, it's highly recommended having the certificate signed by CA (certificate authority). If obtaining the CA-signed certificate is not an option, then we can self-sign a certificate or use the `--insecure-registry` flag.

You can read about creating and using self-signed certificates at `https://docs.docker.com/registry/insecure/#using-self-signed-certificates`.

Having the certificates either signed by CA or self-signed, we can move `domain.crt` and `domain.key` to the `certs` directory and start the registry.

```
$ docker run -d -p 5000:5000 --restart=always --name registry -v
`pwd`/certs:/certs -e REGISTRY_HTTP_TLS_CERTIFICATE=/certs/domain.crt -e
REGISTRY_HTTP_TLS_KEY=/certs/domain.key registry:2
```

In case of a self-signed certificate, clients have to explicitly trust the certificate. In order to do this, they can copy the `domain.crt` file to `/etc/docker/certs.d/<docker_host_domain>:5000/ca.crt`.

Using the `--insecure-registry` flag is not recommended since it provides no security at all.

Adding an access restriction

Unless we use the registry inside a well-secured private network, we should configure the authentication.

The simplest way to do this is to create a user with a password using the `htpasswd` tool from the `registry` image:

```
$ mkdir auth
$ docker run --entrypoint htpasswd registry:2 -Bbn <username> <password> >
auth/passwords
```

The command runs the `htpasswd` tool to create the `auth/passwords` file (with one user inside). Then, we can run the registry with that one user authorized to access it:

```
$ docker run -d -p 5000:5000 --restart=always --name registry -v
`pwd`/auth:/auth -e "REGISTRY_AUTH=htpasswd" -e
"REGISTRY_AUTH_HTPASSWD_REALM=Registry Realm" -e
REGISTRY_AUTH_HTPASSWD_PATH=/auth/passwords -v `pwd`/certs:/certs -e
REGISTRY_HTTP_TLS_CERTIFICATE=/certs/domain.crt -e
REGISTRY_HTTP_TLS_KEY=/certs/domain.key registry:2
```

The command, in addition to setting the certificates, creates the access restriction limited to the users specified in the `auth/passwords` file.

As a result, before using the registry, a client needs to specify the username and password.

 Access restriction doesn't work in the case of the `--insecure-registry` flag.

Other Docker registries

Docker Hub and private registry are not the only possibilities when it comes to Docker-based artifact repositories.

The other options are as follows:

- **General-purpose repositories**: Widely-used general-purpose repositories, such as JFrog Artifactory or Sonatype Nexus, implement the Docker registry API. Their advantage is that one server can store both Docker images and other artifacts (for example, JAR files). These systems are also mature and provide enterprise integration.
- **Cloud-based registries**: Docker Hub is not the only cloud provider. Most cloud-oriented services offer Docker registries in the cloud, for example, Google Cloud or AWS.
- **Custom registries**: The Docker registry API is open, so it's possible to implement custom solutions. What's more, images can be exported to files, so it's feasible to store images simply as files.

Using Docker registry

When the registry is configured, we can show how to work with it in three steps:

- Building an image
- Pushing the image to the registry
- Pulling the image from the registry

Building an image

Let's use the example from Chapter 2, *Introducing Docker*, and build an image with Ubuntu and the Python interpreter installed. In a new directory, we need to create a Dockerfile:

```
FROM ubuntu:16.04
RUN apt-get update && \
    apt-get install -y python
```

Now, we can build the image:

```
$ docker build -t ubuntu_with_python .
```

Pushing the image

In order to push the created image, we need to tag it according to the naming convention:

```
<registry_address>/<image_name>:<tag>
```

The "registry_address" can be:

- User name in case of Docker Hub
- Domain name or IP address with port for a private registry (for example, localhost:5000)

In most cases, <tag> is in the form of image/application version.

Let's tag the image to use Docker Hub:

```
$ docker tag ubuntu_with_python leszko/ubuntu_with_python:1
```

We could have also tagged the image in the build command: "docker build -t leszko/ubuntu_with_python:1 . ".

If the repository has access restriction configured, we need to authorize it first:

```
$ docker login --username <username> --password <password>
```

It's possible to use the `docker login` command without parameters and Docker would ask interactively for the username and password.

Now, we can store the image in the registry using the `push` command:

```
$ docker push leszko/ubuntu_with_python:1
```

Note that there is no need to specify the registry address because Docker uses the naming convention to resolve it. The image is stored, and we can check it using the Docker Hub web interface available at `https://hub.docker.com`.

Pulling the image

To demonstrate how the registry works, we can remove the image locally and retrieve it from the registry:

```
$ docker rmi ubuntu_with_python leszko/ubuntu_with_python:1
```

We can see that the image has been removed using the `docker images` command. Then, let's retrieve the image back from the registry:

```
$ docker pull leszko/ubuntu_with_python:1
```

 If you use the free Docker Hub account, you may need to change the `ubuntu_with_python` repository to public before pulling it.

We can confirm the image is back with the `docker images` command.

When we have the registry configured and understand how it works, we can see how to use it inside the Continuous Delivery pipeline and build the acceptance testing stage.

Acceptance test in pipeline

We already understood the idea behind acceptance testing and know how to configure Docker registry, so we are ready for its first implementation inside the Jenkins pipeline.

Let's look at the figure that presents the process we will use:

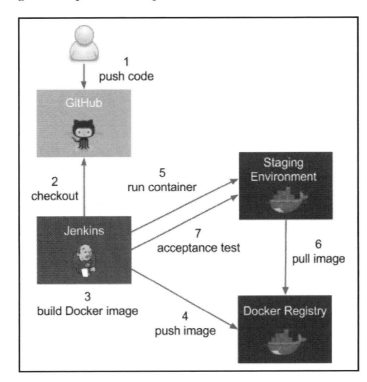

The process goes as follows:

1. The developer pushes a code change to GitHub.
2. Jenkins detects the change, triggers the build, and checks out the current code.
3. Jenkins executes the commit phase and builds the Docker image.
4. Jenkins pushes the image to Docker registry.
5. Jenkins runs the Docker container in the staging environment.
6. Staging the Docker host needs to pull the image from the Docker registry.
7. Jenkins runs the acceptance test suite against the application running in the staging environment.

 For the sake of simplicity, we will run the Docker container locally (and not on a separate staging server). In order to run it remotely, we need to use the -H option or to configure the DOCKER_HOST environment variable. We will cover this part in the next chapter.

Let's continue the pipeline we started in the previous chapter and add three more stages:

- `Docker build`
- `Docker push`
- `Acceptance test`

Keep in mind that you need to have the Docker tool installed on the Jenkins executor (agent slave or master, in the case of slave-less configuration) so that it is able to build Docker images.

> If you use dynamically provisioned Docker slaves, then there is no mature Docker image provided yet. You can build it yourself or use the `leszko/jenkins-docker-slave` image. You also need to mark the `privileged` option in the Docker agent configuration. This solution, however, has some drawbacks, so before using it in production, read the `http://jpetazzo.github.io/2015/09/03/do-not-use-docker-in-docker-for-ci/`.

The Docker build stage

We would like to run the calculator project as a Docker container, so we need to create Dockerfile and add the `"Docker build"` stage to Jenkinsfile.

Adding Dockerfile

Let's create Dockerfile in the root directory of the calculator project:

```
FROM frolvlad/alpine-oraclejdk8:slim
COPY build/libs/calculator-0.0.1-SNAPSHOT.jar app.jar
ENTRYPOINT ["java", "-jar", "app.jar"]
```

> The default build directory for Gradle is `build/libs/`, and `calculator-0.0.1-SNAPSHOT.jar` is the complete application packaged into one JAR file. Note that Gradle automatically versioned the application using the Maven-style version `0.0.1-SNAPSHOT`.

Dockerfile uses a base image that contains JDK 8 (`frolvlad/alpine-oraclejdk8:slim`). It also copies the application JAR (created by Gradle) and runs it. Let's check if the application builds and runs:

```
$ ./gradlew build
$ docker build -t calculator .
$ docker run -p 8080:8080 --name calculator calculator
```

Using the preceding commands, we've built the application, built the Docker image, and run the Docker container. After a while, we should be able to open the browser to `http://localhost:8080/sum?a=1&b=2` and see 3 as a result.

We can stop the container and push the Dockerfile to the GitHub repository:

```
$ git add Dockerfile
$ git commit -m "Add Dockerfile"
$ git push
```

Adding the Docker build to the pipeline

The last step we need is adding the "`Docker build`" stage to Jenkinsfile. Usually, the JAR packaging is also declared as a separate `Package` stage:

```
stage("Package") {
    steps {
        sh "./gradlew build"
    }
}

stage("Docker build") {
    steps {
        sh "docker build -t leszko/calculator ."
    }
}
```

 We don't explicitly version the image, but each image has a unique hash ID. We will cover the explicit versioning in the next chapter.

Note that we used the Docker registry name in the image tag. There is no need to have the image tagged twice `calculator` and `leszko/calculator`.

When we commit and push Jenkinsfile, the pipeline build should start automatically and we should see all boxes green. This means that the Docker image has been built successfully.

 There is also a Gradle plugin for Docker that allows executing the Docker operations within Gradle scripts. You can see an example at: `https://spring.io/guides/gs/spring-boot-docker/`.

The Docker push stage

When the image is ready, we can store it in the registry. The `Docker push` stage is very simple. It's enough to add the following code to Jenkinsfile:

```
stage("Docker push") {
    steps {
        sh "docker push leszko/calculator"
    }
}
```

 If Docker registry has the access restricted, then first we need to log in using the `docker login` command. Needless to say, the credentials must be well secured, for example, using a dedicated credential store as described on the official Docker page: `https://docs.docker.com/engine/reference/commandline/login/#credentials-store`.

As always, pushing changes to the GitHub repository triggers Jenkins to start the build and, after a while, we should have the image automatically stored in the registry.

Acceptance testing stage

To perform acceptance testing, first, we need to deploy the application to the staging environment and then run the acceptance test suite against it.

Adding a staging deployment to the pipeline

Let's add a stage to run the `calculator` container:

```
stage("Deploy to staging") {
    steps {
        sh "docker run -d --rm -p 8765:8080 --name calculator
leszko/calculator"
    }
}
```

After running this stage, the `calculator` container is running as a daemon, publishing its port as `8765` and being removed automatically when stopped.

Adding an acceptance test to the pipeline

Acceptance testing usually requires running a dedicated black-box test suite that checks the behavior of the system. We will cover it in the *Writing acceptance tests* section. At the moment, for the sake of simplicity, let's perform acceptance testing simply by calling the web service endpoint with the `curl` tool and checking the result using the `test` command.

In the root directory of the project, let's create the `acceptance_test.sh` file:

```
#!/bin/bash
test $(curl localhost:8765/sum?a=1\&b=2) -eq 3
```

We call the `sum` endpoint with parameters `a=1` and `b=2` and expect to receive 3 in response.

Then, the `Acceptance test` stage can look as follows:

```
stage("Acceptance test") {
    steps {
        sleep 60
        sh "./acceptance_test.sh"
    }
}
```

Since the `docker run -d` command is asynchronous, we need to wait using the `sleep` operation to make sure the service is already running.

There is no good way to check if the service is already running. An alternative to sleeping could be a script checking every second whether the service has already started.

Adding a cleaning stage environment

As the last step of acceptance testing, we can add the staging environment cleanup. The best place to do this is in the `post` section, to make sure it executes even in case of failure:

```
post {
    always {
        sh "docker stop calculator"
    }
}
```

This statement makes sure that the `calculator` container is no longer running on the Docker host.

Docker Compose

Life is easy without dependencies. In real-life, however, almost every application links to a database, cache, messaging system, or another application. In the case of a (micro) service architecture, each service needs a bunch of other services to do its work. The monolithic architecture does not eliminate the issue, an application usually has some dependencies, at least to the database.

Imagine a newcomer joining your development team; how much time does it take to set up the entire development environment and run the application with all its dependencies?

When it comes to automated acceptance testing, the dependencies issue is no longer only a matter of convenience, but it becomes a necessity. While, during unit testing, we could mock the dependencies, the acceptance testing suite requires a complete environment. How do we set it up quickly and in a repeatable manner? Luckily, Docker Compose is a tool that can help.

What is Docker Compose?

Docker Compose is a tool for defining, running, and managing multi-container Docker applications. Services are defined in a configuration file (a YAML format) and can be created and run all together with a single command.

Docker Compose orchestrates containers using standard Docker mechanisms and provides a convenient way to specify the entire environment.

Docker Compose comes with a lot of features, the most interesting are:

- Building a set of services
- Launching a set of services together
- Managing the state of individual services
- Preserving volume data between runs
- Scaling services up and down
- Showing logs of individual services
- Caching configuration and recreating changed containers between runs

 A detailed description of Docker Compose and its features can be found on the official page at: `https://docs.docker.com/compose/`.

We present the Docker Compose tool starting with the installation process, going through the docker-compose.yml configuration file and the `docker-compose` command, to end up with the building and scaling features.

Installing Docker Compose

The simplest method to install Docker Compose is to use the pip package manager:

 You can find the pip tool installation guide at `https://pip.pypa.io/en/stable/installing/`, or for Ubuntu, at `sudo apt-get install python-pip`.

```
$ pip install docker-compose
```

To check that Docker Compose is installed, we can run:

```
$ docker-compose --version
```

 Installation guidelines for all operating systems can be found at `https://docs.docker.com/compose/install/`.

Defining docker-compose.yml

The `docker-compose.yml` file is used to define the configuration for containers, their relations, and runtime properties.

In other words, when Dockerfile specifies how to create a single Docker image, then `docker-compose.yml` specifies how to set up the entire environment out of Docker images.

 There are three versions of the `docker-compose.yml` file format. In this book, we use version 3, which is the most current and recommended. Read more at: `https://docs.docker.com/compose/compose-file/compose-versioning/`.

The `docker-compose.yml` file has a lot of features and all of them can be found at the official page: `https://docs.docker.com/compose/compose-file/`. We will cover the most important ones in the context of the Continuous Delivery process.

Let's start with an example and imagine that our calculator project uses the Redis server for caching. In this case, we need an environment with two containers, `calculator` and `redis`. In a new directory, let's create the `docker-compose.yml` file.

```
version: "3"
services:
    calculator:
        image: calculator:latest
        ports:
            - 8080
    redis:
        image: redis:latest
```

The environment configuration is presented in the following figure:

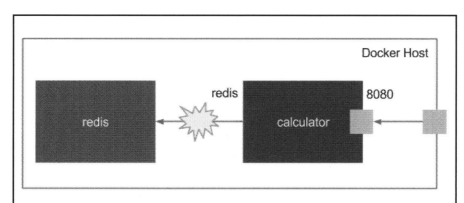

Let's see the definition of the two containers:

- **redis**: A container from the latest version of the `redis` image pulled from the official Docker Hub.
- **calculator**: A container from the latest version of the `calculator` image built locally. It publishes the `8080` port to the Docker host (which is a substitute for the `-p` option of the `docker` command). The container links to the `redis` container, which means that they share the same network and the `redis` IP address is visible under the `redis` hostname from inside the `calculator` container.

 If we like a service to be addressed by a different hostname than its service name (for example, by redis-cache apart from redis), then we can create aliases using the links keyword.

Using the docker-compose command

The `docker-compose` command reads the definition file and creates the environment:

```
$ docker-compose up -d
```

The command started two containers, `calculator` and `redis` in the background (- d option). We can check that the containers are running:

```
$ docker-compose ps
   Name                    Command              State         Ports
   ----------------------------------------------------------------------
   project_calculator_1    java -jar app.jar    Up       0.0.0.0:8080->8080/tcp
   project_redis_1         docker-entrypoint.sh redis ... Up 6379/tcp
```

The container names are prefixed with the project name `project`, which is taken from the name of the directory in which the `docker-compose.yml` file is placed. We could specify the project name manually using the `-p <project_name>` option. Since Docker Compose is run on top of Docker, we can also use the `docker` command to confirm that the containers are running:

```
$ docker ps
CONTAINER ID    IMAGE               COMMAND                    PORTS
360518e46bd3    calculator:latest   "java -jar app.jar"
0.0.0.0:8080->8080/tcp
2268b9f1e14b    redis:latest        "docker-entrypoint..."    6379/tcp
```

When we're done, we can tear down the environment:

```
$ docker-compose down
```

The example is very simple, but the tool itself is extremely powerful. With a short configuration and a bunch of commands, we control the orchestration of all services. Before we use Docker Compose for acceptance testing, let's look at two other Docker Compose features: building images and scaling containers.

Building images

In the preceding example, we had to first build the `calculator` image using the `docker build` command, and then it could be specified inside docker-compose.yml. There is also another approach to let Docker Compose build the image. In that case, we need to specify the `build` property instead of `image` in the configuration.

Let's put the `docker-compose.yml` file in the calculator project's directory. When Dockerfile and Docker Compose configurations are in the same directory, the former can look as follows:

```
version: "3"
services:
    calculator:
        build: .
        ports:
            - 8080
    redis:
        image: redis:latest
```

The `docker-compose build` command builds the image. We can also ask Docker Compose to build images before running the containers with the use of the `docker-compose --build up` command.

Scaling services

Docker Compose provides the functionality to automatically create multiple instances of the same container. We can either specify the `replicas: <number>` parameter inside `docker-compose.yml` or use the `docker-compose scale` command.

As an example, let's run the environment again and replicate the `calculator` container:

```
$ docker-compose up -d
$ docker-compose scale calculator=5
```

We can check which containers are running:

```
$ docker-compose ps
Name                     Command                  State Ports
------------------------------------------------------------------------
calculator_calculator_1  java -jar app.jar        Up    0.0.0.0:32777->8080/tcp
calculator_calculator_2  java -jar app.jar        Up    0.0.0.0:32778->8080/tcp
calculator_calculator_3  java -jar app.jar        Up    0.0.0.0:32779->8080/tcp
calculator_calculator_4  java -jar app.jar        Up    0.0.0.0:32781->8080/tcp
calculator_calculator_5  java -jar app.jar        Up    0.0.0.0:32780->8080/tcp
calculator_redis_1       docker-entrypoint.sh redis ... Up 6379/tcp
```

Five `calculator` containers are exactly the same, apart from the container ID, container name, and published port numbers.

They all use the same instance of the Redis container. We can now stop and remove all the containers:

```
$ docker-compose down
```

Scaling containers is one of the most impressive Docker Compose features. With one command, we can scale up and down the number of clone instances. Docker Compose takes care of cleaning up the containers that are no longer used.

We have seen the most interesting functionalities of the Docker Compose tool.

In the next section, we will focus on how to use it in the context of automated acceptance testing.

Acceptance testing with Docker Compose

Docker Compose fits the acceptance testing process perfectly because it enables setting up the entire environment with one command. What's more, after the testing is performed, the environment can also be cleaned up with one command. If we decide to use Docker Compose on production, then the other benefit is that the acceptance test uses exactly the same configuration, tools, and commands as the released application.

To see how to apply Docker Compose for the Jenkins acceptance testing stage, let's continue the calculator project example and add the Redis-based caching to the application. Then, we will see two different approaches to run acceptance testing: the Jenkins-first method and the Docker-first method.

Using a multi-container environment

Docker Compose provides dependencies between the containers; in other words, it links one container to another container. Technically, this means that containers share the same network and that one container is visible from the other. To continue our example, we need to add this dependency in the code, and we will do this in a few steps.

Adding a Redis client library to Gradle

In the `build.gradle` file, add the following configuration to the `dependencies` section:

```
compile "org.springframework.data:spring-data-redis:1.8.0.RELEASE"
compile "redis.clients:jedis:2.9.0"
```

It adds the Java libraries that take care of the communication with Redis.

Adding a Redis cache configuration

Add a new file `src/main/java/com/leszko/calculator/CacheConfig.java`:

```java
package com.leszko.calculator;
import org.springframework.cache.CacheManager;
import org.springframework.cache.annotation.CachingConfigurerSupport;
import org.springframework.cache.annotation.EnableCaching;
import org.springframework.context.annotation.Bean;
import org.springframework.context.annotation.Configuration;
import org.springframework.data.redis.cache.RedisCacheManager;
import org.springframework.data.redis.connection.RedisConnectionFactory;
import
org.springframework.data.redis.connection.jedis.JedisConnectionFactory;
import org.springframework.data.redis.core.RedisTemplate;

/** Cache config. */
@Configuration
@EnableCaching
public class CacheConfig extends CachingConfigurerSupport {
    private static final String REDIS_ADDRESS = "redis";

    @Bean
    public JedisConnectionFactory redisConnectionFactory() {
        JedisConnectionFactory redisConnectionFactory = new
          JedisConnectionFactory();
        redisConnectionFactory.setHostName(REDIS_ADDRESS);
        redisConnectionFactory.setPort(6379);
        return redisConnectionFactory;
    }

    @Bean
    public RedisTemplate<String, String>
redisTemplate(RedisConnectionFactory cf) {
        RedisTemplate<String, String> redisTemplate = new
RedisTemplate<String,
          String>();
        redisTemplate.setConnectionFactory(cf);
```

```
        return redisTemplate;
    }

    @Bean
    public CacheManager cacheManager(RedisTemplate redisTemplate) {
        return new RedisCacheManager(redisTemplate);
    }
}
```

This a standard Spring cache configuration. Note that for the Redis server address, we use the `redis` hostname that is automatically available thanks to the Docker Compose linking mechanism.

Adding Spring Boot caching

When the cache is configured, we can finally add caching to our web service. In order to do this, we need to change the
`src/main/java/com/leszko/calculator/Calculator.java` file to look as follows:

```
package com.leszko.calculator;
import org.springframework.cache.annotation.Cacheable;
import org.springframework.stereotype.Service;

/** Calculator logic */
@Service
public class Calculator {
    @Cacheable("sum")
    public int sum(int a, int b) {
        return a + b;
    }
}
```

From now on, the sum calculations are cached in Redis, and when we call the
`/sum` endpoint of the `calculator` web service, it will first try to retrieve the result from the cache.

Checking the caching environment

Assuming that we have our docker-compose.yml in the calculator project's directory, we can now start the containers:

```
$ ./gradlew clean build
$ docker-compose up --build -d
```

We can check the port on which the calculator service is published:

```
$ docker-compose port calculator 8080
0.0.0.0:32783
```

If we open the browser on `localhost:32783/sum?a=1&b=2`, the calculator service should reply 3 and, in the meantime, access the `redis` service and store the cached value there. To see that the cache value was really stored in Redis, we can access the `redis` container and look inside the Redis database:

```
$ docker-compose exec redis redis-cli

127.0.0.1:6379> keys *
1)
"\xac\xed\x00\x05sr\x00/org.springframework.cache.interceptor.SimpleKeyL\nW
\x03km\x93\xd8\x02\x00\x02I\x00\bhashCode[\x00\x06paramst\x00\x13[Ljava/lan
g/Object;xp\x00\x00\x03\xe2ur\x00\x13[Ljava.lang.Object;\x90\xceX\x9f\x10s)
l\x02\x00\x00xp\x00\x00\x00\x02sr\x00\x11java.lang.Integer\x12\xe2\xa0\xa4\
xf7\x81\x878\x02\x00\x01I\x00\x05valuexr\x00\x10java.lang.Number\x86\xac\x9
5\x1d\x0b\x94\xe0\x8b\x02\x00\x00xp\x00\x00\x00\x01sq\x00~\x00\x05\x00\x00\
x00\x02"
2) "sum~keys"
```

The `docker-compose exec` command executed the `redis-cli` (the Redis client to browse its database content) command inside the `redis` container. Then, we can run `keys *` to print everything that is stored in Redis.

You can play more with the calculator application and open the browser with different values to see that the Redis service content increases. After this, it's important to tear down the environment with the `docker-compose down` command.

In the next sections, we will see two methods of acceptance tests for the multi-container project. Obviously, before we take any action on Jenkins, we need to commit and push all the changed files (including `docker-compose.yml`) to GitHub.

 Note that, for further steps, Docker Compose has to be installed on Jenkins executors.

Method 1 – Jenkins-first acceptance testing

The first method is to perform acceptance testing in the same way we did in the case of a single container application. The only difference is that now we have two containers running as presented in the following figure:

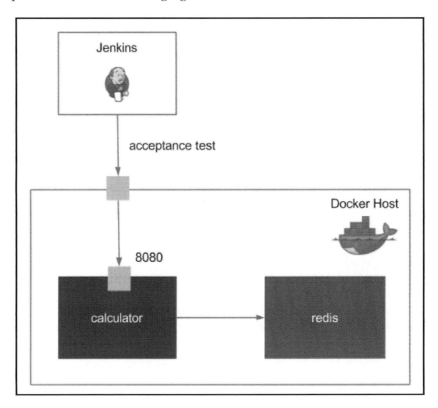

The `redis` container is not visible from a user perspective, so as a result, the only difference between single-container and multi-container acceptance testing is that we use the `docker-compose up` command instead of `docker run`.

Other Docker commands can be also replaced with their Docker Compose equivalents: `docker-compose build` for `docker build` and `docker-compose push` for `docker push`. Nevertheless, if we build just one image, then leaving Docker commands is fine as well.

Changing the staging deployment stage

Let's change the `Deploy to staging` stage to use Docker Compose:

```
stage("Deploy to staging") {
    steps {
        sh "docker-compose up -d"
    }
}
```

We must change the clean up in exactly the same way:

```
post {
    always {
        sh "docker-compose down"
    }
}
```

Changing the acceptance test stage

For the purpose of using `docker-compose scale`, we didn't specify the port number under which our web service would be published. If we did, then the scaling process would fail because all clones would try to publish under the same port number. On the contrary, we let Docker choose the port. Therefore, we need to change the `acceptance_test.sh` script to first find what the port number is and then run `curl` with the correct port number.

```
#!/bin/bash
CALCULATOR_PORT=$(docker-compose port calculator 8080 | cut -d: -f2)
test $(curl localhost:$CALCULATOR_PORT/sum?a=1\&b=2) -eq 3
```

Let's figure out how we found the port number:

1. The `docker-compose port calculator 8080` command checks under which IP and port address the web service is published (it returns, for example, `127.0.0.1:57648`).
2. `cut -d: -f2` selects only port (for example, for `127.0.0.1:57648`, it returns `57648`).

We can push the change to GitHub and observe the Jenkins results. The idea is still the same as with the single-container application, set up the environment, run the acceptance test suite, and tear down the environment. Even though this acceptance testing method is good and works well, let's look at the alternative solution.

Method 2 – Docker-first acceptance testing

In the Docker-first approach, we create an additional `test` container that performs testing from inside the Docker host, as presented in the following figure:

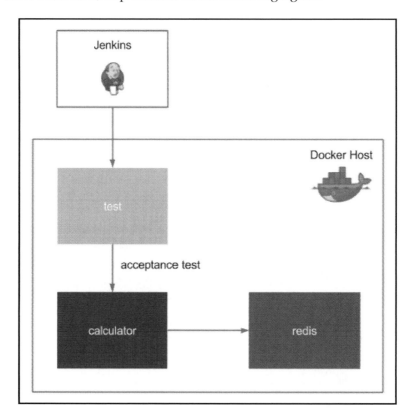

This approach facilitates the acceptance test script in terms of retrieving the port number and can be easily run without Jenkins. It's also much more in the Docker style.

The drawback is that we need to create a separate Dockerfile and Docker Compose configuration for the purpose of testing.

Creating a Dockerfile for acceptance test

We will start by creating a separate Dockerfile for acceptance testing. Let's create a new directory `acceptance` in the calculator project and a Dockerfile inside:

```
FROM ubuntu:trusty
RUN apt-get update && \
    apt-get install -yq curl
COPY test.sh .
CMD ["bash", "test.sh"]
```

It creates an image that runs the acceptance test.

Creating docker-compose.yml for acceptance test

In the same directory, let's create `docker-compose-acceptance.yml` to provide the testing orchestration:

```
version: "3"
services:
    test:
        build: ./acceptance
```

It creates a new container that is linked to the container being tested: `calculator`. What's more, internally it's always 8080 so that eliminates the need for the tricky part of port finding.

Creating an acceptance test script

The last missing part is the test script. In the same directory, let's create the `test.sh` file that represents the acceptance test:

```
#!/bin/bash
sleep 60
test $(curl calculator:8080/sum?a=1\&b=2) -eq 3
```

It's very similar to the previous acceptance test script, the only difference is that we can address the calculator service by the `calculator` hostname and that the port number is always `8080`. Also, in this case, we wait inside the script, not in the Jenkinsfile.

Running the acceptance test

We can run the test locally using the Docker Compose command from the root project directory:

```
$ docker-compose -f docker-compose.yml -f acceptance/docker-compose-
acceptance.yml -p acceptance up -d --build
```

The command uses two Docker Compose configurations to run the `acceptance` project. One of the started containers should be called `acceptance_test_1` and be interested in its result. We can check its logs with the following command:

```
$ docker logs acceptance_test_1
  %    Total %   Received % Xferd Average Speed Time
 100 1      100 1         0 0      1        0     0:00:01
```

The log shows that the `curl` command has been successfully called. If we want to check whether the test succeeded or failed, we can check the exit code of the container:

```
$ docker wait acceptance_test_1
0
```

The 0 exit code means that the test succeeded. Any code other than 0 would mean that the test failed. After the test is done, we should, as always, tear down the environment:

```
$ docker-compose -f docker-compose.yml -f acceptance/docker-compose-
acceptance.yml -p acceptance down
```

Changing the acceptance test stage

As the last step, we can add the acceptance test execution to the pipeline. Let's replace the last three stages in Jenkinsfile with one new **Acceptance test** stage:

```
stage("Acceptance test") {
    steps {
        sh "docker-compose -f docker-compose.yml
                    -f acceptance/docker-compose-acceptance.yml build test"
        sh "docker-compose -f docker-compose.yml
                    -f acceptance/docker-compose-acceptance.yml
                    -p acceptance up -d"
        sh 'test $(docker wait acceptance_test_1) -eq 0'
    }
}
```

This time, we first build the `test` service. There is no need to build the `calculator` image; it's already done by the previous stages. In the end, we should clean up the environment:

```
post {
    always {
        sh "docker-compose -f docker-compose.yml
                    -f acceptance/docker-compose-acceptance.yml
                    -p acceptance down"
    }
}
```

After adding this to Jenkinsfile, we're done with the second method. We can test this by pushing all the changes to GitHub.

Comparing method 1 and method 2

To sum up, let's compare both solutions. The first approach is the real black-box testing from the user perspective in which Jenkins plays the role of a user. The advantage is that it's very close to what will be done in production; in the end, we will access containers via its Docker host. The second approach tests the application from the inside of another container. The solution is somehow more elegant and can be run locally in a simple way; however, it requires more files to create and does not call the application via its Docker host like it will be later done in production.

In the next section, we step away from Docker and Jenkins and take a closer look at the process of writing the acceptance tests themselves.

Writing acceptance tests

So far, we used the `curl` command to perform a suite of acceptance tests. That is obviously a considerable simplification. Technically speaking, if we write a REST web service, then we could write all black-box tests as a big script with a number of "curl" calls. This solution would be, however, very difficult to read, understand, and maintain. What's more, the script would be completely incomprehensible by non-technical, business-related users. How to address this issue and create tests with a good structure, readable by users, and meet its fundamental goal: automatically checking if the system is as expected? I will answer this question throughout this section.

Writing user-facing tests

Acceptance tests are written with users and should be comprehensible to users. This is why the choice of a method for writing them depends on who the customer is.

For example, imagine a purely technical person. If you write a web service that optimizes the database storing, and your system is used only by other systems and read only by other developers, then your tests can be expressed in the same way as unit tests. As a rule, the test is good if understood by both, developer and user.

In real life, most software is written to deliver a specific business value, and that business value is defined by non-developers. Therefore, we need a common language to collaborate. On one side, there is the business who understands what is needed but not how to do it; on the other side, the development team who knows how but doesn't know what. Luckily, there are a number of frameworks that help to connect these two worlds, for instance, Cucumber, FitNesse, JBehave, Capybara, and many more. They differ from each other, and each of them may be a subject for a separate book; however, the general idea of writing acceptance tests is the same and can be presented in the following figure:

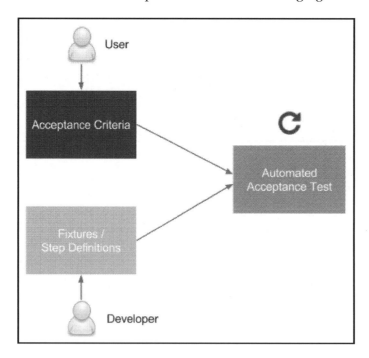

The **Acceptance Criteria** are written by users (or a product owner as their representative) with the help of developers. They are usually written in the form of the following scenarios:

```
Given I have two numbers: 1 and 2
When the calculator sums them
Then I receive 3 as a result
```

Developers write the testing implementation called **fixtures** or **step definitions** that integrates the human-friendly DSL specification with the programming language. As a result, we have an automated test that can be well-integrated into the Continuous Delivery pipeline.

Needless to add, writing acceptance tests is a continuous agile process, not a waterfall one. It requires constant collaboration during which the test specifications are improved and maintained by both, developers and business.

 In the case of an application with a user interface, it can be tempting to perform the acceptance testing directly via the interface (for example, by recording Selenium scripts); however, this approach when not done properly can lead to tests that are slow and tightly coupled to the interface layer.

Let's see how writing acceptance tests look in practice and how to bind them to the Continuous Delivery pipeline.

Using the acceptance testing framework

Let's use the Cucumber framework and create an acceptance test for the calculator project. As previously described, we will do this in three steps:

- Creating acceptance criteria
- Creating step definitions
- Running an automated acceptance test

Creating acceptance criteria

Let's put the business specification in
`src/test/resources/feature/calculator.feature`:

```
Feature: Calculator
    Scenario: Sum two numbers
        Given I have two numbers: 1 and 2
        When the calculator sums them
        Then I receive 3 as a result
```

This file should be created by users with the help of developers. Note that it is written in a way that non-technical people can understand it.

Creating step definitions

The next step is to create the Java bindings so that the feature specification would be executable. In order to do this, we create a new file
`src/test/java/acceptance/StepDefinitions.java`:

```java
package acceptance;

import cucumber.api.java.en.Given;
import cucumber.api.java.en.Then;
import cucumber.api.java.en.When;
import org.springframework.web.client.RestTemplate;

import static org.junit.Assert.assertEquals;

/** Steps definitions for calculator.feature */
public class StepDefinitions {
    private String server = System.getProperty("calculator.url");

    private RestTemplate restTemplate = new RestTemplate();

    private String a;
    private String b;
    private String result;

    @Given("^I have two numbers: (.*) and (.*)$")
    public void i_have_two_numbers(String a, String b) throws Throwable {
        this.a = a;
        this.b = b;
    }

    @When("^the calculator sums them$")
```

```
public void the_calculator_sums_them() throws Throwable {
    String url = String.format("%s/sum?a=%s&b=%s", server, a, b);
    result = restTemplate.getForObject(url, String.class);
}

@Then("^I receive (.*) as a result$")
public void i_receive_as_a_result(String expectedResult) throws
Throwable {
    assertEquals(expectedResult, result);
}
}
```

Each line (Given, When, and Then) from the feature specification file is matched by regular expressions with the corresponding method in the Java code. The wildcards (.*) are passed as parameters. Note that the server address is passed as the Java property calculator.url. The method performs the following actions:

- i_have_two_numbers: Saves parameters as fields
- the_calculator_sums_them: Calls the remote calculator service and stores the result in a field
- i_receive_as_a_result: Asserts that the result is as expected

Running an automated acceptance test

To run an automated test, we need to make a few configurations:

1. **Add Java cucumber libraries**: In the build.gradle file, add the following code to the dependencies section:

   ```
   testCompile("info.cukes:cucumber-java:1.2.4")
   testCompile("info.cukes:cucumber-junit:1.2.4")
   ```

2. **Add Gradle target**: In the same file, add the following code:

   ```
   task acceptanceTest(type: Test) {
       include '**/acceptance/**'
       systemProperties System.getProperties()
   }

   test {
       exclude '**/acceptance/**'
   }
   ```

> This splits the tests into unit (run with `./gradlew test`) and acceptance (run with `./gradlew acceptanceTest`).

3. **Add JUnit runner**: Add a new file `src/test/java/acceptance/AcceptanceTest.java`:

```
package acceptance;

import cucumber.api.CucumberOptions;
import cucumber.api.junit.Cucumber;
import org.junit.runner.RunWith;

/** Acceptance Test */
@RunWith(Cucumber.class)
@CucumberOptions(features = "classpath:feature")
public class AcceptanceTest { }
```

This is the entry point to the acceptance test suite.

After this configuration, if the server is running on the localhost, we can test it by executing the following code:

```
$ ./gradlew acceptanceTest –Dcalculator.url=http://localhost:8080
```

Obviously, we can add this command to our `acceptance_test.sh` instead of the `curl` command. This would make the Cucumber acceptance test run in the Jenkins pipeline.

Acceptance test-driven development

Acceptance tests, like most aspects of the Continuous Delivery process, are less about technology and more about people. The test quality depends on, of course, the engagement of users and developers, but also, what is maybe less intuitive, the time when the tests are created.

The last question to ask is, during which phase of the software development life cycle should the acceptance tests be prepared? Or to rephrase it, should we create acceptance tests before or after writing the code?

Technically speaking, the result is the same; the code is well-covered with both, unit and acceptance tests. However, it's tempting to consider writing tests first. The idea of TDD (test-driven development) can be well adapted for acceptance testing. If unit tests are written before the code, the result code is cleaner and better structured. Analogously, if acceptance tests are written before the system feature, the resulting feature corresponds better to the customer's requirements. This process, often called acceptance test-driven development, is presented in the following figure:

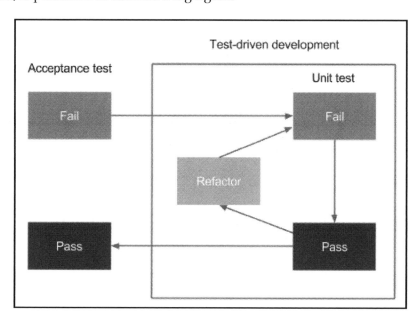

Users, with developers, write the acceptance criteria specification in the human-friendly DSL format. Developers write the fixtures and the tests fail. Then, the feature development starts using the TDD methodology internally. After the feature is completed, the acceptance test should pass, and this is a sign that the feature is completed.

A very good practice is to attach the Cucumber feature specification to the request ticket in the issue tracking tool (for example, JIRA) so that the feature would be always requested together with its acceptance test. Some development teams take an even more radical approach and refuse to start the development process if no acceptance tests are prepared. There is a lot of sense in that, after all, *how can you develop something that the client can't test?*

Exercises

We covered a lot of new material throughout this chapter, so to better understand, we recommend doing the exercises and creating your own project with acceptance tests:

1. Create a Ruby-based web service `book-library` to store books:

   The acceptance criteria is delivered in the form of the following Cucumber feature:

   ```
   Scenario: Store book in the library
   Given: Book "The Lord of the Rings" by "J.R.R. Tolkien" with ISBN
   number
   "0395974682"
   When: I store the book in library
   Then: I am able to retrieve the book by the ISBN number
   ```

   - Write step definitions for the Cucumber test
   - Write the web service (the simplest is to use the Sinatra framework: `http://www.sinatrarb.com/`, but you can also use Ruby on Rails).
   - The book should have the following attributes: name, author, and ISBN.
   - The web service should have the following endpoints:
     - POST "`/books/`" to add a book
     - GET "`books/<isbn>`" to retrieve the book
   - The data can be stored in the memory.
   - In the end, check if the acceptance test is green.

2. Add "book-library" as a Docker image to the Docker registry:
   - Create an account on Docker Hub.
   - Create Dockerfile for the application.
   - Build the Docker image and tag it according to the naming convention.
   - Push the image to Docker Hub.

3. Create the Jenkins pipeline to build Docker image, push it to the Docker registry, and perform acceptance testing:

    - Create a `"Docker build"` stage.
    - Create the `Docker login` and `Docker push` stages.
    - Create a `test` container that performs acceptance testing and use Docker Compose to perform the test.
    - Add an `Acceptance test` stage to the pipeline.
    - Run the pipeline and observe the result.

Summary

In this chapter, you learned how to build a complete and functional acceptance test stage, which is an essential part of the Continuous Delivery process. The key takeaway from the chapter:

- Acceptance tests can be difficult to create because they combine technical challenges (application dependencies, environment set up) with personal challenges (developers-business collaboration).
- Acceptance testing frameworks provide a way to write tests in a human-friendly language that makes them comprehensible to non-technical people.
- Docker registry is an artifact repository for Docker images.
- Docker registry fits well with the Continuous Delivery process because it provides a way to use exactly the same Docker image throughout the stages and environments.
- Docker Compose orchestrates a group of Docker container interacting together. It can also build images and scale containers.
- Docker Compose can help with setting up a complete environment before running a suite of acceptance tests.
- Acceptance tests can be written as a Docker image, and Docker Compose can run the complete environment together with the tests and provide the results.

In the next chapter, we will cover the missing stages necessary to complete the Continuous Delivery pipeline.

6

Configuration Management with Ansible

We have already covered the two most crucial phases of the Continuous Delivery process: the commit phase and the automated acceptance testing. In this chapter, we will focus on the configuration management, which connects the virtual containerized environment to the real server infrastructure.

This chapter covers the following points:

- Introducing the concept of configuration management
- Explaining the most popular configuration management tools
- Discussing Ansible requirements and the installation process
- Using Ansible with ad hoc commands
- Showing the power of Ansible automation with playbooks
- Explaining Ansible roles and Ansible Galaxy
- Implementing a use case of the deployment process
- Using Ansible together with Docker and Docker Compose

Introducing configuration management

Configuration management is a process of controlling configuration changes in a way that the system maintains integrity over time. Even though the term did not originate in the IT industry, currently it is broadly used to refer to the software and the hardware. In this context, it concerns the following aspects:

- **Application configuration**: This involves software properties that decide how the system works, which are usually expressed in the form of flags or properties files passed to the application, for example, the database address, the maximum chunk size for file processing, or the logging level. They can be applied during different development phases: build, package, deploy, or run.
- **Infrastructure configuration**: This involves server infrastructure and environment configuration, which takes care of the deployment process. It defines what dependencies should be installed on each server and specifies the way applications are orchestrated (which application is run on which server and in how many instances).

As an example, we can think of the calculator web service, which uses the Redis server. Let's look at the diagram presenting how the configuration management tool works.

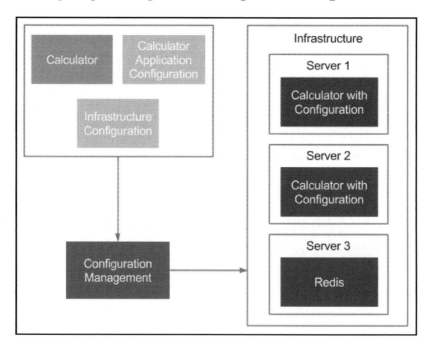

The configuration management tool reads the configuration file and prepares the environment respectively (installs dependent tools and libraries, deploys the applications to multiple instances).

In the preceding example, the **Infrastructure Configuration** specifies that the **Calculator** service should be deployed in two instances on **Server 1** and **Server 2** and that the **Redis** service should be installed on **Server 3**. **Calculator Application Configuration** specifies the port and the address of the **Redis** server so that the services can communicate.

 Configuration can differ depending on the type of the environment (QA, staging, production), for example, server addresses can be different.

There are many approaches to configuration management, but before we look into concrete solutions, let's comment on what characteristics a good configuration management tool should have.

Traits of good configuration management

What should the modern configuration management solution look like? Let's walk through the most important factors:

- **Automation**: Each environment should be automatically reproducible, including the operating system, the network configuration, the software installed, and the applications deployed. In such an approach, fixing production issues means nothing more than an automatic rebuild of the environment. What's more, that simplifies server replications and ensures that the staging and production environments are exactly the same.
- **Version control**: Every change in the configuration should be tracked, so that we know who made it, why, and when. Usually, that means keeping the configuration in the source code repository either together with the code or in a separate place. The former solution is recommended because configuration properties have a different lifecycle than the application itself. Version control also helps with fixing production issues—the configuration can always be rolled back to the previous version and the environment automatically rebuilt. The only exception to the version control-based solution is storing credentials and other sensitive information-these should be never checked in.

- **Incremental changes**: Applying a change in the configuration should not require rebuilding the whole environment. On the contrary, a small change in the configuration should change only the related part of the infrastructure.
- **Server provisioning**: Thanks to automation, adding a new server should be as quick as adding its address to the configuration (and executing one command).
- **Security**: The access to both, the configuration management tool and the machines under its control, should be well secured. When using the SSH protocol for communication, the access to the keys or credentials needs to be well protected.
- **Simplicity**: Every member of the team should be able to read the configuration, make a change, and apply it to the environment. The properties themselves should also be kept as simple as possible and the ones that are not subjected to change are better off kept hardcoded.

It is important to keep these points in mind while creating the configuration and, even before, while choosing the right configuration management tool.

Overview of configuration management tools

The most popular configuration management tools are Ansible, Puppet, and Chef. Each of them is a good choice; they are all open source products with free basic versions and paid enterprise editions. The most important differences between them are:

- **Configuration Language**: Chef uses Ruby, Puppet uses its own DSL (based on Ruby), and Ansible uses YAML.
- **Agent-based**: Puppet and Chef use agents for communication, which means that each managed server needs to have a special tool installed. Ansible, on the contrary, is agentless and uses the standard SSH protocol for communication.

The agentless feature is a significant advantage because it implies no need to install anything on servers. What's more, Ansible is quickly trending upwards, which is why it was chosen for this book. Nevertheless, other tools can also be successfully used for the Continuous Delivery process.

Installing Ansible

Ansible is an open source, agentless automation engine for software provisioning, configuration management, and application deployment. Its first release was in 2012 and its basic version is free for both, personal and commercial use. The enterprise version, called Ansible Tower, provides GUI management and dashboards, REST API, role-based access control, and some more features.

We present the installation process and a description of how it can be used separately as well as together with Docker.

Ansible server requirements

Ansible uses the SSH protocol for communication and has no special requirements regarding the machine it manages. There is also no central master server, so it's enough to install the Ansible client tool anywhere and we can already use it to manage the whole infrastructure.

> The only requirement for the machines being managed is to have the Python tool and, obviously, the SSH server installed. These tools are, however, almost always available by default on any server.

Ansible installation

The installation instructions differ depending on the operating system. In the case of Ubuntu, it's enough to run the following commands:

```
$ sudo apt-get install software-properties-common
$ sudo apt-add-repository ppa:ansible/ansible
$ sudo apt-get update
$ sudo apt-get install ansible
```

> You can find the installation guides for all operating systems on the official Ansible page at: http://docs.ansible.com/ansible/intro_installation.html.

After the installation process is completed, we can execute the Ansible command to check that everything was installed successfully.

```
$ ansible --version
ansible 2.3.2.0
    config file = /etc/ansible/ansible.cfg
    configured module search path = Default w/o overrides
```

Docker-based Ansible client

It's also possible to use Ansible as a Docker container. We can do it by running the following command:

```
$ docker run williamyeh/ansible:ubuntu14.04
ansible-playbook 2.3.2.0
    config file = /etc/ansible/ansible.cfg
    configured module search path = Default w/o overrides
```

 The Ansible Docker image is no longer officially supported, so the only solution is to use the community-driven version. You can read more on its usage on the Docker Hub page.

Using Ansible

In order to use Ansible, first we need to define the inventory, which represents the available resources. Then, we will be able to either execute a single command or define a set of tasks using the Ansible playbook.

Creating inventory

An inventory is a list of all the servers that are managed by Ansible. Each server requires nothing more than the Python interpreter and the SSH server installed. By default, Ansible assumes that the SSH keys are used for authentication; however, it is also possible to use the username and the password by adding the --ask-pass option to the Ansible commands.

SSH keys can be generated with the `ssh-keygen` tool and are usually stored in the `~/.ssh` directory.

The inventory is defined in the `/etc/ansible/hosts` file and it has the following structure:

```
[group_name]
<server1_address>
<server2_address>
...
```

The inventory syntax also accepts ranges of servers, for example, `www[01-22].company.com`. The SSH port should also be specified if it's anything other than 22 (the default one). You can read more on the official Ansible page at: `http://docs.ansible.com/ansible/intro_inventory.html`.

There may be 0 or many groups in the inventory file. As an example, let's define two machines in one group of servers.

```
[webservers]
192.168.0.241
192.168.0.242
```

We can also create the configuration with server aliases and specify the remote user:

```
[webservers]
web1 ansible_host=192.168.0.241 ansible_user=admin
web2 ansible_host=192.168.0.242 ansible_user=admin
```

The preceding file defines a group called `webservers`, which consists of two servers. The Ansible client will log in as the user `admin` to both of them. When we have the inventory created, let's discover how we can use it to execute the same command on many servers.

Ansible offers a possibility to dynamically pull the inventory from the cloud provider (for example, Amazon EC2/Eucalyptus), LDAP, or Cobbler. Read more about dynamic inventories at: `http://docs.ansible.com/ansible/intro_dynamic_inventory.html`.

Ad hoc commands

The simplest command we can run is a ping on all servers.

```
$ ansible all -m ping
web1 | SUCCESS => {
      "changed": false,
      "ping": "pong"
}
web2 | SUCCESS => {
      "changed": false,
      "ping": "pong"
}
```

We used the -m <module_name> option, which allows specifying the module that should be executed on the remote hosts. The result is successful, which means that the servers are reachable and the authentication is configured correctly.

> A full list of modules available in Ansible can be found on the page:
> http://docs.ansible.com/ansible/modules.html.

Note that we used all, so that all servers would be addressed, but we could also call them by the group name webservers or by the single host alias. As a second example, let's execute a shell command only on one of the servers.

```
$ ansible web1 -a "/bin/echo hello"
web1 | SUCCESS | rc=0 >>
hello
```

The -a <arguments> option specifies the arguments that are passed to the Ansible module. In this case, we didn't specify the module, so the arguments are executed as a shell Unix command. The result was successful and hello was printed.

> If the ansible command is connecting to the server for the first time (or the server is reinstalled), then we are prompted with the key confirmation message (SSH message when the host is not present in known_hosts). Since it may interrupt an automated script, we can disable the prompt message by uncommenting host_key_checking = False in the /etc/ansible/ansible.cfg file or by setting the environment variable ANSIBLE_HOST_KEY_CHECKING=False.

In its simplistic form, the Ansible ad hoc command syntax looks as follows:

```
ansible <target> -m <module_name> -a <module_arguments>
```

The purpose of ad hoc commands is to do something quickly when it is not necessary to repeat it. For example, we may want to check if a server is alive or to power off all the machines for the Christmas break. This mechanism can be seen as a command execution on a group of machines with the additional syntax simplification provided by the modules. The real power of Ansible automation, however, lies in playbooks.

Playbooks

An Ansible playbook is a configuration file, which describes how servers should be configured. It provides a way to define a sequence of tasks that should be performed on each of the machines. A playbook is expressed in the YAML configuration language, which makes it human-readable and easy to understand. Let's start with a sample playbook and then see how we can use it.

Defining a playbook

A playbook is composed of one or many plays. Each play contains a host group name, tasks to perform, and configuration details (for example, remote username or access rights). An example playbook might look like this:

```
---
- hosts: web1
  become: yes
  become_method: sudo
  tasks:
  - name: ensure apache is at the latest version
    apt: name=apache2 state=latest
  - name: ensure apache is running
    service: name=apache2 state=started enabled=yes
```

This configuration contains one play which:

- Is executed only on the host `web1`
- Gains root access using the `sudo` command

- Executes two tasks:
  - Installing the latest version of `apache2`: The Ansible module `apt` (called with two parameters `name=apache2` and `state=latest`) checks whether the `apache2` package is installed on the server, and if not, then it uses the `apt-get` tool to install `apache2`
  - Running the `apache2` service: The Ansible module `service` (called with three parameters `name=apache2`, `state=started`, and `enabled=yes`) checks whether the Unix service `apache2` is started, and if not, it uses the `service` command to start it

 While addressing the hosts, you can also use patterns, for example, we could use `web*` to address both `web1` and `web2`. You can read more about Ansible patterns at: `http://docs.ansible.com/ansible/intro_patterns.html`.

Note that each task has a human-readable name, which is used in the console output such that `apt` and `service` are Ansible modules and `name=apache2`, `state=latest`, and `state=started` are module arguments. We have already seen Ansible modules and arguments while using ad hoc commands. In the preceding playbook, we defined only one play, but there can be many of them and each can be related to different groups of hosts.

For example, we could define two groups of servers in the inventory: `database` and `webservers`. Then, in the playbook, we could specify tasks that should be executed on all database-hosting machines and some different tasks that should be executed on all the web servers. By using one command, we could set up the whole environment.

Executing the playbook

When playbook.yml is defined, we can execute it using the `ansible-playbook` command.

```
$ ansible-playbook playbook.yml

PLAY [web1] ********************************************************************

TASK [setup] ******************************************************************
ok: [web1]

TASK [ensure apache is at the latest version] *********************************
changed: [web1]
```

```
TASK [ensure apache is running] *****************************************

ok: [web1]

PLAY RECAP *************************************************************
web1: ok=3 changed=1 unreachable=0 failed=0
```

> If the server requires entering the password for the `sudo` command, then we need to add the `--ask-sudo-pass` option to the `ansible-playbook` command. It's also possible to pass the `sudo` password (if required) by setting the extra variable `-e ansible_become_pass=<sudo_password>`.

The playbook configuration was executed, and, therefore, the `apache2` tool was installed and started. Note that if the task changed something on the server, it is marked as `changed`. On the contrary, if there was no change, it's marked as `ok`.

> It is possible to run tasks in parallel using the `-f <num_of_threads>` option.

Playbook's idempotency

We can execute the command again.

```
$ ansible-playbook playbook.yml

PLAY [web1] ***********************************************************

TASK [setup] **********************************************************
ok: [web1]

TASK [ensure apache is at the latest version] ************************
ok: [web1]

TASK [ensure apache is running] *************************************
ok: [web1]

PLAY RECAP ***********************************************************
web1: ok=3 changed=0 unreachable=0 failed=0
```

Note that the output is slightly different. This time the command didn't change anything on the server. That is because each Ansible module is designed to be idempotent. In other words, executing the same module many times in a sequence should have the same effect as executing it only once.

The simplest way to achieve idempotency is to always first check if the task hasn't been executed yet, and execute it only if it hasn't. Idempotency is a powerful feature and we should always write our Ansible tasks this way.

If all tasks are idempotent, then we can execute them as many times as we want. In that context, we can think of the playbook as a description of the desired state of remote machines. Then, the `ansible-playbook` command takes care of bringing the machine (or group of machines) into that state.

Handlers

Some operations should be executed only if some other task changed. For example, imagine that you copy the configuration file to the remote machine and the Apache server should be restarted only if the configuration file has changed. How to approach such a case?

For example, imagine that you copy the configuration file to the remote machine and the Apache server should be restarted only if the configuration file has changed. How to approach such a case?

Ansible provides an event-oriented mechanism to notify about the changes. In order to use it, we need to know two keywords:

- `handlers`: This specifies the tasks executed when notified
- `notify`: This specifies the handlers that should be executed

```
tasks:
- name: copy configuration
  copy:
    src: foo.conf
    dest: /etc/foo.conf
  notify:
  - restart apache
handlers:
- name: restart apache
  service:
    name: apache2
    state: restarted
```

Now, we can create the `foo.conf` file and run the `ansible-playbook` command.

```
$ touch foo.conf
$ ansible-playbook playbook.yml

...
TASK [copy configuration] ***********************************************
changed: [web1]

RUNNING HANDLER [restart apache] ****************************************
changed: [web1]

PLAY RECAP **************************************************************
web1: ok=5 changed=2 unreachable=0 failed=0
```

> Handlers are executed always at the end of the play and only once, even if triggered by multiple tasks.

Ansible copied the file and restarted the Apache server. It's important to understand that if we run the command again, nothing will happen. However, if we change the content of the `foo.conf` file and then run the `ansible-playbook` command, the file will be copied again (and the Apache server will be restarted).

```
$ echo "something" > foo.conf
$ ansible-playbook playbook.yml

...

TASK [copy configuration] ***********************************************
```

```
changed: [web1]

RUNNING HANDLER [restart apache] ****************************************
changed: [web1]

PLAY RECAP ***************************************************************
web1: ok=5 changed=2 unreachable=0 failed=0
```

We used the `copy` module, which is smart enough to detect if the file has changed, and then in such a case, make a change on the server.

> There is also a publish-subscribe mechanism in Ansible. Using it means assigning a topic to many handlers. Then, a task notifies the topic to execute all related handlers. You can read more about it at: `http://docs.ansible.com/ansible/playbooks_intro.html`.

Variables

While the Ansible automation makes things identical and repeatable for multiple hosts, it is inevitable that servers may require some differences. For example, think of the application port number. It can be different depending on the machine. Luckily, Ansible provides variables, which is a good mechanism to deal with server differences. Let's create a new playbook and define a variable.

For example, think of the application port number. It can be different depending on the machine. Luckily, Ansible provides variables, which is a good mechanism to deal with server differences. Let's create a new playbook and define a variable.

```
---
- hosts: web1
  vars:
    http_port: 8080
```

The configuration defines the `http_port` variable with the value `8080`. Now, we can use it using the Jinja2 syntax.

```
tasks:
- name: print port number
  debug:
    msg: "Port number: {{http_port}}"
```

> The Jinja2 language allows doing way more than just getting a variable. We can use it to create conditions, loops, and many more. You can find more details on the Jinja page at: `http://jinja.pocoo.org/`.

The `debug` module prints the message while executing. If we run the `ansible-playbook` command, we can see the variable usage.

```
$ ansible-playbook playbook.yml

...

TASK [print port number] ***********************************************
ok: [web1] => {
      "msg": "Port number: 8080"
}
```

 Variables can also be defined in the inventory filing using the `[group_name:vars]` section. You can read more about it at: http://docs.ansible.com/ansible/intro_inventory.html#host-variables.

Apart from user-defined variables, there are also predefined automatic variables. For example, the `hostvars` variable stores a map with the information regarding all hosts from the inventory. Using the Jinja2 syntax, we could iterate and print the IP addresses of all hosts in the inventory.

```
---
- hosts: web1
  tasks:
  - name: print IP address
    debug:
      msg: "{% for host in groups['all'] %} {{
              hostvars[host]['ansible_host'] }} {% endfor %}"
```

Then, we can execute the `ansible-playbook` command.

```
$ ansible-playbook playbook.yml

...

TASK [print IP address] ***********************************************
ok: [web1] => {
      "msg": " 192.168.0.241  192.168.0.242 "
}
```

Note that with the use of the Jinja2 language, we can specify the flow control operations inside the Ansible playbook file.

An alternative to the Jinja2 templating language, for the conditionals and loops, is to use the Ansible built-in keywords: `when` and `with_items`. You can read more about it at: `http://docs.ansible.com/ansible/playbooks_conditionals.html`.

Roles

We can install any tool on the remote server using Ansible playbooks. Imagine we would like to have a server with MySQL. We could easily prepare a playbook similar to the one with the `apache2` package. However, if you think about it, a server with MySQL is quite a common case and, for sure, someone has already prepared a playbook for it, so maybe we could just reuse it? Here comes Ansible roles and Ansible Galaxy.

Understanding roles

The Ansible role is a well-structured playbook part prepared to be included in the playbooks. Roles are separate units that always have the following directory structure:

```
templates/
tasks/
handlers/
vars/
defaults/
meta/
```

You can read more about roles and what each directory means on the official Ansible page at: `http://docs.ansible.com/ansible/playbooks_roles.html`.

In each of the directories, we can define the `main.yml` file, which contains the playbook parts that can be included in the `playbook.yml` file. Continuing the MySQL case, there is a role defined on GitHub: `https://github.com/geerlingguy/ansible-role-mysql`. This repository contains kind-of task templates that can be used in our playbook. Let's look at a part of the `tasks/main.yml` file, which installs the `mysql` package.

```
...
- name: Ensure MySQL Python libraries are installed.
  apt: "name=python-mysqldb state=installed"

- name: Ensure MySQL packages are installed.
  apt: "name={{ item }} state=installed"
```

```
    with_items: "{{ mysql_packages }}"
    register: deb_mysql_install_packages
...
```

This is only one of the tasks defined in the `tasks/main.yml` file. Others are responsible for the MySQL configuration.

 The `with_items` keyword is used to create a loop over all the items. The `when` keyword means that the task is executed only under a certain condition.

If we use this role, then in order to install the MySQL on the server, it's enough to create the following playbook.yml:

```
---
- hosts: all
  become: yes
  become_method: sudo
  roles:
  - role: geerlingguy.mysql
    become: yes
```

Such configuration installs the MySQL database to all servers using the `geerlingguy.mysql` role.

Ansible Galaxy

Ansible Galaxy is to Ansible what Docker Hub is for Docker-it stores common roles, so that they can be reused by others. You can browse the available roles on the Ansible Galaxy page at: `https://galaxy.ansible.com/`.

To install the role from Ansible Galaxy, we can use the `ansible-galaxy` command.

```
$ ansible-galaxy install username.role_name
```

This command automatically downloads the role. In the case of the MySQL example, we could download the role by executing:

```
$ ansible-galaxy install geerlingguy.mysql
```

The command downloads the `mysql` role, which can be later used in the playbook file.

 If you need to install a lot of roles at the same time, you can define them in the `requirements.yml` file and use `ansible-galaxy install -r requirements.yml`. Read more about that approach and about Ansible Galaxy at: `http://docs.ansible.com/ansible/galaxy.html`.

Deployment with Ansible

We have covered the most fundamental features of Ansible. Let's now forget, just for a little while, about Docker and configure a complete deployment step using Ansible. We will run the calculator service on one server and the Redis service on the second server.

Installing Redis

We can specify a play in the new playbook. Let's create the `playbook.yml` file with the following content:

```
---
- hosts: web1
  become: yes
  become_method: sudo
  tasks:
  - name: install Redis
    apt:
      name: redis-server
      state: present
  - name: start Redis
    service:
      name: redis-server
      state: started
  - name: copy Redis configuration
    copy:
      src: redis.conf
      dest: /etc/redis/redis.conf
    notify: restart Redis
  handlers:
  - name: restart Redis
    service:
      name: redis-server
      state: restarted
```

The configuration is executed on one server `web1`. It installs the `redis-server` package, copies the Redis configuration, and starts Redis. Note that each time we change the content of the `redis.conf` file and re-run the `ansible-playbook` command, the configuration is updated on the server and the Redis service is restarted.

We also need to create the `redis.conf` file with the following content:

```
daemonize yes
pidfile /var/run/redis/redis-server.pid
port 6379
bind 0.0.0.0
```

This configuration runs Redis as a daemon and exposes it to all network interfaces under port number 6379. Let's now define the second play, which sets up the calculator service.

Deploying a web service

We prepare the calculator web service in three steps:

1. Configure the project to be executable.
2. Change the Redis host address.
3. Add calculator deployment to the playbook.

Configuring a project to be executable

First, we need to make the build JAR executable, so that it can be easily run on the server as a Unix service. In order to do it, it's enough to add the following code to the `build.gradle` file:

```
bootRepackage {
    executable = true
}
```

Changing the Redis host address

Previously, we've hardcoded the Redis host address as `redis`, so now we should change it in the `src/main/java/com/leszko/calculator/CacheConfig.java` file to `192.168.0.241`.

 In real-life projects, the application properties are usually kept in the properties file. For example, for the Spring Boot framework, it's a file called `application.properties` or `application.yml`.

Adding calculator deployment to the playbook

Finally, we can add the deployment configuration as a new play in the `playbook.yml` file.

```
- hosts: web2
  become: yes
  become_method: sudo
  tasks:
  - name: ensure Java Runtime Environment is installed
    apt:
      name: default-jre
      state: present
  - name: create directory for Calculator
    file:
      path: /var/calculator
      state: directory
  - name: configure Calculator as a service
    file:
      path: /etc/init.d/calculator
      state: link
      force: yes
      src: /var/calculator/calculator.jar
  - name: copy Calculator
    copy:
      src: build/libs/calculator-0.0.1-SNAPSHOT.jar
      dest: /var/calculator/calculator.jar
      mode: a+x
    notify:
    - restart Calculator
  handlers:
  - name: restart Calculator
    service:
      name: calculator
      enabled: yes
      state: restarted
```

Let's walk through the steps we defined:

- **Prepare the environment**: This task ensures that the Java Runtime Environment is installed. Basically, it prepares the server environment, so that the calculator application would have all the necessary dependencies. With more complex applications, the list of dependent tools and libraries can be way longer.
- **Configure application as a service**: We would like to have the calculator application running as a Unix service, so that it will be manageable in the standard way. In this case, it's enough to create a link to our application in the `/etc/init.d/` directory.
- **Copy the new version**: The new version of the application is copied into the server. Note that if the source file didn't change, then the file won't be copied and therefore the service won't be restarted.
- **Restart the service**: As a handler, every time the new version of the application is copied, the service is restarted.

Running deployment

As always, we can execute the playbook using the `ansible-playbook` command. Before that, we need to build the calculator project with Gradle.

```
$ ./gradlew build
$ ansible-playbook playbook.yml
```

After the successful deployment, the service should be available and we can check it's working at `http://192.168.0.242:8080/sum?a=1&b=2`. As expected, it should return 3 as the output.

Note that we have configured the whole environment by executing one command. What's more, if we need to scale the service, then it's enough to add a new server to the inventory and re-run the `ansible-playbook` command.

We have showed how to use Ansible for environment configuration and application deployment. The next step is to use Ansible together with Docker.

Ansible with Docker

As you may have noticed, Ansible and Docker address similar software deployment issues:

- **Environment configuration**: Both Ansible and Docker provide a way to configure the environment; however, they use different means. While Ansible uses scripts (encapsulated inside the Ansible modules), Docker encapsulates the whole environment inside a container.
- **Dependencies**: Ansible provides a way to deploy different services on the same or different hosts and let them be deployed together. Docker Compose has a similar functionality, which allows running multiple containers at the same time.
- **Scalability**: Ansible helps to scale services providing the inventory and host groups. Docker Compose has a similar functionality to automatically increase or decrease the number of running containers.
- **Automation with configuration files**: Both Docker and Ansible store the whole environment configuration and service dependencies in files (stored in the source control repository). For Ansible, this file is called `playbook.yml`. In the case of Docker, we have Dockerfile for the environment and docker-compose.yml for the dependencies and scaling.
- **Simplicity**: Both tools are very simple to use and provide a way to set up the whole running environment with a configuration file and just one command execution.

If we compare the tools, then Docker does a little more, since it provides the isolation, portability, and some kind of security. We could even imagine using Docker without any other configuration management tool. Then, why do we need Ansible at all?

Benefits of Ansible

Ansible may seem redundant; however, it brings additional benefits to the delivery process:

- **Docker environment**: The Docker host itself has to be configured and managed. Every container is ultimately running on Linux machines, which needs kernel patching, Docker engine updates, network configuration, and so on. What's more, there may be different server machines with different Linux distributions and the responsibility of Ansible is to make sure the Docker engine is up and running.

- **Non-Dockerized applications**: Not everything is run inside a container. If part of the infrastructure is containerized and part is deployed in the standard way or in the cloud, then Ansible can manage it all with the playbook configuration file. There may be different reasons for not running an application as a container, for example performance, security, specific hardware requirements, Windows-based software, or working with the legacy software.
- **Inventory**: Ansible offers a very friendly way to manage the physical infrastructure using inventories, which store the information about all servers. It can also split the physical infrastructure into different environments: production, testing, development.
- **GUI**: Ansible offers a (commercial) GUI manager called Ansible Tower, which aims to improve the infrastructure management for the enterprises.
- **Improve testing process**: Ansible can help with the integration and acceptance testing and can encapsulate the testing scripts in a similar way that Docker Compose does.

We can look at Ansible as the tool that takes care of the infrastructure, while Docker as a tool that takes care of the environment configuration. The overview is presented in the following diagram:

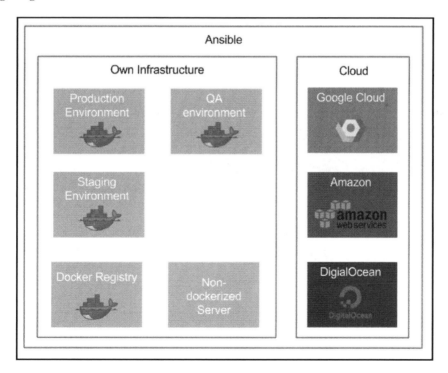

Ansible manages the infrastructure: Docker servers, Docker registry, servers without Docker, and cloud providers. It also takes care of the physical location of the servers. Using the inventory host groups, it can link the web services to the databases that are close to their geographic location.

Ansible Docker playbook

Ansible integrates smoothly with Docker because it provides a set of Docker-dedicated modules. If we create an Ansible playbook for Docker-based deployment, then the first tasks need to make sure that the Docker engine is installed on every machine. Then, it should run a container using Docker or a set of interacting containers using Docker Compose.

 There are a few very useful Docker-related modules provided by Ansible: `docker_image` (build/manage images), `docker_container` (run containers), `docker_image_facts` (inspect images), `docker_login` (log into Docker registry), `docker_network` (manage Docker networks), and `docker_service` (manage Docker Compose).

Installing Docker

We can install the Docker engine using the following task in the Ansible playbook.

```
tasks:
- name: add docker apt keys
  apt_key:
    keyserver: hkp://p80.pool.sks-keyservers.net:80
    id: 9DC858229FC7DD38854AE2D88D81803C0EBFCD88
- name: update apt
  apt_repository:
    repo: deb [arch=amd64] https://download.docker.com/linux/ubuntu xenial
main stable
    state: present
- name: install Docker
  apt:
    name: docker-ce
    update_cache: yes
    state: present
- name: add admin to docker group
  user:
    name: admin
    groups: docker
    append: yes
```

```
- name: install python-pip
  apt:
    name: python-pip
    state: present
- name: install docker-py
  pip:
    name: docker-py
- name: install Docker Compose
  pip:
    name: docker-compose
    version: 1.9.0
```

The playbook looks slightly different for each operating system. The one presented here is for Ubuntu 16.04.

This configuration installs the Docker engine, enables the `admin` user to work with Docker, and installs Docker Compose with dependent tools.

Alternatively, you may also use the `docker_ubuntu` role as described here: `https://www.ansible.com/2014/02/12/installing-and-building-docker-with-ansible`.

When Docker is installed, we can add a task, which will run a Docker container.

Running Docker containers

Running Docker containers is done with the use of the `docker_container` module and it looks very similar to what we presented for the Docker Compose configuration. Let's add it to the `playbook.yml` file.

```
- name: run Redis container
  docker_container:
    name: redis
    image: redis
    state: started
    exposed_ports:
    - 6379
```

You can read more about all of the options of the `docker_container` module on the official Ansible page at: `https://docs.ansible.com/ansible/docker_container_module.html`.

We can now execute the playbook to observe that Docker has been installed and the Redis container started. Note that it's a very convenient way of using Docker, since we don't need to manually install Docker engine on every machine.

Using Docker Compose

The Ansible playbook is very similar to the Docker Compose configuration. They even both share the same YAML file format. What's more, it is possible to use `docker-compose.yml` directly from Ansible. We will show how to do it, but first, let's define the `docker-compose.yml` file.

```
version: "2"
services:
  calculator:
    image: leszko/calculator:latest
    ports:
    - 8080
  redis:
    image: redis:latest
```

It is almost the same as what we defined in the previous chapter. This time we get the calculator image directly from the Docker Hub registry, and do not build it in `docker-compose.yml`, since we want to build the image once, push it to the registry, and then reuse it in every deployment step (on every environment), to make sure the same image is deployed on each Docker host machine. When we have `docker-compose.yml`, we are ready to add new tasks to `playbook.yml`.

```
- name: copy docker-compose.yml
  copy:
    src: ./docker-compose.yml
    dest: ./docker-compose.yml
- name: run docker-compose
  docker_service:
    project_src: .
    state: present
```

We first copy the docker-compose.yml file into the server and then execute `docker-compose`. As a result, Ansible creates two containers: calculator and redis.

We have seen the most important features of Ansible. In the next sections, we write a little bit about the infrastructure and application versioning. At the end of this chapter, we will present how to use Ansible in order to complete the Continuous Delivery pipeline.

Exercises

In this chapter, we have covered the fundamentals of Ansible and the way to use it together with Docker. As an exercise, we propose the following tasks:

1. Create the server infrastructure and use Ansible to manage it.
   - Connect a physical machine or run a VirtualBox machine to emulate the remote server
   - Configure SSH access to the remote machine (SSH keys)
   - Install Python on the remote machine
   - Create an Ansible inventory with the remote machine
   - Run the Ansible ad hoc command (with the `ping` module) to check that the infrastructure is configured correctly
2. Create a Python-based "hello world" web service and deploy it in a remote machine using Ansible playbook.
   - The service can look exactly the same as described in the exercises for the chapter
   - Create a playbook, which deploys the service into the remote machine
   - Run the `ansible-playbook` command and check whether the service was deployed

Summary

We have covered the configuration management process and its relation to Docker. The key takeaway from the chapter is as follows:

- Configuration management is a process of creating and applying the configurations of the infrastructure and the application
- Ansible is one of the best trending configuration management tools. It is agentless and therefore requires no special server configuration
- Ansible can be used with ad hoc commands, but the real power lies in Ansible playbooks
- The Ansible playbook is a definition of how the environment should be configured

- The purpose of Ansible roles is to reuse parts of playbooks.
- Ansible Galaxy is an online service to share Ansible roles
- Ansible integrates well with Docker and brings additional benefits compared to using Docker and Docker Compose alone

In the next chapter, we will wrap up the Continuous Delivery process and complete the final Jenkins pipeline.

7
Continuous Delivery Pipeline

We have already covered the most crucial parts of the Continuous Delivery process: the commit phase, the artifact repository, automated acceptance testing, and configuration management.

In this chapter, we will focus on the missing parts of the final pipeline, which are the environments and infrastructure, application versioning, and nonfunctional testing.

This chapter covers the following points:

- Designing different software environments and their infrastructures
- Securing the connection between Jenkins agents and servers
- Introducing various kinds of nonfunctional tests
- Presenting the challenges of nonfunctional tests in the Continuous Delivery process
- Explaining different types of application versioning
- Completing the Continuous Delivery pipeline
- Introducing the concept of smoke testing and adding it to the final pipeline

Environments and infrastructure

So far, we have always used one Docker host for everything and treated it as the virtualization of endless resources where we can deploy everything. Obviously, the Docker host can actually be a cluster of machines and we will show how to create it using Docker Swarm in the next chapters. However, even if the Docker host were unlimited in terms of resources, we still need to think about the underlying infrastructure for at least two reasons:

- Physical location of the machines matters
- No testing should be done on the production physical machines

Taking these facts into consideration, in this section, we will discuss different types of environment, their role in the Continuous Delivery process, and infrastructure security aspects.

Types of environment

There are four most common environment types: production, staging, QA (testing), and development. Let's discuss each of them and its infrastructure.

Production

Production is the environment that is used by the end user. It exists in every company and, of course, it is the most important environment.

Let's look at the following diagram and see how most production environments are organized:

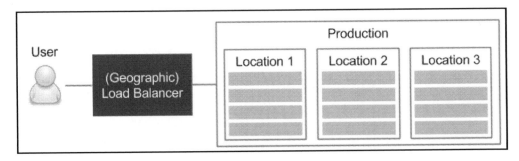

Users access the service through the load balancer, which chooses the exact machine. If the application is released in multiple physical locations, then the (first) device is usually a DNS-based geographic load balancer. In each location, we have a cluster of servers. If we use Docker, then that cluster of servers can be hidden behind one or multiple Docker hosts (which are internally composed of many machines using Docker Swarm).

The physical location of machines matters because the request-response time can differ significantly depending on the physical distance. Moreover, the database and other dependent services should be located on a machine that is close to where the service is deployed. What's even more important is that the database should be sharded in a way that the replication overhead between different locations is minimized. Otherwise, we may end up waiting a lot for the databases to reach consensus between its instances located far away from each other. More details on the physical aspects are beyond the scope of this book, but it's important to remember that Docker is not always a silver bullet.

Containerization and virtualization allow you to think about servers as an infinite resource; however, some physical aspects such as location are still relevant.

Staging

The staging environment is the place where the release candidate is deployed in order to perform the final tests before going live. Ideally, this environment is a mirror of the production.

Let's look at the following to see how such an environment should look in the context of the delivery process:

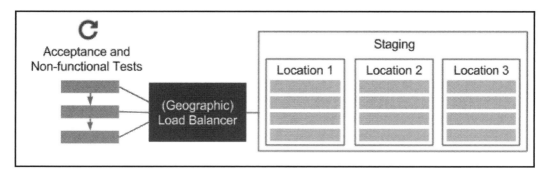

Note that the staging environment an exact a production clone. If the application is deployed in multiple locations, then the staging should also have multiple locations.

In the Continuous Delivery process, all automated acceptance functional and nonfunctional tests are run against this environment. While most functional tests don't usually require identical production-like infrastructure, in the case of nonfunctional (especially performance) tests, it's a must.

It is not uncommon that, for the purpose of cost saving, the staging infrastructure differs from the production (usually it contains fewer machines). Such an approach can, however, lead to many production issues. *Michael T. Nygard,* in his great book *Release It!*, gives an example of a real-life scenario in which fewer machines were used in the staging environment than in production.

The story goes like this: in one company, the system was stable until a certain code change, which caused the production to be extremely slow, even though all stress tests passed. How was it possible? It happened that there was a synchronization point, in which each server communicated with each other. In the case of the staging, there was one server, so actually there was no blocker. In production, however, there were many servers, which resulted in servers waiting for each other. This example is just the tip of the iceberg and many production issues may fail to be tested by acceptance tests if the staging environment is different from the production environment.

QA

The QA environment (also called the testing environment) is intended for the QA team to perform exploratory testing and for external applications (which depend on our service) to perform integration testing. The use cases and the infrastructure of the QA environment are presented in the following diagram:

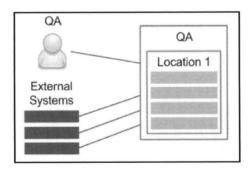

While staging does not need to be stable (in the case of Continuous Delivery, it is changed after every code change committed to the repository), the QA instance needs to provide a certain stability and expose the same (or backward compatible) API as the production. Contrary to the staging environment, the infrastructure can be different from the production, since its purpose is not to ensure that the release candidate works properly.

A very common case is to allocate fewer machines (for example, only from one location) for the purpose of the QA instance.

> Deploying to the QA environment is usually done in a separate pipeline, so that it will be independent from the automatic release process. Such an approach is convenient, because the QA instance has a different life cycle than production (for instance, the QA team may want to perform testing on the experimental code branched from the trunk).

Development

The development environment can be created as a shared server for all developers or each developer can have his/her own development environment. A simple diagram is presented here:

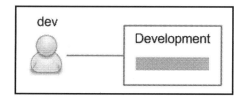

The development environment always contains the latest version of the code. It is used to enable integration between developers and can be treated the same way as the QA environment, but is used by developers, not QAs.

Environments in Continuous Delivery

For the purpose of the Continuous Delivery process, the staging environment is indispensable. In some very rare cases, when the performance is not important and the project does not have many dependencies, we could perform the acceptance tests on the local (development) Docker host (like we did in the previous chapter), but that should be an exception, not a rule. In such a case, we always risk some production issues related to the environment.

The other environments are usually not important with regard to Continuous Delivery. If we would like to deploy to the QA or development environment with every commit, then we can create separate pipelines for that purpose (being careful not to obscure the main release pipeline). In many cases, deployment to the QA environment is triggered manually, because it can have different life cycles from production.

Securing environments

All environments need to be well secured. That's clear. What's even more obvious is that the most important requirement is to keep the production secure, because our business depends on it and the consequences of any security flaw can be highest there.

 Security is a broad topic. In this section, we focus only on the topics related to the Continuous Delivery process. Nevertheless, setting up a complete server infrastructure requires much more knowledge about security.

In the Continuous Delivery process, the slave must have access to servers, so that it can deploy the application.

There are different approaches for providing slaves with the server's credentials:

- **Put SSH key into slave**: If we don't use dynamic Docker slave provisioning, then we can configure Jenkins slave machines to contain private SSH keys.
- **Put SSH key into slave image**: If we use dynamic Docker slave provisioning, we could add the SSH private key into the Docker slave image. However, it creates a possible security hole, since anyone who has access to that image would have access to the production servers.
- **Jenkins credentials**: We can configure Jenkins to store credentials and use them in the pipeline.
- **Copy to Slave Jenkins plugin**: We can copy the SSH key dynamically into the slave while starting the Jenkins build.

Each solution has some advantages and drawbacks. While using any of them we have to take extra caution, since, when a slave has access to the production, then anyone breaking into the slave breaks into the production.

The most risky solution is to put SSH private keys into the Jenkins slave image, since then all the places where the image is stored (the Docker registry or Docker host with Jenkins) need to be well secured.

Nonfunctional testing

We learned a lot about functional requirements and automated acceptance testing in the previous chapter. However, what should we do with nonfunctional requirements? Or even more challenging, what if there are no requirements? Should we skip them at all in the Continuous Delivery process? Let's answer these questions throughout this section.

Nonfunctional aspects of the software are always important, because they can cause a significant risk to the operation of the system.

For example, many applications fail, because they are not able to bear the load of a sudden increase in the number of users. In the book *Usability Engineering, Jakob Nielsen,* writes that 1.0 second is about the limit for the user's flow of thought to stay uninterrupted. Imagine that our system, with the growing load, starts to exceed that limit. Users can stop using the service just because of its performance. Taking it into consideration, nonfunctional testing is as important as functional testing.

To cut a long story short, we should always take the following steps for nonfunctional testing:

- Decide which nonfunctional aspects are crucial to our business
- For each of them:
    - Specify the tests the same way we did for acceptance testing
    - Add a stage to the Continuous Delivery pipeline (after acceptance testing, while the application is still deployed on the staging environment)
- The application comes to the release stage only after all nonfunctional tests pass

Irrespective of the type of the nonfunctional test, the idea is always the same. The approach, however, may slightly differ. Let's examine different test types and the challenges they pose.

Types of nonfunctional test

Functional test are always related to the same aspect—the behavior of the system. On the contrary, nonfunctional tests concern a lot of different aspects. Let's discuss the most common system properties and how they can be tested inside the Continuous Delivery process.

Performance testing

Performance tests are the most widely used nonfunctional tests. They measure the responsiveness and stability of the system. The simplest performance test we could create is to send a request to the web service and measure its **round-trip time (RTT)**.

There are different definitions of performance testing. In many places, they are meant to include load, stress, and scalability testing. Sometimes they are also described as white-box tests. In this book, we define performance testing as the most basic form of black-box test to measure the latency of the system.

For the purpose of performance testing, we can use a dedicated framework (for Java the most popular is JMeter) or just use the same tool we used for acceptance tests. A simple performance test is usually added as a pipeline stage just after Acceptance tests. Such a test should fail if the RTT exceeds the given limit and it detects bugs that definitely slow down the service.

The JMeter plugin for Jenkins can show performance trends over the time.

Load testing

Load tests are used to check how the system functions when there are a lot of concurrent requests. While a system can be very fast with a single request, it does not mean that it works fast enough with 1,000 requests at the same time. During load testing, we measure the average request-response time of many concurrent calls, usually performed from many machines. Load testing is a very common QA phase in the release cycle. To automate it, we can use the same tools as with the simple performance test; however, in the case of larger systems, we may need a separate client environment to perform a large number of concurrent requests.

Stress testing

Stress testing, also called capacity testing or throughput testing, is a test that determines how many concurrent users can access our service. It may sound the same as load testing; however, in the case of load testing, we set the number of concurrent users (throughput) to a given number, check the response time (latency), and make the build fail if the limit is exceeded. During stress testing, however, we keep the latency constant and increase the throughput to discover the maximum number of concurrent calls when the system is still operable. So the result of a stress test may be notification that our system can handle 10,000 concurrent users, which helps us prepare for the peak usage time.

Stress testing is not well suited for the Continuous Delivery process, because it requires long tests with an increasing number of concurrent requests. It should be prepared as a separate script of a separate Jenkins pipeline and triggered on demand, when we know that the code change can cause performance issues.

Scalability testing

Scalability testing explains how latency and throughput change when we add more servers or services. The perfect characteristic would be linear, which means if we have one server and the average request-response time is 500 ms when used by 100 parallel users, then adding another server would keep the response time the same and allow us to add another 100 parallel users. In reality, it's often hard to achieve thsi because of keeping data consistency between servers.

Scalability testing should be automated and should provide the graph presenting the relationship between the number of machines and the number of concurrent users. Such data is helpful in determining the limits of the system and the point at which adding more machines does not help.

Scalability tests, similar to stress tests, are hard to put into the Continuous Delivery pipeline and should rather be kept separate.

Endurance testing

Endurance tests, also called longevity tests, run the system for a long time to see if the performance drops after a certain period of time. They detect memory leaks and stability issues. Since they require a system running for a long time, it doesn't make sense to run them inside the Continuous Delivery pipeline.

Security testing

Security testing deals with different aspects related to security mechanisms and data protection. Some security aspects are purely functional requirements such as authentication, authorization, or role assignment. These parts should be checked the same way as any other functional requirement—during the acceptance test phase. There are also other security aspects that are nonfunctional; for example, the system should be protected against SQL injection. No client would probably specify such a requirement, but it's implicit.

Security tests should be included in Continuous Delivery as a pipeline stage. They can be written using the same frameworks as the acceptance tests or with dedicated security testing frameworks, for example, BDD security.

 Security should also always be a part the explanatory testing process, in which testers and security experts detect security holes and add new testing scenarios.

Maintainability testing

Maintainability tests explain how simple a system is to maintain. In other words, they judge code quality. We already have related stages in the commit phase that check the test coverage and perform static code analysis. The Sonar tool can also give some overview of the code quality and the technical debt.

Recovery testing

Recovery testing is a technique to determine how quickly the system can recover after it crashed because of a software or hardware failure. The best case would be if the system does not fail at all, even if a part of its services is down. Some companies even perform production failures on purpose to check if they can survive a disaster. The best known example is Netflix and their Chaos Monkey tool, which randomly terminates random instances of the production environment. Such an approach forces engineers to write code that makes systems resilient to failures.

Recovery testing is obviously not part of the Continuous Delivery process, but rather a periodic event to check the overall health.

 You can read more about Chaos Monkey at `https://github.com/Netflix/chaosmonkey`.

There are many more nonfunctional test types, which are closer to or further from the code and the Continuous Delivery process. Some of them relate to the law such as compliance testing; others are related to the documentation or internationalization. There are also usability testings and volume testings (which check whether the system behaves well in the case of large amounts of data). Most of these tests, however, have no part in the Continuous Delivery process.

Nonfunctional challenges

Nonfunctional aspects pose new challenges to the software development and delivery:

- **Long test run**: The tests can take a long time to run and may need a special execution environment.
- **Incremental nature**: It's hard to set the limit value when the test should fail (unless SLA is well defined). Even if the edge limit is set, the application would probably incrementally approach the limit. In most cases, actually, no one code change caused the test failure.
- **Vague requirements**: Users usually don't have much input concerning nonfunctional requirements. They may provide some guidelines concerning the request-response time or the number of users; however, they won't probably know much about maintainability, security, or scalability.
- **Multiplicity**: There are a lot of different nonfunctional tests and choosing which should be implemented requires making some compromises.

The best approach to address nonfunctional aspects is to take the following steps:

1. Make a list of all nonfunctional test types.
2. Cross out explicitly the test you don't need for your system. There may be a lot of reasons you don't need one kind of test, for example:
   - The service is super small and a simple performance test is enough
   - The system is internal only and available only for read-only, so it may not need any security checks
   - The system is designed for one machine only and does not need any scaling
   - The cost of creating certain tests is too high

3. Split your tests into two groups:
   - **Continuous Delivery**: It is possible to add it to the pipeline
   - **Analysis**: It is not possible to add to the pipeline because of their execution time, their nature, or the associated cost

4. For the Continuous Delivery group, implement the related pipeline stages.
5. For the Analysis group:
   - Create automated tests
   - Schedule when they should be run
   - Schedule meetings to discuss their results and take action points

A very good approach is to have a nightly build with the long tests that don't fit the Continuous Delivery pipeline. Then, it's possible to schedule a weekly meeting to monitor and analyze the trends of system performance.

As presented, there are many types of nonfunctional test and they pose additional challenges to the delivery process. Nevertheless, for the sake of the stability of our system, these tests should never be blankly skipped. The technical implementation differs depending on the test type, but in most cases they can be implemented in a similar manner to functional acceptance tests and should be run against the staging environment.

If you're interested in the topic of nonfunctional testing, system properties, and system stability, then read the book *Release It!* by *Michael T. Nygard*.

Application versioning

So far, during every Jenkins build, we have created a new Docker image, pushed it into the Docker registry, and used the **latest** version throughout the process. However, such a solution has at least three disadvantages:

- If, during the Jenkins build, after the acceptance tests, someone pushes a new version of the image, then we can end up releasing the untested version
- We always push an image named in the same way; thus, so effectively, it is overwritten in the Docker registry
- It's very hard to manage images without versions just by their hashed-style IDs

What is the recommended way of managing Docker image versions together with the Continuous Delivery process? In this section, we get to see different versioning strategies and learn different ways of creating versions in the Jenkins pipeline.

Versioning strategies

There are different ways to version applications.

Let's discuss these most popular solutions, which can be applied together with the Continuous Delivery process (when each commit creates a new version).

- **Semantic versioning**: The most popular solution is to use sequence-based identifiers (usually in the form of x.y.z). This method requires a commit to the repository done by Jenkins in order to increase the current version number, which is usually stored in the build file. This solution is well supported by Maven, Gradle, and other build tools. The identifier usually consists of three numbers:
  - **x**: This is the major version; the software does not need to   be backward-compatible when this version is incremented
  - **y**: This is the minor version; the software needs to be backward compatible when the version is incremented
  - **z**: This is the build number; this is sometimes also considered as a backward and forward-compatible change

- **Timestamp**: Using the date and time of the build for the application version is less verbose than sequential numbers, but very convenient in the case of the Continuous Delivery process, because it does not require committing back to the repository by Jenkins.
- **Hash**: A randomly generated hash version shares the benefit of the datetime and is probably the simplest solution possible. The drawback is that it's not possible to look at two versions and tell which is the latest one.
- **Mixed**: There are many variations of the solutions described earlier, for example, major and minor versions with the datetime.

All solutions are fine to use with the Continuous Delivery process. Semantic versioning requires, however, a commit to the repository from the build execution, so that the version is increased in the source code repository.

 Maven (and the other build tools) popularized version snapshotting, which added a suffix SNAPSHOT to the versions that are not released, but kept just for the development process. Since Continuous Delivery means releasing every change, there are no snapshots.

Versioning in the Jenkins pipeline

As described earlier, there are different possibilities when it comes to using software versioning and each of them can be implemented in Jenkins.

As an example, let's use the datetime.

 In order to use the timestamp information from Jenkins, you need to install the Build Timestamp Plugin and set the timestamp format in the Jenkins configuration (for example, to "yyyyMMdd-HHmm").

In every place where we use the Docker image, we need to add the tag suffix: `${BUILD_TIMESTAMP}`.

For example, the `Docker build` stage should look like this:

```
sh "docker build -t leszko/calculator:${BUILD_TIMESTAMP} ."
```

After the changes, when we run the Jenkins build, we should have the image tagged with the timestamp version in our Docker registry.

> Note that after explicitly tagging the image, it's no longer implicitly tagged as the latest.

With versioning completed, we are finally ready to complete the Continuous Delivery pipeline.

Complete Continuous Delivery pipeline

After discussing all the aspects of Ansible, environments, nonfunctional testing, and versioning, we are ready to extend the Jenkins pipeline and finalize a simple, but complete, Continuous Delivery pipeline.

We will do it in a few steps as follows:

- Create the inventory of staging and production environments
- Update acceptance tests to use the remote host (instead of local)
- Release the application to the production environment
- Add a smoke test which makes sure the application was successfully released

Inventory

In their simplest form, we can have two environments: staging and production, each having one Docker host machine. In real life, we may want to add more host groups for each environment if we want to have servers in different locations or having different requirements.

Let's create two Ansible inventory files. Starting from the staging, we can define the `inventory/staging` file. Assuming the staging address is `192.168.0.241`, it would have the following content:

```
[webservers]
web1 ansible_host=192.168.0.241 ansible_user=admin
```

By analogy, if the production IP address is `192.168.0.242`, then the `inventory/production` should look like this:

```
[webservers]
web2 ansible_host=192.168.0.242 ansible_user=admin
```

 It may look oversimplified to have just one machine for each environment; however, using Docker Swarm (which we show later in this book), a cluster of hosts can be hidden behind one Docker host.

Having the inventory defined, we can change acceptance testing to use the staging environment.

Acceptance testing environment

Depending on our needs, we could test the application by running it on the local Docker host (like we did in the previous chapter) or using the remote staging environment. The former solution is closer to what happens in production, so it can be considered as a better one. This is very close to what was presented in the *Method 1: Jenkins-first acceptance testing* section of the previous chapter. The only difference is that now we deploy the application on a remote Docker host.

In order to do this, we could use `docker` (or the `docker-compose` command) with the `–H` parameter, which specifies the remote Docker host address. This would be a good solution and if you don't plan to use Ansible or any other configuration management tool, then that is the way to go. Nevertheless, for the reasons already mentioned in this chapter, it is beneficial to use Ansible. In that case, we can use the `ansible-playbook` command inside the Continuous Delivery pipeline.

```
stage("Deploy to staging") {
    steps {
        sh "ansible-playbook playbook.yml -i inventory/staging"
    }
}
```

If `playbook.yml` and docker-compose.yml look the same as in the *Ansible with Docker* section, then it should be enough to deploy the application with dependencies into the staging environment.

The `Acceptance test` stage looks exactly the same as in the previous chapter. The only adjustment can be the hostname of the staging environment (or its load balancer). It's also possible to add stages for performance testing or other nonfunctional tests against the application running on the staging environment.

After all tests are passed, it's high time to release the application.

Release

The production environment should be as close to the staging environment as possible. The Jenkins step for the release should also be very similar to the stage that deploys the application to the staging environment.

In the simplest scenario, the only differences are the inventory file and the application configuration (for example, in case of a Spring Boot application, we would set a different Spring profile, which results in taking a different properties file). In our case, there are no application properties, so the only difference is the inventory file.

```
stage("Release") {
    steps {
        sh "ansible-playbook playbook.yml -i inventory/production"
    }
}
```

In reality, the release step can be a little more complex if we want to provide zero downtime deployment. More on that topic is presented in the next chapters.

After the release is done, we might think that everything is completed; however, there is one more missing stage, a smoke test.

Smoke testing

A smoke test is a very small subset of acceptance tests whose only purpose is to check that the release process is completed successfully. Otherwise, we could have a situation in which the application is perfectly fine; however, there is an issue in the release process, so we may end up with a non-working production.

The smoke test is usually defined in the same way as the acceptance test. So the `Smoke test` stage in the pipeline should look like this:

```
stage("Smoke test") {
    steps {
        sleep 60
        sh "./smoke_test.sh"
    }
}
```

After everything is set up, the Continuous Delivery build should run automatically and the application should be released to production. With this step, we have completed the Continuous Delivery pipeline in its simplest, but fully productive, form.

Complete Jenkinsfile

To sum up, throughout the recent chapters we have created quite a few stages, which results in a complete Continuous Delivery pipeline that could be successfully used in many projects.

Next we see the complete Jenkins file for the calculator project:

```
pipeline {
  agent any

  triggers {
    pollSCM('* * * * *')
  }

  stages {
    stage("Compile") { steps { sh "./gradlew compileJava" } }
    stage("Unit test") { steps { sh "./gradlew test" } }

    stage("Code coverage") { steps {
      sh "./gradlew jacocoTestReport"
      publishHTML (target: [
            reportDir: 'build/reports/jacoco/test/html',
            reportFiles: 'index.html',
            reportName: "JaCoCo Report" ])
      sh "./gradlew jacocoTestCoverageVerification"
    } }

    stage("Static code analysis") { steps {
      sh "./gradlew checkstyleMain"
      publishHTML (target: [
            reportDir: 'build/reports/checkstyle/',
```

```
                reportFiles: 'main.html',
                reportName: "Checkstyle Report" ])
    } }

    stage("Build") { steps { sh "./gradlew build" } }


    stage("Docker build") { steps {
      sh "docker build -t leszko/calculator:${BUILD_TIMESTAMP} ."
    } }

    stage("Docker push") { steps {
      sh "docker push leszko/calculator:${BUILD_TIMESTAMP}"
    } }

    stage("Deploy to staging") { steps {
      sh "ansible-playbook playbook.yml -i inventory/staging"
      sleep 60
    } }

    stage("Acceptance test") { steps { sh "./acceptance_test.sh" } }

    // Performance test stages

    stage("Release") { steps {
      sh "ansible-playbook playbook.yml -i inventory/production"
      sleep 60
    } }

    stage("Smoke test") { steps { sh "./smoke_test.sh" } }
  }
}
```

 You can find this Jenkinsfile on GitHub at `https://github.com/leszko/` `calculator/blob/master/Jenkinsfile`.

Exercises

In this chapter, we have covered a lot of new aspects for the Continuous Delivery pipeline; to better understand the concept, we recommend you perform the following exercises:

1. Add a performance test, which tests the "hello world" service:
   - The "hello world" service can be taken from the previous chapter
   - Create a `performance_test.sh` script, which makes 100 calls in parallel and checks whether the average request-response time is below 1 second
   - You can use Cucumber or the `curl` command for the script

2. Create a Jenkins pipeline that builds the "hello world" web service as a versioned Docker image and performs performance test:
   - Create the `Docker build` stage, which builds the Docker image with the "hello world" service and adds a timestamp as a version tag
   - Create an Ansible playbook that uses the Docker image
   - Add the `Deploy to staging` stage, which deploys the image into the remote machine
   - Add the `Performance testing` stage, which executes `performance_test.sh`
   - Run the pipeline and observe the results

Summary

In this chapter, we have completed the Continuous Delivery pipeline, which finally releases the application. The following are the key takeaways from the chapter:

- For the purpose of Continuous Delivery, two environments are indispensable: staging and production.
- Nonfunctional tests are an essential part of the Continuous Delivery process and should always be considered as pipeline stages.
- Nonfunctional tests that don't fit the Continuous Delivery process should be considered as periodic tasks in order to monitor the overall performance trends.
- Applications should always be versioned; however, the versioning strategy depends on the type of the application.

- The minimal Continuous Delivery pipeline can be implemented as a sequence of scripts that ends with two stages: release and smoke test.
- The smoke test should always be added as the last stage of the Continuous Delivery pipeline in order to check whether the release was successful.

In the next chapter, we will have a look at the Docker Swarm tool, which helps us to create a cluster of Docker hosts.

8
Clustering with Docker Swarm

We have already covered all the fundamental aspects of the Continuous Delivery pipeline. In this chapter, we will see how to change the Docker environment from a single Docker host into a cluster of machines and how to use it all together with Jenkins.

This chapter covers the following points:

- Explaining the concept of server clustering
- Introducing Docker Swarm and its most important features
- Presenting how to build a swarm cluster from multiple Docker hosts
- Running and scaling Docker images on a cluster
- Exploring advanced swarm features: rolling updates, draining nodes, multiple manager nodes, and tuning the scheduling strategy
- Deploying the Docker Compose configuration on a cluster
- Introducing Kubernetes and Apache Mesos as alternatives to Docker Swarm
- Dynamically scaling Jenkins agents on a cluster

Server clustering

So far, we have have interacted with each of the machines individually. Even when we used Ansible to repeat the same operations on multiple servers, we had to explicitly specify on which host the given service should be deployed. In most cases, however, if servers share the same physical location, we are not interested on which particular machine the service is deployed. All we need is to have it accessible and replicated in many instances. How can we configure a set of machines to work together so that adding a new one would require no additional setup? This is the role of clustering.

In this section, you will be introduced to the concept of server clustering and the Docker Swarm toolkit.

Introducing server clustering

A server cluster is a set of connected computers that work together in a way that they can be used similarly to a single system. Servers are usually connected through the local network with a connection fast enough to ensure a small influence of the fact that services are distributed. A simple server cluster is presented in the following image:

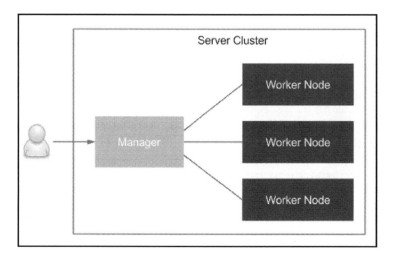

A user accesses the cluster via a host called the manager, whose interface should be similar to a usual Docker host. Inside the cluster, there are multiple worker nodes that receive tasks, execute them, and notify the manager of their current state. The manager is responsible for the orchestration process, including task dispatching, service discovery, load balancing, and worker failure detection.

> The manager can also execute tasks, which is the default configuration in Docker Swarm. However, for large clusters, the manager should be configured for management purposes only.

Introducing Docker Swarm

Docker Swarm is a native clustering system for Docker that turns a set of Docker hosts into one consistent cluster, called a swarm. Each host connected to the swarm plays the role of a manager or a worker (there must be at least one manager in a cluster). Technically, the physical location of the machines does not matter; however, it's reasonable to have all Docker hosts inside one local network, otherwise, managing operations (or reaching consensus between multiple managers) can take a significant amount of time.

 Since Docker 1.12, Docker Swarm is natively integrated into Docker Engine as swarm mode. In older versions, it was necessary to run the swarm container on each of the hosts to provide the clustering functionality.

Regarding the terminology, in swarm mode, a running image is called a **service,** as opposed to a **container**, which is run on a single Docker host. One service runs a specified number of **tasks.** A task is an atomic scheduling unit of the swarm that holds the information about the container and the command that should be run inside the container. A **replica** is each container that is run on the node. The number of replicas is the expected number of all containers for the given service.

Let's look at an image presenting the terminology and the Docker Swarm clustering process:

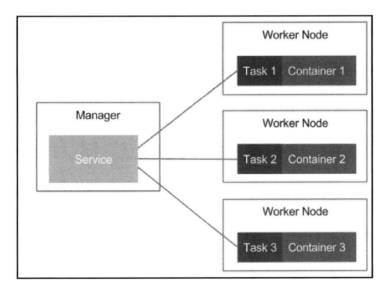

We start by specifying a service, the Docker image and the number of replicas. The manager automatically assigns tasks to worker nodes. Obviously, each replicated container is run from the same Docker image. In the context of the presented flow, Docker Swarm can be viewed as a layer on top of the Docker Engine mechanism that is responsible for container orchestration.

In the preceding sample image, we have three tasks, and each of them is run on a separate Docker host. Nevertheless, it may also happen that all containers would be started on the same Docker host. Everything depends on the manager node that allocates tasks to worker nodes using the scheduling strategy. We will show how to configure that strategy later, in a separate section.

Docker Swarm features overview

Docker Swarm provides a number interesting features. Let's walk through the most important ones:

- **Load balancing**: Docker Swarm takes care of the load balancing and assigning unique DNS names so that the application deployed on the cluster can be used in the same way as deployed on a single Docker host. In other words, a swarm can publish ports in a similar manner as the Docker container, and then the swarm manager distributes requests among the services in the cluster.
- **Dynamic role management**: Docker hosts can be added to the swarm at runtime, so there is no need for a cluster restart. What's more, the role of the node (manager or worker) can also be dynamically changed.
- **Dynamic service scaling**: Each service can be dynamically scaled up or down with the Docker client. The manager node takes care of adding or removing containers from the nodes.
- **Failure recovery**: Nodes are constantly monitored by the manager and, if any of them fails, new tasks are started on different machines so that the declared number of replicas would be constant. It's also possible to create multiple manager nodes in order to prevent a breakdown in case one of them fails.
- **Rolling updates**: An update to services can be applied incrementally; for example, if we have 10 replicas and we would like to make a change, we can define a delay between the deployment to each replica. In such a case, when anything goes wrong, we never end up with a scenario where no replica is working correctly.

- **Two service modes:** There are two modes in which can be run:
  - **Replicated services**: The specified number of replicated containers are distributed among the nodes based on the scheduling strategy algorithm
  - **Global services**: One container is run on every available node in the cluster
- **Security:** As everything is in Docker, Docker Swarm enforces the TLS authentication and the communication encryption. It's also possible to use CA (or self-signed) certificates.

Let's see how all of this looks in practice.

Docker Swarm in practice

Docker Engine includes the Swarm mode by default, so there is no additional installation process required. Since Docker Swarm is a native Docker clustering system, managing cluster nodes is done by the `docker` command and is therefore very simple and intuitive. Let's start by creating a manager node with two worker nodes. Then, we will run and scale a service from a Docker image.

Setting up a Swarm

In order to set up a Swarm, we need to initialize the manager node. We can do this using the following command on a machine that is supposed to become the manager:

```
$ docker swarm init

Swarm initialized: current node (qfqzhk2bumhd2h0ckntrysm81) is now a
manager.

To add a worker to this swarm, run the following command:
docker swarm join \
--token SWMTKN-1-253vezc1pqqgb93c5huc9g3n0hj4p7xik1ziz5c4rsdo3f7iw2-
df098e2jpe8uvwe2ohhhcxd6w \
192.168.0.143:2377

To add a manager to this swarm, run 'docker swarm join-token manager' and
follow the instructions.
```

TIP

A very common practice is to use the `--advertise-addr` `<manager_ip>` parameter, because if the manager machine has more than one potential network interfaces, then `docker swarm init` can fail.

In our case, the manager machine has the IP address `192.168.0.143` and, obviously, it has to be reachable from the worker nodes (and vice versa). Note that the command to execute on worker machines was printed to the console. Also note that a special token has been generated. From now on, it will be used to connect a machine to the cluster and should be kept secret.

We can check that the Swarm has been created using the `docker node` command:

```
$ docker node ls
ID                          HOSTNAME         STATUS  AVAILABILITY  MANAGER
STATUS
qfqzhk2bumhd2h0ckntrysm81 * ubuntu-manager Ready    Active        Leader
```

When the manager is up and running, we are ready to add worker nodes to the Swarm.

Adding worker nodes

In order to add a machine to the Swarm, we have to log in to the given machine and execute the following command:

```
$ docker swarm join \
--token SWMTKN-1-253vezc1pqqgb93c5huc9g3n0hj4p7xik1ziz5c4rsdo3f7iw2-
df098e2jpe8uvwe2ohhhcxd6w \
192.168.0.143:2377

This node joined a swarm as a worker.
```

We can check that the node has been added to the Swarm with the `docker node ls` command. Assuming that we've added two node machines, the output should look as follows:

```
$ docker node ls
ID                          HOSTNAME         STATUS  AVAILABILITY  MANAGER
STATUS
cr7vin5xzu0331fvxkdxla22n   ubuntu-worker2 Ready    Active
md4wx15t87nn0c3pyv24kewtz   ubuntu-worker1 Ready    Active
qfqzhk2bumhd2h0ckntrysm81 * ubuntu-manager Ready    Active        Leader
```

At this point, we have a cluster that consists of three Docker hosts, `ubuntu-manager`, `ubuntu-worker1`, and `ubuntu-worker2`. Let's see how we can run a service on this cluster.

Deploying a service

In order to run an image on a cluster, we don't use `docker run` but the Swarm-dedicated `docker service` command (which is executed on the manager node). Let's start a single `tomcat` application and give it the name `tomcat`:

```
$ docker service create --replicas 1 --name tomcat tomcat
```

The command created the service and therefore sent a task to start a container on one of the nodes. Let's list the running services:

```
$ docker service ls
ID              NAME       MODE          REPLICAS   IMAGE
x65aeojumj05    tomcat     replicated    1/1        tomcat:latest
```

The log confirms that the `tomcat` service is running, and it has one replica (one Docker container is running). We can examine the service even more closely:

```
$ docker service ps tomcat
ID              NAME       IMAGE           NODE             DESIRED STATE CURRENT
STATE
kjy1udwcnwmi tomcat.1   tomcat:latest   ubuntu-manager   Running         Running
about a minute ago
```

> If you are interested in the detailed information about a service, you can use the `docker service inspect <service_name>` command.

From the console output, we can see that the container is running on the manager node (`ubuntu-manager`). It could have been started on any other node as well; the manager automatically chooses the worker node using the scheduling strategy algorithm. We can confirm that the container is running using the well-known `docker ps` command:

```
$ docker ps
CONTAINER ID       IMAGE
COMMAND            CREATED           STATUS              PORTS
NAMES
6718d0bcba98
tomcat@sha256:88483873b279aaea5ced002c98dde04555584b66de29797a4476d5e94874e
```

```
6de
"catalina.sh run" About a minute ago Up About a minute    8080/tcp
tomcat.1.kjy1udwcnwmiosiw2qn71nt1r
```

> If we don't want a task to be executed on the manager node, we can constrain the service with the `--constraint node.role==worker` option. The other possibility is to disable the manager completely from executing tasks with `docker node update --availability drain <manager_name>`.

Scaling service

When the service is running, we can scale it up or down so that it will be running in many replicas:

```
$ docker service scale tomcat=5
tomcat scaled to 5
```

We can check that the service has been scaled:

```
$ docker service ps tomcat
ID              NAME        IMAGE           NODE            DESIRED STATE
CURRENT STATE
kjy1udwcnwmi  tomcat.1  tomcat:latest  ubuntu-manager  Running     Running 2
minutes ago
536p5zc3kaxz  tomcat.2  tomcat:latest  ubuntu-worker2  Running       Preparing
18 seconds ago npt6ui1g9bdp  tomcat.3  tomcat:latest  ubuntu-manager
Running      Running 18 seconds ago zo2kger1rmqc  tomcat.4  tomcat:latest
ubuntu-worker1  Running       Preparing 18 seconds ago 1fb24nf94488  tomcat.5
tomcat:latest  ubuntu-worker2  Running       Preparing 18 seconds ago
```

Note that this time, two containers are running on the `manager` node, one on the `ubuntu-worker1` node, and the other on the `ubuntu-worker2` node. We can check that they are really running by executing `docker ps` on each of the machines.

If we want to remove the services, it's enough to execute the following command:

```
$ docker service rm tomcat
```

You can check with the `docker service ls` command that the service has been removed, and therefore all related `tomcat` containers were stopped and removed from all the nodes.

Publishing ports

Docker services, similar to the containers, have a port forwarding mechanism. We use it by adding the `-p <host_port>:<container:port>` parameter. Here's what starting a service could look like:

```
$ docker service create --replicas 1 --publish 8080:8080 --name tomcat
tomcat
```

Now, we can open a browser and see the Tomcat's main page under the address `http://192.168.0.143:8080/`.

The application is available on the manager host that acts as a load balancer and distributes requests to worker nodes. What may sound a little less intuitive is the fact that we can access Tomcat using the IP address of any worker, for example, if worker nodes are available under `192.168.0.166` and `192.168.0.115`, we can access the same running container with `http://192.168.0.166:8080/` and `http://192.168.0.115:8080/`. This is possible because Docker Swarm creates a routing mesh, in which each node has the information how to forward the published port.

 You can read more about how the load balancing and routing are done by Docker Swarm at `https://docs.docker.com/engine/swarm/ingress/`.

By default, the internal Docker Swarm load balancing is used. Therefore, it's enough to address all requests to the manager's machine, and it will take care of its distribution between nodes. The other option is to configure an external load balancer (for example, HAProxy or Traefik).

We have discussed the basic usage of Docker Swarm. Let's now dive into more challenging features.

Advanced Docker Swarm

Docker Swarm offers a lot of interesting features that are useful in the Continuous Delivery process. In this section, we will walk through the most important ones.

Rolling updates

Imagine you deploy a new version of your application. You need to update all replicas in the cluster. One option would be to stop the whole Docker Swarm service and to run a new one from the updated Docker image. Such approach, however, causes downtime between the moment when the service is stopped and the moment when the new one is started. In the Continuous Delivery process, downtime is not acceptable, since the deployment can take place after every source code change, which is simply often. Then, how can we provide zero-downtime deployment in a cluster? This is the role of rolling updates.

A rolling update is an automatic method for replacing a service, replica by a replica, in a way that some of the replicas are working all the time. Docker Swarm uses rolling updates by default, and they can be steered with two parameters:

- update-delay: Delay between starting one replica and stopping the next one (0 seconds by default)
- update-parallelism: Maximum number of replicas updated at the same time (one by default)

The Docker Swarm rolling update process looks as follows:

1. Stop the <update-parallelism> number of tasks (replicas).
2. In their place, run the same number of updated tasks.
3. If a task returns the **RUNNING** state, then wait for the <update-delay> period.
4. If, at any time, any task returns the **FAILED** state, then pause the update.

> The value of the update-parallelism parameter should be adapted to the number of replicas we run. If the number is small and booting the service is fast, it's reasonable to keep the default value of 1. The update-delay parameter should be set to the period longer than the expected boot time of our application so that we will notice the failure, and therefore pause the update.

Let's look at an example and change the Tomcat application from version 8 to version 9. Suppose we have the tomcat:8 service with five replicas:

```
$ docker service create --replicas 5 --name tomcat --update-delay 10s
tomcat:8
```

We can check that all replicas are running with the docker service ps tomcat command. Another useful command that helps examine the service is the docker service inspect command:

```
$ docker service inspect --pretty tomcat

ID:        au1nu396jzdewyq2y8enm0b6i
Name:      tomcat
Service Mode:      Replicated
  Replicas:      5
Placement:
UpdateConfig:
  Parallelism:      1
  Delay:      10s
  On failure:      pause
  Max failure ratio: 0
ContainerSpec:
  Image:
tomcat:8@sha256:835b6501c150de39d2b12569fd8124eaebc53a899e2540549b6b6f86765
38484
Resources:
Endpoint Mode:      vip
```

We can see that the service has five replicas created out of the image tomcat:8. The command output also includes the information about the parallelism and the delay time between updates (as set by the options in the docker service create command).

Now, we can update the service into the tomcat:9 image:

```
$ docker service update --image tomcat:9 tomcat
```

Let's check what happens:

```
$ docker service ps tomcat
ID               NAME       IMAGE      NODE            DESIRED STATE   CURRENT
STATE
4dvh6ytn4lsq     tomcat.1   tomcat:8   ubuntu-manager  Running         Running 4
minutes ago
2mop96j5q4aj     tomcat.2   tomcat:8   ubuntu-manager  Running         Running 4
minutes ago
owurmusr1c48     tomcat.3   tomcat:9   ubuntu-manager  Running         Preparing 13
seconds ago
r9drfjpizuxf     \_ tomcat.3  tomcat:8  ubuntu-manager  Shutdown       Shutdown
12 seconds ago
0725ha5d8p4v     tomcat.4   tomcat:8   ubuntu-manager  Running         Running 4
minutes ago
wl25m2vrqgc4     tomcat.5   tomcat:8   ubuntu-manager  Running         Running 4
minutes ago
```

Note that the first replica of `tomcat:8` has been shut down and the first `tomcat:9` is already running. If we kept on checking the output of the `docker service ps tomcat` command, we would notice that after every 10 seconds, another replica is in the shutdown state and a new one is started. If we also monitored the `docker inspect` command, we would see that the value **UpdateStatus: State** will change to **updating** and then, when the update is done, to **completed**.

A rolling update is a very powerful feature that allows zero downtime deployment and it should always be used in the Continuous Delivery process.

Draining nodes

When we need to stop a worker node for maintenance, or we would just like to remove it from the cluster, we can use the Swarm draining node feature. Draining the node means asking the manager to move all tasks out of a given node and exclude it from receiving new tasks. As a result, all replicas are running only on the active nodes and the drained nodes are idle.

Let's look how this works in practice. Suppose we have three cluster nodes and a Tomcat service with five replicas:

```
$ docker node ls
ID                            HOSTNAME          STATUS   AVAILABILITY   MANAGER
STATUS
4mrrmibdrpa3yethhmy13mwzq     ubuntu-worker2    Ready    Active
kzgm7erw73tu2rjjninxdb4wp *   ubuntu-manager    Ready    Active         Leader
```

```
yllusy42jp08w8fmze43rmqqs    ubuntu-worker1   Ready    Active

$ docker service create --replicas 5 --name tomcat tomcat
```

Let's check on which nodes the replicas are running:

```
$ docker service ps tomcat
ID                  NAME         IMAGE           NODE              DESIRED STATE
CURRENT STATE
zrnawwpupuql  tomcat.1  tomcat:latest  ubuntu-manager  Running     Running
17 minutes ago
x6rqhyn7mrot  tomcat.2  tomcat:latest  ubuntu-worker1  Running     Running
16 minutes ago
rspgxcfv3is2  tomcat.3  tomcat:latest  ubuntu-worker2  Running     Running 5
weeks ago
cf00k61vo7xh  tomcat.4  tomcat:latest  ubuntu-manager  Running     Running
17 minutes ago
otjo08e06qbx  tomcat.5  tomcat:latest  ubuntu-worker2  Running     Running 5
weeks ago
```

There are two replicas running on the `ubuntu-worker2` node. Let's drain that node:

```
$ docker node update --availability drain ubuntu-worker2
```

The node is put into the **drain** availability, so all replicas should be moved out of it:

```
$ docker service ps tomcat
ID                  NAME         IMAGE           NODE              DESIRED STATE
CURRENT STATE
zrnawwpupuql  tomcat.1  tomcat:latest  ubuntu-manager  Running     Running
18 minutes ago
x6rqhyn7mrot  tomcat.2  tomcat:latest  ubuntu-worker1  Running     Running
17 minutes ago qrptjztd777i  tomcat.3  tomcat:latest  ubuntu-worker1
Running     Running less than a second ago
rspgxcfv3is2    \_ tomcat.3  tomcat:latest  ubuntu-worker2  Shutdown
Shutdown less than a second ago
cf00k61vo7xh  tomcat.4  tomcat:latest  ubuntu-manager  Running     Running
18 minutes ago k4c14tyo7leq  tomcat.5  tomcat:latest  ubuntu-worker1
Running     Running less than a second ago
otjo08e06qbx    \_ tomcat.5  tomcat:latest  ubuntu-worker2  Shutdown
Shutdown less than a second ago
```

We can see that new tasks were started on the `ubuntu-worker1` node and the old replicas were shut down. We can check the status of the nodes:

```
$ docker node ls
ID                         HOSTNAME         STATUS   AVAILABILITY   MANAGER
STATUS
4mrrmibdrpa3yethhmy13mwzq    ubuntu-worker2   Ready    Drain
kzgm7erw73tu2rjjninxdb4wp *  ubuntu-manager   Ready    Active                 Leader
yllusy42jp08w8fmze43rmqqs    ubuntu-worker1   Ready    Active
```

As expected, the `ubuntu-worker2` node is available (status `Ready`), but its availability is set to drain, which means it doesn't host any tasks. If we would like to get the node back, we can check its availability to `active`:

```
$ docker node update --availability active ubuntu-worker2
```

 A very common practice is to drain the manager node and, as a result, it will not receive any tasks, but do management work only.

An alternative method to draining the node would be to execute the `docker swarm leave` command from the worker. This approach, however, has two drawbacks:

- For a moment, there are fewer replicas than expected (after leaving the swarm and before the master starts new tasks on other nodes)
- The master does not control if the node is still in the cluster

For these reasons, if we plan to stop the worker for some time and then get it back, it's recommended to use the draining node feature.

Multiple manager nodes

Having a single manager node is risky because when the manager machine is down, the whole cluster is down. This situation is, obviously, not acceptable in the case of business-critical systems. In this section, we present how to manage multiple master nodes.

In order to add a new manager node to the system, we need to first execute the following command on the (currently single) manager node:

```
$ docker swarm join-token manager

To add a manager to this swarm, run the following command:
```

```
docker swarm join \
--token SWMTKN-1-5blnptt38eh9d3s8lk8po3069vbjmz7k7r3falkm20y9v9hefx-
a4v5olovq9mnvy7v8ppp63r23 \
192.168.0.143:2377
```

The output shows the token and the entire command that needs to be executed on the machine that is supposed to become the manager. After executing it, we should see that a new manager was added.

 Another option to add a manager is to promote it from the worker role using the `docker node promote <node>` command. In order to get it back to the worker role, we can use the `docker node demote <node>` command.

Suppose we have added two additional managers; we should see the following output:

```
$ docker node ls
ID                             HOSTNAME           STATUS   AVAILABILITY   MANAGER
STATUS
4mrrmibdrpa3yethhmy13mwzq      ubuntu-manager2    Ready    Active
kzgm7erw73tu2rjjninxdb4wp *    ubuntu-manager     Ready    Active         Leader
pkt4sjjsbxx4ly1lwetieuj2n      ubuntu-manager1    Ready    Active
Reachable
```

Note that the new managers have the manager status set to reachable (or left empty), while the old manager is the leader. The reason for this is the fact that there is always one primary node responsible for all Swarm management and orchestration decisions. The leader is elected from the managers using the Raft consensus algorithm, and when it is down, a new leader is elected.

 Raft is a consensus algorithm that is used to make decisions in distributed systems. You can read more about how it works (and see a visualization) at `https://raft.github.io/`. A very popular alternative algorithm for the same goal is called Paxos.

Suppose we shut down the `ubuntu-manager` machine; let's have a look at how the new leader was elected:

```
$ docker node ls
ID                             HOSTNAME           STATUS   AVAILABILITY   MANAGER
STATUS
4mrrmibdrpa3yethhmy13mwzq      ubuntu-manager2    Ready    Active
Reachable
kzgm7erw73tu2rjjninxdb4wp      ubuntu-manager     Ready    Active
Unreachable
pkt4sjjsbxx4ly1lwetieuj2n *    ubuntu-manager1    Ready    Active         Leader
```

Note that even when one of the managers is down, the swarm can work correctly.

There is no limit for the number of managers, so it may sound that the more managers the better fault tolerance. It's true, however, having a lot of managers has an impact on the performance because all Swarm-state-related decisions (for example, adding a new node or leader election) have to be agreed between all managers using the Raft algorithm. As a result, the number of managers is always a tradeoff between the fault tolerance and the performance.

The Raft algorithm itself has a constraint on the number of managers. Distributed decisions have to be approved by the majority of nodes, called a quorum. This fact implies that an odd number of managers is recommended.

To understand why, let's see what would happen if we had two managers. In that case, the majority is two, so if any of the managers is down, then it's not possible to reach the quorum and therefore elect the leader. As a result, losing one machine makes the whole cluster out of order. We added a manager, but the whole cluster became less fault tolerant. The situation would be different in the case of three managers. Then, the majority is still two, so losing one manager does not stop the whole cluster. This is the fact that even though it's not technically forbidden, only odd number of managers makes sense.

> The more the managers in the cluster, the more the Raft-related operations are involved. Then, the `manager` nodes should be put into the drain availability in order to save their resources.

Scheduling strategy

So far, we have learned that the manager automatically assigns a worker node to a task. In this section, we dive deeper into what automatically means. We present the Docker Swarm scheduling strategy and a way to configure it according to our needs.

Docker Swarm uses two criteria for choosing the right worker node:

- **Resource availability**: Scheduler is aware of the resources available on nodes. It uses the so-called **spread strategy** that attempts to schedule the task on the least loaded node, provided it meets the criteria specified by labels and constraints.
- **Labels and constraints**:
    - Label is an attribute of a node. Some labels are assigned automatically, for example, `node.id` or `node.hostname`; others can be defined by the cluster admin, for example, `node.labels.segment`
    - Constraint is a restriction applied by the creator of the service, for example, choosing only nodes with the given label

 Labels are divided into two categories, `node.labels` and `engine.labels`. The first one is added by the operational team; the second one is collected by Docker Engine, for example, operating system or hardware specifics.

As an example, if we would like to run the Tomcat service on the concrete node, `ubuntu-worker1`, then we need to use the following command:

```
$ docker service create --constraint 'node.hostname == ubuntu-worker1' tomcat
```

We can also add a custom label to the node:

```
$ docker node update --label-add segment=AA ubuntu-worker1
```

The preceding command added a label, `node.labels.segment`, with the value AA. Then, we can use it while running the service:

```
$ docker service create --constraint 'node.labels.segment == AA' tomcat
```

This command runs the `tomcat` replicas only on the nodes that are labeled with the given segment, AA.

Labels and constraints give us the flexibility to configure the nodes on which service replicas would be run. This approach, even though valid in many cases, should not be overused, since it's best to keep the replicas distributed on multiple nodes and let Docker Swarm take care of the right scheduling process.

Docker Compose with Docker Swarm

We have described how to use Docker Swarm in order to deploy a service, which in turn runs multiple containers from the given Docker image. On the other hand, there is Docker Compose, which provides a method to define the dependencies between containers and enables scaling containers, but everything is done within one Docker host. How do we merge both technologies so that we can specify the `docker-compose.yml` file and automatically distribute the containers on a cluster? Luckily, there is Docker Stack.

Introducing Docker Stack

Docker Stack is a method to run multiple-linked containers on a Swarm cluster. To understand better how it links Docker Compose with Docker Swarm, let's take a look at the following figure:

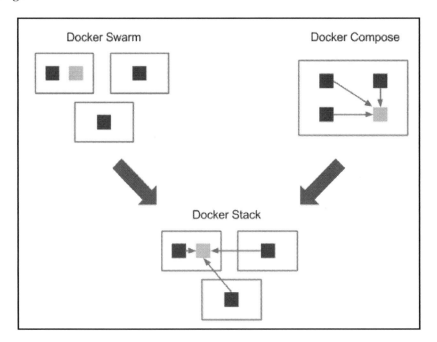

Docker Swarm orchestrates which container is run on which physical machine. The containers, however, don't have any dependencies between themselves, so in order for them to communicate, we would need to link them manually. Docker Compose, in contrast, provides linking between the containers. In the example from the preceding figure, one Docker image (deployed in three replicated containers) depends on another Docker image (deployed as one container). All containers, however, run on the same Docker host, so the horizontal scaling is limited to the resources of one machine. Docker Stack connects both technologies and allows using the `docker-compose.yml` file to run the complete environment of linked containers deployed on a cluster of Docker hosts.

Using Docker Stack

As an example, let's use the `calculator` image that depends on the `redis` image. Let's split the process into four steps:

1. Specifying `docker-compose.yml`.
2. Running the Docker Stack command.
3. Verifying the services and containers.
4. Removing the stack.

Specifying docker-compose.yml

We already defined the `docker-compose.yml` file in the previous chapters and it looked similar to the following one:

```
version: "3"
services:
    calculator:
        deploy:
            replicas: 3
        image: leszko/calculator:latest
        ports:
        - "8881:8080"
    redis:
        deploy:
            replicas: 1
        image: redis:latest
```

Note that all images must be pushed to the registry before running the `docker stack` command so that they would be accessible from all nodes. It is therefore not possible to build images inside `docker-compose.yml`.

With the presented docker-compose.yml configuration, we will run three `calculator` containers and one `redis` container. The endpoint of the calculator service will be exposed on port `8881`.

Running the docker stack command

Let's use the `docker stack` command to run the services, which in turn will start containers on the cluster:

```
$ docker stack deploy --compose-file docker-compose.yml app
Creating network app_default
Creating service app_redis
Creating service app_calculator
```

Docker plans to simplify the syntax so that the `stack` word would not be needed, for example, `docker deploy --compose-file docker-compose.yml app`. At the time of writing, it's only available in the experimental version.

Verifying the services and containers

The services have started. We can check that they are running with the `docker service ls` command:

```
$ docker service ls
ID            NAME            MODE         REPLICAS   IMAGE
5jbdzt9wolor  app_calculator  replicated   3/3
leszko/calculator:latest
zrr4pkh3n13f  app_redis       replicated   1/1        redis:latest
```

We can look even closer at the services and check on which Docker hosts they have been deployed:

```
$ docker service ps app_calculator
ID            NAME              IMAGE                    NODE    DESIRED
STATE    CURRENT STATE
jx0ipdxwdilm  app_calculator.1  leszko/calculator:latest  ubuntu-manager
Running      Running 57 seconds ago
```

```
psweuemtb2wf  app_calculator.2  leszko/calculator:latest  ubuntu-worker1
Running      Running about a minute ago
iuas0dmi7abn  app_calculator.3  leszko/calculator:latest  ubuntu-worker2
Running      Running 57 seconds ago

$ docker service ps app_redis
ID             NAME           IMAGE          NODE           DESIRED STATE
CURRENT STATE
8sg1ybbggx31  app_redis.1  redis:latest  ubuntu-manager  Running   Running
about a minute ago
```

We can see that one of the `calculator` containers and the `redis` containers are started on the `ubuntu-manager` machine. Two other `calculator` containers run on the `ubuntu-worker1` and `ubuntu-worker2` machines.

Note that we explicitly specified the port number under which the `calculator` web service should be published. Therefore, we are able to access the endpoint via the manager's IP address `http://192.168.0.143:8881/sum?a=1&b=2`. The operation returns 3 as a result and caches it in the Redis container.

Removing the stack

When we're done with the stack, we can remove everything using the convenient `docker stack rm` command:

```
$ docker stack rm app
Removing service app_calculator
Removing service app_redis
Removing network app_default
```

Using Docker Stack allows running the Docker Compose specification on the Docker Swarm cluster. Note that we used the exact `docker-compose.yml` format, which is a great benefit, because there is no need to specify anything extra for the Swarm.

The merger of both technologies gives us the real power of deploying applications on Docker because we don't need to think about individual machines. All we need to specify is how our (micro) services are dependent on each other, express it in the docker-compose.yml format, and let Docker take care of everything else. The physical machines can be then treated simply as a set of resources.

Alternative cluster management systems

Docker Swarm is not the only system for clustering Docker containers. Even though it's the one available out of the box, there may be some valid reasons to install a third-party cluster manager. Let's walk through the most popular alternatives.

Kubernetes

Kubernetes is an open source cluster management system originally designed by Google. Even though it's not Docker-native, the integration is smooth, and there are many additional tools that help with this process; for example, **kompose** can translate the `docker-compose.yml` files into Kubernetes configuration files.

Let's take a look at the simplified architecture of Kubernetes:

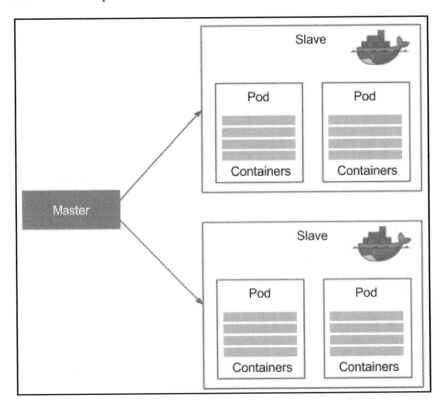

Kubernetes is similar to Docker Swarm in a way that it also has master and worker nodes. Additionally, it introduces the concept of a **pod** that represents a group of containers deployed and scheduled together. Most pods have a few containers that make up a service. Pods are dynamically built and removed depending on the changing requirements.

Kubernetes is relatively young. Its development started in 2014; however, it's based on Google's experience, and this is one of the reasons why it's one of the most popular cluster management systems available on the market. There are more and more organizations that migrated to Kubernetes, such as eBay, Wikipedia, and Pearson.

Apache Mesos

Apache Mesos is an open source scheduling and clustering system started at the University of California, Berkeley, in 2009, long before Docker emerged. It provides an abstraction layer over CPU, disk space, and RAM. One of the great advantages of Mesos is that it supports any Linux application, not necessarily (Docker) containers. This is why it's possible to create a cluster out of thousands of machines and use it for both Docker containers and other programs, for example, Hadoop-based calculations.

Let's look at the figure presenting the Mesos architecture:

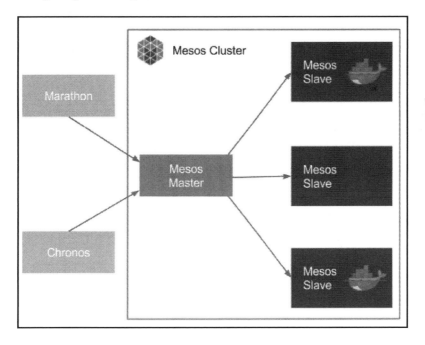

Apache Mesos, similar to other clustering systems, has the master-slave architecture. It uses node agents installed on every node for communication, and it provides two types of schedulers, Chronos - for cron-style repeating tasks and Marathon - providing a REST API to orchestrate services and containers.

Apache Mesos is very mature compared to other clustering systems, and it has been adopted in a large number of organizations, such as Twitter, Uber, and CERN.

Comparing features

Kubernetes, Docker Swarm, and Mesos are all good choices for the cluster management system. All of them are free and open source, and all of them provide important cluster management features such as load balancing, service discovery, distributed storage, failure recovery, monitoring, secret management, and rolling updates. All of them can also be used in the Continuous Delivery process without huge differences. This is because, in the Dockerized infrastructure, they all address the same issue, the clustering of Docker containers. Nevertheless, obviously, the systems are not exactly the same. Let's have a look at a table presenting the differences:

	Docker Swarm	**Kubernetes**	**Apache Mesos**
Docker support	Native	Supports Docker as one of the container types in the pod	Mesos agents (slaves) can be configured to host Docker containers
Application types	Docker images	Containerized applications (Docker, rkt, and hyper)	Any application that can be run on Linux (also containers)
Application definition	Docker Compose configuration	Pods configuration, replica sets, replication controllers, services, and deployments	Application groups formed in the tree structure
Setup process	Very simple	Depending on the infrastructure, it may require running one command or many complex operations	Fairly involved, it requires configuring Mesos, Marathon, Chronos, Zookeeper, and Docker support
API	Docker REST API	REST API	Chronos/Marathon REST API

User Interface	Docker console client, third-party web applications, such as Shipyard	Console tools, native Web UI (Kubernetes Dashboard)	Official web interfaces for Mesos, Marathon, and Chronos
Cloud integration	Manual installation required	Cloud-native support from most providers (Azure, AWS, Google Cloud, and others)	Support from most cloud providers
Maximum cluster size	1,000 nodes	1,000 nodes	50,000 nodes
Autoscaling	Not available	Provides horizontal pod autoscaling based on the observed CPU usage	Marathon provides autoscaling based on resource (CPU/Memory) consumption, number of requests per second, and queue length

Obviously, apart from Docker Swarm, Kubernetes, and Apache Mesos, there are other clustering systems available in the market. They are, however, not that popular and their usage decreases over time.

No matter which system you choose, you can use it not only for the staging/production environments but also to scale Jenkins agents. Let's have a look at how to do it.

Scaling Jenkins

The obvious use cases for server clustering are the staging and production environments. When used, it's enough to attach a physical machine in order to increase the capacity of the environment. Nevertheless, in the context of Continuous Delivery, we may also want to improve the Jenkins infrastructure by running Jenkins agent (slave) nodes on a cluster. In this section, we take a look at two different methods to achieve this goal.

Dynamic slave provisioning

We saw dynamic slave provisioning in Chapter 3, *Configuring Jenkins*. With Docker Swarm, the idea stays exactly the same. When the build is started, the Jenkins master runs a container from the Jenkins slave Docker image, and the Jenkinsfile script is executed inside the container. Docker Swarm, however, makes the solution more powerful since we are not limited to a single Docker host machine but can provide real horizontal scaling. Adding a new Docker host to the cluster effectively scales up the capacity of the Jenkins infrastructure.

At the time of writing, the Jenkins Docker plugin does not support Docker Swarm. One of the solutions is to use Kubernetes or Mesos as the cluster management system. Each of them has a dedicated Jenkins plugin: Kubernetes Plugin (https://wiki.jenkins.io/display/JENKINS/Kubernetes+Plugin) and Mesos Plugin (https://wiki.jenkins.io/display/JENKINS/Mesos+Plugin).

No matter how the slaves are provisioned, we always configure them by installing the appropriate plugin and adding the entry to the **Cloud** section in **Manage Jenkins | Configure System**.

Jenkins Swarm

If we don't want to use the dynamic slave provisioning, then another solution for clustering Jenkins slaves is to use Jenkins Swarm. We described how to use it in Chapter 3, *Configuring Jenkins*. Here, we add the description for Docker Swarm.

First, let's have a look at how to run the Jenkins Swarm slave using the Docker image built from the swarm-client.jar tool. There are a few of them available on Docker Hub; we can use the csanchez/jenkins-swarm-slave image:

```
$ docker run csanchez/jenkins-swarm-slave:1.16 -master -username -password -name jenkins-swarm-slave-2
```

This command execution should have exactly the same effect as the on presented in Chapter 3, *Configuring Jenkins*; it dynamically adds a slave to the Jenkins master.

Then, to get the most of Jenkins Swarm, we can run the slave containers on the Docker Swarm cluster:

```
$ docker service create --replicas 5 --name jenkins-swarm-slave
csanchez/jenkins-swarm-slave -master -disableSslVerification -username -
password -name jenkins-swarm-slave
```

The preceding command starts five slaves on the cluster and attaches them to the Jenkins master. Please note that it is very simple to scale Jenkins horizontally by executing the docker service scale command.

Comparison of dynamic slave provisioning and Jenkins Swarm

Dynamic slave provisioning and Jenkins Swarm can be both run on a cluster that results in the architecture presented in the following diagram:

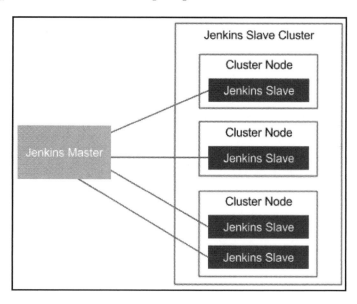

Jenkins slaves are run on the cluster and therefore are very easily scaled up and down. If we need more Jenkins resources, we scale up Jenkins slaves. If we need more cluster resources, we add more physical machines to the cluster.

The difference between the two solutions is that the dynamic slave provisioning automatically adds a Jenkins slave to the cluster before each build. The benefit of such approach is that we don't even have to think about how many Jenkins slaves should be running at the moment since the number automatically adapts to the number of pipeline builds. This is why, in most cases, the dynamic slave provisioning is the first choice. Nevertheless, Jenkins Swarm also carries a few significant benefits:

- **Control of the number of slaves**: Using Jenkins Swarm, we explicitly decide how many Jenkins slaves should be running at the moment.
- **Stateful slaves**: Many builds share the same Jenkins slave, which may sound like a drawback; however, it becomes an advantage when a build requires downloading a lot of dependent libraries from the internet. In the case of dynamic slave provisioning, to cache the dependencies, we would need to set up a shared volume.
- **Control of where the slaves are running**: Using Jenkins Swarm, we can decide not to run slaves on the cluster but to choose the host machine dynamically; for example, for many startups, when the cluster infrastructure is costly, slaves can be dynamically run on the laptop of a developer who is starting the build.

Clustering Jenkins slaves bring a lot of benefits and it is what the modern Jenkins architecture should look like. This way, we can provide the dynamic horizontal scaling of the infrastructure for the Continuous Delivery process.

Exercises

In this chapter, we have covered Docker Swarm and the clustering process in detail. In order to enhance this knowledge, we recommend the following exercises:

1. Set up a swarm cluster that consists of three nodes:

    - Use one machine as the manager node and two machines as worker nodes
    - You can use physical machines connected to one network, machines from the cloud provider, or VirtualBox machines with the shared network
    - Check that the cluster is configured properly using the `docker node` command

2. Run/scale a hello world service on the cluster:

- The service can look exactly the same as described in the exercises for `Chapter 2`, *Introducing Docker*
- Publish the port so that it will be accessible from outside of the cluster
- Scale the service to five replicas
- Make a request to the "hello world" service and check which of the containers is serving the request

3. Scale Jenkins using slaves deployed on the Swarm cluster:

- Use Jenkins Swarm or dynamic slave provisioning
- Run a pipeline build and check that it is executed on one of the clustered slaves

Summary

In this chapter, we took a look at the clustering methods for Docker environments that enable setting up the complete staging/production/Jenkins environment. Here are the key takeaways from the chapter:

- Clustering is a method of configuring a set of machines in a way that, in many respects, can be viewed as a single system
- Docker Swarm is the native clustering system for Docker
- Docker Swarm clusters can be dynamically configured using built-in Docker commands
- Docker images can be run and scaled on the cluster using the docker service command
- Docker Stack is a method to run the Docker Compose configuration on a Swarm cluster
- The most popular clustering systems that support Docker are Docker Swarm, Kubernetes, and Apache Mesos
- Jenkins agents can be run on a cluster using the dynamic slave provisioning or the Jenkins Swarm plugin

In the next chapter, we will describe the more advanced aspects of the Continuous Delivery process and present the best practices for building pipelines

9
Advanced Continuous Delivery

In the last chapter, we covered how server clustering works and how we can use it together with Docker and Jenkins. In this chapter, we will see a mixture of different aspects that are very important in the Continuous Delivery process but have not been described yet.

This chapter covers the following points:

- Explaining how to approach database changes in the context of Continuous Delivery
- Introducing the idea of database migration and related tools
- Exploring different approaches to backwards-compatible and backwards-incompatible database updates
- Using parallel steps in the Jenkins pipeline
- Creating a Jenkins shared library
- Presenting a way to roll back production changes
- Introducing Continuous Delivery for legacy systems
- Exploring how to prepare zero-downtime deployments
- Presenting Continuous Delivery best practices

Managing database changes

So far, we have focused on the Continuous Delivery process, which was applied to a web service. A simple part of this was that web services are inherently stateless. This fact means that they can be easily updated, restarted, cloned in many instances, and recreated from the given source code. A web service, however, is usually linked to its stateful part, a database that poses new challenges to the delivery process. These challenges can be grouped into the following categories:

- **Compatibility**: The database schema and the data itself must be compatible with the web service all the time
- **Zero-downtime deployment**: In order to achieve zero-downtime deployment, we use rolling updates, which means that a database must be compatible with two different web service versions at the same time
- **Rollback**: A rollback of a database can be difficult, limited, or sometimes even impossible because not all operations are reversible (for example, removing a column that contains data)
- **Test data**: Database-related changes are difficult to test because we need test data that is very similar to production

In this section, I will explain how to address these challenges so that the Continuous Delivery process will be as safe as possible.

Understanding schema updates

If you think about the delivery process, it's not really the data itself that cause difficulties because we don't usually change the data when we deploy an application. The data is something that is collected while the system is live in the production; whereas, during deployment, we only change the way we store and interpret this data. In other words, in the context of the Continuous Delivery process, we are interested in the structure of the database, not exactly in its content. This is why this section concerns mainly relational databases (and their schemas) and focuses less on other types of storage such as NoSQL databases, where there is no structure definition.

To understand this better, we think of Redis, which we have already used in this book. It stored the cached data, so effectively it was a database. Nevertheless, it required zero effort from the Continuous Delivery perspective since it didn't have any data structure. All it stored was the key-value entries, which does not evolve over time.

NoSQL databases usually don't have any restricting schema and therefore simplify the Continuous Delivery process because there is no additional schema update step required. This is a huge benefit; however, it doesn't necessarily mean that writing applications with NoSQL databases is simpler because we have put more effort into data validation in the source code.

Relational databases have static schemas. If we would like to change it, for example, to add a new column to the table, we need to write and execute a SQL DDL (data definition language) script. Doing this manually for every change requires a lot of work and leads to error-prone solutions, in which the operations team has to keep in sync the code and the database structure. A much better solution is to automatically update the schema in an incremental manner. Such a solution is called database migration.

Introducing database migrations

Database schema migration is a process of incremental changes to the relational database structure. Let's have a look at the following diagram to understand it better:

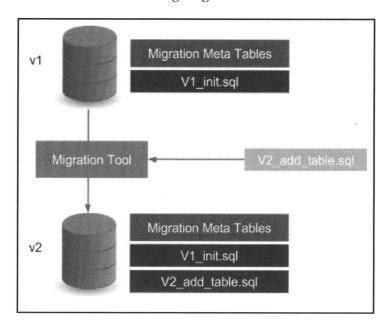

The database in the version **v1** has the schema defined by the `V1_init.sql` file. Additionally, it stores the metadata related to the migration process, for example, its current schema version and the migration changelog. When we want to update the schema, we provide the changes in the form of a SQL file, such as `V2_add_table.sql`. Then, we need to run the migration tool that executes the given SQL file on the database (it also updates the metatables). In effect, the database schema is a result of all subsequently executed SQL migration scripts. Next, we will see an example of a migration.

Migration scripts should be stored in the version control system, usually in the same repository as the source code.

Migration tools and the strategies they use can be divided into two categories:

- **Upgrade and downgrade**: This approach, for example, used by the Ruby on Rails framework, means that we can migrate up (from v1 to v2) and down (from v2 to v1). It allows the database schema to roll back, which may sometimes end up in data loss (if the migration is logically irreversible).
- **Upgrade only**: This approach, for example, used by the Flyway tool, only allows us to migrate up (from v1 to v2). In many cases, the database updates are not reversible, for example, removing a table from the database. Such a change cannot be rolled back because even if we recreate the table, we have already lost all the data.

There are many database migration tools available on the market, out of which the most popular are Flyway, Liquibase, and Rail Migrations (from the Ruby on Rails framework). As a next step to understand how such tools work, we will see an example based on the Flyway tool.

There are also commercial solutions provided for the particular databases, for example, Redgate (for SQL Server) and Optim Database Administrator (for DB2).

Using Flyway

Let's use Flyway to create a database schema for the calculator web service. The database will store the history of all operations that were executed on the service: the first parameter, the second parameter, and the result.

We show how to use the SQL database and Flyway in three steps:

1. Configuring the Flyway tool to work together with Gradle.
2. Defining the SQL migration script to create the calculation history table.
3. Using the SQL database inside the Spring Boot application code.

Configuring Flyway

In order to use Flyway together with Gradle, we need to add the following content to the build.gradle file:

```
buildscript {
    dependencies {
        classpath('com.h2database:h2:1.4.191')
    }
}
...
plugins {
    id "org.flywaydb.flyway" version "4.2.0"
}
...
flyway {
    url = 'jdbc:h2:file:/tmp/calculator'
    user = 'sa'
}
```

Here's a quick comment on the configuration:

- We used the H2 database, which is an in-memory (and file-based) database
- We store the database in the /tmp/calculator file
- The default database user is called sa (system administrator)

In the case of other SQL databases (for example, MySQL), the configuration would be very similar. The only difference is in the Gradle dependencies and the JDBC connection.

After this configuration is applied, we should be able to run the Flyway tool by executing the following command:

```
$ ./gradlew flywayMigrate -i
```

The command created the database in the file `/tmp/calculator.mv.db`. Obviously, it has no schema since we haven't defined anything yet.

 Flyway can be used as a command-line tool, via Java API, or as a plugin for the popular building tools Gradle, Maven, and Ant.

Defining the SQL migration script

The next step is to define the SQL file that adds the calculation table into the database schema. Let's create the `src/main/resources/db/migration/V1__Create_calculation_table.sql` file with the following content:

```
create table CALCULATION (
    ID      int not null auto_increment,
    A       varchar(100),
    B       varchar(100),
    RESULT  varchar(100),
    primary key (ID)
);
```

Note the migration file naming convention, `<version>__<change_description>.sql`. The SQL file creates a table with four columns, `ID`, `A`, `B`, `RESULT`. The `ID` column is an automatically incremented primary key of the table. Now, we are ready to run the Flyway command to apply the migration:

```
$ ./gradlew flywayMigrate -i
...
Successfully applied 1 migration to schema "PUBLIC" (execution time
00:00.028s).
:flywayMigrate (Thread[Daemon worker Thread 2,5,main]) completed. Took
1.114 secs.
```

The command automatically detected the migration file and executed it on the database.

 The migration files should be always kept in the version control system, usually, together with the source code.

Accessing database

We executed our first migration, so the database is prepared. To see the complete example, we should also adapt our project so that it would access the database.

Let's first configure the Gradle dependencies to use the H2 database from the Spring Boot project. We can do this by adding the following lines to the `build.gradle` file:

```
dependencies {
    compile("org.springframework.boot:spring-boot-starter-data-jpa")
    compile("com.h2database:h2")
}
```

The next step is to set up the database location and the startup behavior in the `src/main/resources/application.properties` file:

```
spring.datasource.url=jdbc:h2:file:/tmp/calculator;DB_CLOSE_ON_EXIT=FALSE
spring.jpa.hibernate.ddl-auto=validate
```

The second line means that Spring Boot will not try to automatically generate the database schema from the source code model. On the contrary, it will only validate if the database schema is consistent with the Java model.

Now, let's create the Java ORM entity model for the calculation in the new `src/main/java/com/leszko/calculator/Calculation.java` file:

```java
package com.leszko.calculator;
import javax.persistence.Entity;
import javax.persistence.GeneratedValue;
import javax.persistence.GenerationType;
import javax.persistence.Id;

@Entity
public class Calculation {
    @Id
    @GeneratedValue(strategy= GenerationType.AUTO)
    private Integer id;
    private String a;
    private String b;
    private String result;

    protected Calculation() {}

    public Calculation(String a, String b, String result) {
        this.a = a;
        this.b = b;
        this.result = result;
```

```
        }
    }
```

The entity class represents the database mapping in the Java code. A table is expressed as a class and each column as a field. The next step is to create the repository for loading and storing the `Calculation` entities.

Let's create the `src/main/java/com/leszko/calculator/CalculationRepository.java` file:

```
package com.leszko.calculator;
import org.springframework.data.repository.CrudRepository;

public interface CalculationRepository extends CrudRepository<Calculation,
Integer> {}
```

Finally, we can use the `Calculation` and `CalculationRepository` classes to store the calculation history. Let's add the following code to the `src/main/java/com/leszko/calculator/CalculatorController.java` file:

```
...
class CalculatorController {
    ...

    @Autowired
    private CalculationRepository calculationRepository;

    @RequestMapping("/sum")
    String sum(@RequestParam("a") Integer a, @RequestParam("b") Integer b) {
        String result = String.valueOf(calculator.sum(a, b));
        calculationRepository.save(new Calculation(a.toString(),
b.toString(), result));
        return result;
    }
}
```

Now, when we start the service and execute the /sum endpoint, each summing operation is logged into the database.

If you would like to browse the database content, then you can add `spring.h2.console.enabled=true` to the `application.properties` file, and then browse the database via the `/h2-console` endpoint.

We explained how the database schema migration works and how to use it inside a Spring project, built with Gradle. Now, let's have a look at how it integrates within the Continuous Delivery process.

Changing database in Continuous Delivery

The first approach to use database updates inside the Continuous Delivery pipeline could be to add a stage within the migration command execution. This simple solution would work correctly for many cases; however, it has two significant drawbacks:

- **Rollback**: As mentioned before, it's not always possible to roll back the database change (Flyway doesn't support downgrades at all). Therefore, in the case of service rollback, the database becomes incompatible.
- **Downtime**: The service update and the database update are not executed exactly at the same time, which causes downtime.

This leads us to two constraints that we will need to address:

- The database version needs to be compatible with the service version all the time
- The database schema migration is not reversible

We will address these constraints for two different cases: backwards-compatible updates and non-backwards-compatible updates.

Backwards-compatible changes

Backwards-compatible changes are simpler. Let's look at the following figure to see how they work:

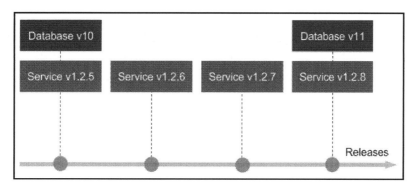

Suppose the schema migration `Database v10` is backwards-compatible. If we need to roll back the `Service v1.2.8` release, then we deploy `Service v1.2.7`, and there is no need to do anything with the database (database migrations are not reversible, so we keep `Database v11`). Since the schema update is backwards-compatible, `Service v.1.2.7` works perfectly fine with `Database v11`. The same applies if we need to roll back to `Service v1.2.6`, and so on. Now, suppose `Database v10` and all other migrations are backwards-compatible, then we could roll back to any service version and everything would work correctly.

There is also no problem with the downtime. If the database migration is zero-downtime itself, then we can execute it first and then use the rolling updates for the service.

Let's look at an example of a backwards-compatible change. We will create a schema update that adds a `created_at` column to the calculation table. The migration file `src/main/resources/db/migration/V2__Add_created_at_column.sql` looks as follows:

```
alter table CALCULATION
add CREATED_AT timestamp;
```

Besides the migration script, the calculator service requires a new field in the `Calculation` class:

```
...
private Timestamp createdAt;
...
```

We also need to adjust its constructor and then its usage in the `CalculatorController` class:

```
calculationRepository.save(new Calculation(a.toString(), b.toString(),
result, Timestamp.from(Instant.now())));
```

After running the service, the calculation history is stored together with the `created_at` column. Note that the change is backwards-compatible because even if we revert the Java code and leave the `created_at` column in the database, everything would work perfectly fine (the reverted code does not address the new column at all).

Non-backwards-compatible changes

Non-backwards-compatible changes are way more difficult. Looking at the previous figure, if database change v11 was backwards-incompatible, it would be impossible to roll back the service to 1.2.7. In this case, how can we approach non-backwards-compatible database migrations so that rollbacks and zero-downtime deployments would be possible?

To make a long story short, we can address this issue by converting a non-backwards-compatible change into a change that is backwards-compatible for a certain period of time. In other words, we need to put in the extra effort and split the schema migration into two parts:

- Backwards-compatible update executed now, which usually means keeping some redundant data
- Non-backwards-compatible update executed after the rollback period time that defines how far back we can revert our code

To illustrate this better, let's look at the following image:

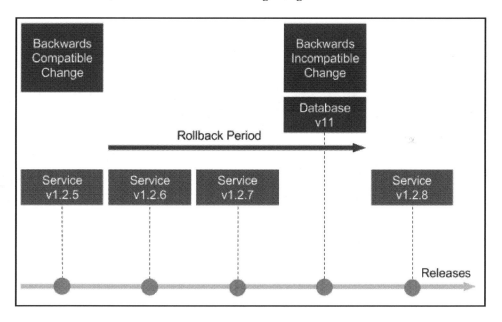

Let's think about an example of dropping a column. A proposed method would include two steps:

1. Stop using the column in the source code (v1.2.5, backwards-compatible update, executed first).
2. Drop the column from the database (v11, non-backwards-compatible update, executed after the rollback period).

All service versions until `Database v11` can be rolled back to any previous version, the services starting from `Service v1.2.8` can be rolled back only within the rollback period. Such approach may sound trivial because all we did was delay the column removal from the database. However, it addresses both the rollback issue and the zero-downtime deployment issue. As a result, it reduces the risk associated with the release. If we adjust the rollback period to a reasonable amount of time, for example, in the case of multiple releases per day to two weeks, then the risk is negligible. We don't usually roll many versions back.

Dropping a column was a very simple example. Let's have a look at a more difficult scenario and rename the result column in our calculator service. We present how to do this in a few steps:

1. Adding a new column to the database.
2. Changing the code to use both columns.
3. Merging the data in both columns.
4. Removing the old column from the code.
5. Dropping the old column from the database.

Adding a new column to the database

Let's say we need to rename the `result` column to `sum`. The first step is to add a new column that will be a duplicate. We must create a `src/main/resources/db/migration/V3__Add_sum_column.sql` migration file:

```
alter table CALCULATION
add SUM varchar(100);
```

As a result, after executing the migration, we have two columns: `result` and `sum`.

Changing the code to use both columns

The next step is to rename the column in the source code model and to use both database columns for the set and get operations. We can change it in the Calculation class:

```
public class Calculation {
    ...
    private String sum;
    ...
    public Calculation(String a, String b, String sum, Timestamp createdAt)
{
        this.a = a;
        this.b = b;
        this.sum = sum;
        this.result = sum;
        this.createdAt = createdAt;
    }

    public String getSum() {
        return sum != null ? sum : result;
    }
}
```

To be 100% accurate, in the getSum() method, we should compare something like the last modification column date (not exactly necessary to always take the new column first).

From now on, every time we add a row into the database, the same value is written to both the result and sum columns. While reading sum, we first check if it exists in the new column, and if not, we read it from the old column.

The same result can be achieved with the use of database triggers that would automatically write the same values into both columns.

All the changes we made so far were backwards-compatible, so we can roll back the service anytime we want, to any version we want.

Merging the data in both columns

This step is usually done after some time when the release is stable. We need to copy the data from the old `result` column into the new `sum` column. Let's create a migration file called `V4__Copy_result_into_sum_column.sql`:

```
update CALCULATION
set CALCULATION.sum = CALCULATION.result
where CALCULATION.sum is null;
```

We still have no limits for the rollback; however, if we need to deploy the version before the change in step 2, then this database migration needs to be repeated.

Removing the old column from the code

At this point, we already have all data in the new column, so we can start using it without the old column in the data model. In order to do this, we need to remove all code related to `result` in the `Calculation` class so that it would look as follows:

```
public class Calculation {
    ...
    private String sum;
    ...
    public Calculation(String a, String b, String sum, Timestamp createdAt)
{
        this.a = a;
        this.b = b;
        this.sum = sum;
        this.createdAt = createdAt;
    }

    public String getSum() {
        return sum;
    }
}
```

After this operation, we no longer use the `result` column in the code. Note that this operation is only backwards-compatible up to step 2. If we need to roll back to step 1, then we could lose the data stored after this step.

Dropping the old column from the database

The last step is to drop the old column from the database. This migration should be performed after the rollback period when we are sure we won't need to roll back before step 4.

 The rollback period can be very long since we aren't using the column from the database anymore. This task can be treated as a cleanup task, so even though it's non-backwards-compatible, there is no associated risk.

Let's add the final migration, `V5__Drop_result_column.sql`:

```
alter table CALCULATION
drop column RESULT;
```

After this step, we finally completed the column renaming procedure. Note that all we did was complicate the operation a little bit, in order to stretch it in time. This reduced the risk of backwards-incompatible database changes and allowed zero-downtime deployments.

Separating database updates from code changes

So far, in all figures, we presented that database migrations are run together with service releases. In other words, each commit (which implies each release) took both database changes and code changes. However, the recommended approach is to make a clear separation that a commit to the repository is either a database update or a code change. This method is presented in the following image:

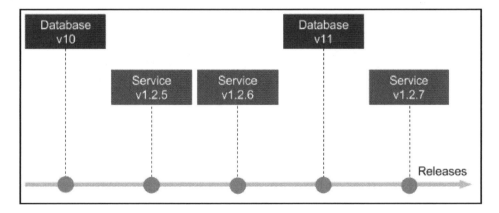

The benefit of database-service change separation is that we get the backwards-compatibility check for free. Imagine that the changes v11 and v1.2.7 concern one logical change, for example, adding a new column to the database. Then, we first commit database v11, so the tests in the Continuous Delivery pipeline check if database v11 works correctly with service v.1.2.6. In other words, they check if database update v11 is backwards-compatible. Then, we commit the v1.2.7 change, so the pipeline checks if database v11 works fine with service v1.2.7.

 The database-code separation does not mean that we must have two separate Jenkins pipelines. The pipeline can always execute both, but we should keep it as a good practice that a commit is either a database update or a code change.

To sum up, the database schema changes should be never done manually. Instead, we should always automate them using a migration tool, executed as a part of the Continuous Delivery pipeline. We should also avoid non-backwards-compatible database updates and the best way to assure this is to commit separately the database and code changes into the repository.

Avoiding shared database

In many systems, we can spot that the database becomes the central point that is shared between multiple services. In such a case, any update to the database becomes much more challenging because we need to coordinate it between all services.

For example, imagine we develop an online shop and we have a Customers table that contains the following columns: first name, last name, username, password, email, and discount. There are three services that are interested in the customer's data:

- **Profile manager**: This enables editing user's data
- **Checkout processor**: This processes the checkout (reads username and email)
- **Discount manager**: This analyzes the customer's orders and sets the suitable discount

Let's look at the following image that presents this situation:

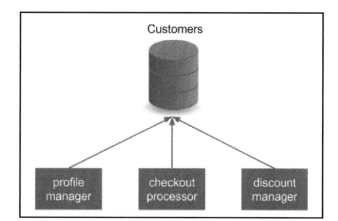

They are dependent on the same database schema. There are at least two issues with such an approach:

- When we want to update the schema, it must be compatible with all three services. While all backwards-compatible changes are fine, any non-backwards-compatible update becomes way more difficult or even impossible.
- Each service has a separate delivery cycle and a separate Continuous Delivery pipeline. Then, which pipeline should we use for the database schema migrations? Unfortunately, there is no good answer to this question.

For the reasons mentioned previously, each service should have its own database and the services should communicate via their APIs. Following our example, we could apply the following refactoring:

- The checkout processor should communicate with the profile manager's API to fetch the customer's data
- The discount column should be extracted to a separate database (or schema), and the discount manager should take the ownership

The refactored version is presented in the following image:

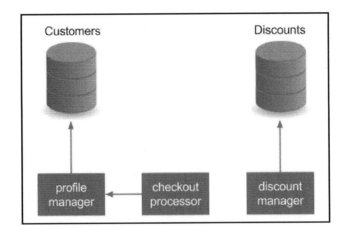

Such an approach is consistent with the principles of the microservice architecture and should always be applied. The communication over APIs is way more flexible than the direct database access.

 In the case of monolithic systems, a database is usually the integration point. Since such an approach causes a lot of issues, it's considered as an anti-pattern.

Preparing test data

We have already presented database migrations that keep the database schema consistent between the environments as a side effect. This is due to the fact that if we run the same migration scripts on the development machine, in the staging environment, or in the production, then we would always get the result in the same schema. However, the data values inside the tables differ. How can we prepare the test data so that it would effectively test our system? This is the topic of this section.

The answer to this question depends on the type of the test, and it is different for unit testing, integration/acceptance testing, and performance testing. Let's examine each case.

Unit testing

In the case of unit testing, we don't use the real database. We either mock the test data on the level of the persistence mechanism (repositories, data access objects) or we fake the real database with an in-memory database (for example, H2 database). Since unit tests are created by developers, the exact data values are usually invented by developers and they don't matter much.

Integration/acceptance testing

Integration and acceptance tests usually use the test/staging database, which should be as similar as possible to the production. One approach, taken by many companies, is to snapshot the production data into staging that guarantees that it is exactly the same. This approach, however, is treated as an anti-pattern for the following reasons:

- **Test isolation**: Each test operates on the same database, so the result of one test may influence the input of the others
- **Data security**: Production instances usually store sensitive information and are therefore better secured
- **Reproducibility**: After every snapshot, the test data is different, which may result in flaky tests

For the preceding reasons, the preferred approach is to manually prepare the test data by selecting a subset of the production data, together with the customer or the business analyst. When the production database grows, it's worth revisiting its content to see if there are any reasonable cases that should be added.

The best way to add data to the staging database is to use the public API of a service. This approach is consistent with acceptance tests, which are usually black-box. What's more, using the API guarantees that the data itself is consistent and simplifies database refactoring by limiting direct database operations.

Performance testing

Test data for the performance testing is usually similar to acceptance testing. One significant difference is the amount of data. In order to test the performance correctly, we need to provide sufficient volume of input data, at least as large as available on the production (during the peak time). For this purpose, we can create data generators, which are usually shared between acceptance and performance tests.

Pipeline patterns

We already know everything that is necessary to start a project and set up the Continuous Delivery pipeline with Jenkins and Docker. This section is intended to extend this knowledge with a few of the recommended general Jenkins pipeline practices.

Parallelizing pipelines

Throughout this book, we have always executed the pipeline sequentially, stage by stage, step by step. This approach makes it easy to reason the state and the result of the build. If there is first the acceptance test stage and then the release stage, it means that the release won't ever happen until the acceptance tests are successful. Sequential pipelines are simple to understand and usually do not cause any surprises. This is why the first method to solve any problem is to do it sequentially.

However, in some cases, the stages are time-consuming and it's worth running them in parallel. A very good example is performance tests. They usually take a lot of time, so assuming they are independent and isolated, it makes sense to run them in parallel. In Jenkins, we can parallelize the pipeline on two different levels:

- **Parallel steps**: Within one stage, parallel processes run on the same agent. This method is simple because all Jenkins workspace-related files are located on one physical machine, however, as always with the vertical scaling, the resources are limited to that single machine.
- **Parallel stages**: Each stage can be run in parallel on a separate agent machine that provides horizontal scaling of resources. We need to take care of the file transfer between the environments (using the `stash` Jenkinsfile keyword) if a file created in the previous stage is needed on the other physical machine.

 By the time of writing this book, parallel stages are not available in the declarative pipeline. The feature is supposed to be added in Jenkins Blue Ocean v1.3. In the meantime, the only possibility is to use the deprecated feature in the Groovy-based scripting pipeline, as described here at `https://jenkins.io/doc/book/pipeline/jenkinsfile/#executing-in-parallel`.

Let's look at how it looks in practice. If we would like to run two steps in parallel, the Jenkinsfile script should look as follows:

```
pipeline {
    agent any
    stages {
        stage('Stage 1') {
            steps {
                parallel (
                        one: { echo "parallel step 1" },
                        two: { echo "parallel step 2" }
                )
            }
        }
        stage('Stage 2') {
            steps {
                echo "run after both parallel steps are completed"
            }
        }
    }
}
```

In `Stage 1`, with the use of the `parallel` keyword, we execute two parallel steps, `one` and `two`. Note that `Stage 2` is executed only after both parallel steps are completed. This is why such solutions are perfectly safe to run tests in parallel; we can always be sure that the deployment stage is run only after all parallelized tests have already passed.

 There is a very useful plugin called `Parallel Test Executor` that helps to automatically split tests and run them in parallel. Read more at `https:/ /jenkins.io/doc/pipeline/steps/parallel-test-executor/`.

The preceding description concerned the parallel steps level. The other solution would be to use parallel stages and therefore run each stage on a separate agent machine. The decision on which type of parallelism to use usually depends on two factors:

- How powerful the agent machines are
- How much time the given stage takes

As a general recommendation, unit tests are fine to run in parallel steps, but performance tests are usually better off on separate machines.

Reusing pipeline components

When the Jenkinsfile script grows in size and becomes more complex, we may want to reuse its parts between similar pipelines.

For example, we may want to have separate, but similar, pipelines for different environments (dev, QA, prod). Another common example in the microservice world is that each service has a very similar Jenkinsfile. Then, how do we write Jenkinsfile scripts so that we don't repeat the same code all over again? There are two good patterns for this purpose, parameterized build and shared libraries. Let's describe them one by one.

Build parameters

We already mentioned in Chapter 4, *Continuous Integration Pipeline*, that a pipeline can have input parameters. We can use them to provide different use cases with the same pipeline code. As an example, let's create a pipeline parametrized with the environment type:

```
pipeline {
    agent any

    parameters {
        string(name: 'Environment', defaultValue: 'dev', description: 'Which
            environment (dev, qa, prod)?')
    }

    stages {
        stage('Environment check') {
            steps {
                echo "Current environment: ${params.Environment}"
            }
        }
    }
}
```

The build takes one input parameter, `Environment`. Then, all we do in this step is print the parameter. We can also add a condition to execute different code for different environments.

With this configuration, when we start the build, we will see a prompt for the input parameter, as follows:

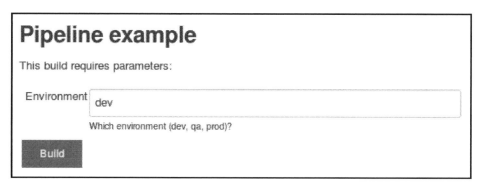

Parametrized build can help reuse the pipeline code for scenarios when it differs just a little bit. This feature, however, should not be overused because too many conditions can make the Jenkinsfile difficult to understand.

Shared libraries

The other solution to reuse the pipeline is to extract its parts into a shared library.

A shared library is a Groovy code that is stored as a separate source-controlled project. This code can be later used in many Jenkinsfile scripts as pipeline steps. To make it clear, let's have a look at an example. A shared library technique always requires three steps:

1. Create a shared library project.
2. Configure the shared library in Jenkins.
3. Use the shared library in Jenkins file.

Creating a shared library project

We start by creating a new Git project, in which we put the shared library code. Each Jenkins step is expressed as a Groovy file located in the `vars` directory.

Let's create a `sayHello` step that takes the `name` parameter and echoes a simple message. This should be stored in the `vars/sayHello.groovy` file:

```
/**
 * Hello world step.
 */
def call(String name) {
```

```
    echo "Hello $name!"
}
```

 Human-readable descriptions for shared library steps can be stored in the `*.txt` files. In our example, we could add the `vars/sayHello.txt` file with the step documentation.

When the library code is done, we need to push it to the repository, for example, as a new GitHub project.

Configure the shared library in Jenkins

The next step is to register the shared library in Jenkins. We open **Manage Jenkins | Configure System**, and find the **Global Pipeline Libraries** section. There, we can add the library giving it a name chosen, as follows:

We specified the name under which the library is registered and the library repository address. Note that the latest version of the library will be automatically downloaded during the pipeline build.

> We presented importing the Groovy code as *Global Shared Library*, but there are also other alternative solutions. Read more at `https://jenkins.io/doc/book/pipeline/shared-libraries/`.

Use shared library in Jenkinsfile

Finally, we can use the shared library in the Jenkinsfile script.

Let's have a look at the example:

```
pipeline {
    agent any
    stages {
        stage("Hello stage") {
            steps {
            sayHello 'Rafal'
            }
        }
    }
}
```

> If "Load implicitly" hadn't been checked in the Jenkins configuration, then we would need to add "`@Library('example')` _" at the beginning of the Jenkinsfile script.

As you can see, we can use the Groovy code as a pipeline step `sayHello`. Obviously, after the pipeline build completes, in the console output, we should see `Hello Rafal!`.

> Shared libraries are not limited to one step. Actually, with the power of the Groovy language, they can even act as templates for entire Jenkins pipelines.

Rolling back deployments

I remember the words of my colleague, a senior architect, *You don't need more QAs, you need a faster rollback.* While this statement is oversimplified and the QA team is often of great value, there is a lot of truth in this sentence. Think about it; if you introduce a bug in the production but roll it back soon after the first user reports an error, then usually nothing bad happens. On the other hand, if production errors are rare but no rollback is applied, then the process to debug the production usually ends up in long sleepless nights and a number of dissatisfied users. This is why we need to think about the rollback strategy up front while creating the Jenkins pipeline.

In the context of Continuous Delivery, there are two moments when the failure can happen:

- During the release process, in the pipeline execution
- After the pipeline build is completed, in production

The first scenario is pretty simple and harmless. It concerns a case when the application is already deployed to production but the next stage fails, for example, the smoke test. Then, all we need to do is execute a script in the `post` pipeline section for the `failure` case, which downgrades the production service to the older Docker image version. If we use blue-green deployment (as described later in this chapter), the risk of any downtime is minimal since we usually execute the load-balancer switch as the last pipeline stage, after the smoke test.

The second scenario, when we notice a production bug after the pipeline is successfully completed, is more difficult and requires a few comments. Here, the rule is that we should always release the rolled back service using exactly the same process as the standard release. Otherwise, if we try to do something manually, in a faster way, we are asking for trouble. Any nonrepetitive task is risky, especially under stress, when the production is out of order.

 As a side note, if the pipeline completes successfully but there is a production bug, then it means that our tests are not good enough. So, the first thing after rollback is to extend the unit/acceptance test suites with the corresponding scenarios.

The most common Continuous Delivery process is one fully automated pipeline that starts by checking out the code and ends up with release to the production.

The following figure presents how this works:

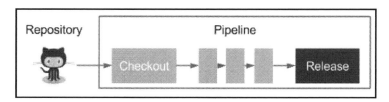

We already presented the classic Continuous Delivery pipeline throughout this book. If the rollback should use exactly the same process, then all we need to do is revert the latest code change from the repository. As a result, the pipeline automatically builds, tests, and finally, releases the right version.

 Repository reverts and emergency fixes should never skip the testing stages in the pipeline. Otherwise, we may end up with a release that is still not working correctly because of another issue that makes debugging even harder.

The solution is very simple and elegant. The only drawback is the downtime that we need to spend on the complete pipeline build. This downtime can be avoided if we use blue-green deployment or canary releases, in which cases, we only change the load balancer setting to address the healthy environment.

The rollback operation becomes way more complex in the case of orchestrated releases, during which many services are deployed at the same time. This is one of the reasons why orchestrated releases are treated as an anti-pattern, especially in the microservice world. The correct approach is to always maintain backwards compatibility, at least for some time (like we presented for the database at the beginning of this chapter). Then, it's possible to release each service independently.

Adding manual steps

In general, the Continuous Delivery pipelines should be fully automated, triggered by a commit to the repository, and end up after the release. Sometimes, however, we can't avoid having manual steps. The most common example is the release approval, which means that the process is fully automated, but there is a manual step to approve the new release. Another common example is manual tests. Some of them may exist because we operate on the legacy system; some others may occur when a test simply cannot be automated. No matter what the reason is, sometimes there is no choice but to add a manual step.

Jenkins syntax offers a keyword `input` for manual steps:

```
stage("Release approval") {
    steps {
        input "Do you approve the release?"
    }
}
```

The pipeline will stop execution on the `input` step and wait until it's manually approved.

Remember that manual steps quickly become a bottleneck in the delivery process, and this is why they should always be treated as a solution that's inferior to complete automation.

 It is sometimes useful to set a timeout for the input in order to avoid waiting forever for the manual interaction. After the configured time is elapsed, the whole pipeline is aborted.

Release patterns

In the last section, we discussed the Jenkins pipeline patterns used to speed up the build execution (parallel steps), help with the code reuse (shared libraries), limit the risk of production bugs (rollback), and deal with manual approvals (manual steps). This section presents the next group of patterns, this time related to the release process. They are designed to reduce the risk of updating the production to a new software version.

We already described one of the release patterns, rolling updates, in Chapter 8, *Clustering with Docker Swarm*. Here, we present two more: blue-green deployment and canary releases.

Blue-green deployment

Blue-green deployment is a technique to reduce the downtime associated with the release. It concerns having two identical production environments, one called green, the other called blue, as presented in the following figure:

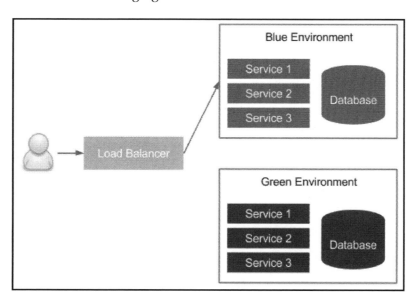

In the figure, the currently accessible environment is blue. If we want to make a new release, then we deploy everything to the green environment and, at the end of the release process, change the load balancer to the green environment. As a result, a user, all of a sudden, starts using the new version. The next time we want to make a release, we make changes to the blue environment and, at the end, we change the load balancer to blue. We proceed the same every time, switching from one environment to another.

 The blue-green deployment technique works correctly with two assumptions: environment isolation and no orchestrated releases.

This solution gives two significant benefits:

- **Zero downtime**: All the downtime from the user perspective is a moment of changing the load balance switch, which is negligible
- **Rollback**: In order to roll back one version, it's enough to change back the load balance switch blue-green deployment include:

- **Database**: Schema migrations can be tricky in case of a rollback, so it's worth using the patterns presented at the beginning of this chapter
- **Transactions**: Running database transactions must be handed over to the new database
- **Redundant infrastructure/resources**: We need to have double the resources

There are techniques and tools to overcome these challenges, so the blue-green deployment pattern is highly recommended and widely used in the IT industry.

 You can read more about the blue-green deployment technique on the excellent Martin Fowler's blog `https://martinfowler.com/bliki/BlueGreenDeployment.html`.

Canary release

Canary releasing is a technique to reduce the risk associated with introducing a new version of the software. Similar to blue-green deployment, it uses two identical environments, as presented in the following figure:

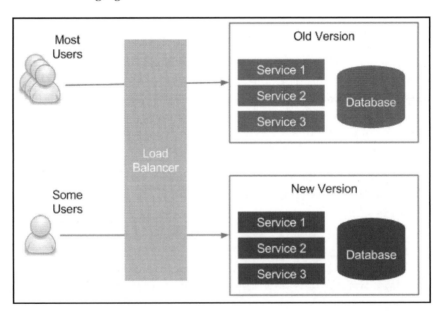

Also, similar to the blue-green deployment technique, the release process starts by deploying a new version in the environment that is currently unused. Here, however, the similarities end. The load balancer, instead of switching to the new environment, is set to link only a selected group of users to the new environment. All the rest still use the old version. This way, a new version can be tested by some users and in case of a bug, only a small group is affected. After the testing period, all users are switched to the new version.

This approach has some great benefits:

- **Acceptance and performance testing**: If the acceptance and performance testing is difficult to run in the staging environment, then it's possible to test it in production, minimizing the impact on a small group of users.
- **Simple rollback**: If a new change causes a failure, then rolling back is done by switching back all users to the old version.
- **A/B testing**: If we are not sure whether the new version is better than the UX or the performance perspective, then it's possible to compare it with the old version.

Canary releasing shares the same drawbacks as blue-green deployment. The additional challenge is that we have two production systems running at the same time. Nevertheless, canary releasing is an excellent technique used in most companies to help with the release and testing.

 You can read more about the canary releasing technique on the excellent Martin Fowler's blog `https://martinfowler.com/bliki/CanaryRelease.html`.

Working with legacy systems

All we have described so far applies smoothly to greenfield projects, for which setting up a Continuous Delivery pipeline is relatively simple.

Legacy systems are, however, way more challenging because they usually depend on manual tests and manual deployment steps. In this section, we will walk through the recommended scenario to incrementally apply Continuous Delivery to a legacy system.

As a step zero, I recommend reading an excellent book by Michael Feathers, *Working Effectively with Legacy Code*. His ideas on how to deal with testing, refactoring, and adding new features clear most of the concerns about how to automate the delivery process for legacy systems.

For many developers, it may be tempting to completely rewrite a legacy system, rather than refactor it. While the idea is interesting from a developer's perspective, it is usually a bad business decision that results in product failure. You can read more about the history of rewriting the Netscape browser in an excellent blog post by Joel Spolsky, *Things You Should Never Do,* at `https://www.joelonsoftware.com/2000/04/06/ things-you-should-never-do-part-i`.

The way to apply the Continuous Delivery process depends a lot on the current project's automation, the technologies used, the hardware infrastructure, and the current release process. Usually, it can be split into three steps:

1. Automating build and deployment.
2. Automating tests.
3. Refactoring and introducing new features.

Let's look at them in detail.

Automating build and deployment

The first step includes automating the deployment process. The good news is that in most legacy systems I have worked with, there was already some automation in place, for example, in the form of shell scripts.

In any case, the activities for automated deployment includes the following:

- **Build and package**: Some automation usually already exists in the form of Makefile, Ant, Maven, any other build tool configuration, or a custom script.
- **Database migration**: We need to start managing the database schema in an incremental manner. It requires putting the current schema as an initial migration and making all the further changes with tools such as Flyway or Liquibase, as already described in this chapter.
- **Deployment**: Even if the deployment process is fully manual, then there is usually a text/wiki page description that needs to be converted into an automated script.
- **Repeatable configuration**: In legacy systems, configuration files are usually changed manually. We need to extract the configuration and use a configuration management tool, as described in `Chapter 6`, *Configuration Management with Ansible.*

After the preceding steps, we can put everything into a deployment pipeline and use it as an automated phase after a manual UAT (user acceptance testing) cycle.

From the process perspective, it's worth already starting releasing more often. For example, if the release is yearly, try to do it quarterly, then monthly. The push for that factor will later result in faster-automated delivery adoption.

Automating tests

The next step, usually much more difficult, is to prepare the automated tests for the system. It requires communicating with the QA team in order to understand how they currently test the software so that we can move everything into an automated acceptance test suite. This phase requires two steps:

- **Acceptance/sanity test suite**: We need to add automated tests that replace some of the regression activities of the QA team. Depending on the system, they can be provided as a black-box Selenium test or Cucumber test.
- **(Virtual) test environments**: At this point, we should be already thinking of the environments in which our tests would be run. Usually, the best solution to save resources and limit the number of machines required is to virtualize the testing environment using Vagrant or Docker.

The ultimate goal is to have an automated acceptance test suite that will replace the whole UAT phase from the development cycle. Nevertheless, we can start with a sanity test that will shortly check if the system is correct from the regression perspective.

 While adding test scenarios, remember that the test suite should execute in reasonable time. For sanity tests, it is usually less than 10 minutes.

Refactoring and introducing new features

When we have at least the fundamental regression testing suite, we are ready to add new features and refactor the old code. It's always better to do it in small pieces, step by step because refactoring everything at once usually ends up in a chaos that leads to production failures (not clearly related to any particular change).

This phase usually includes the following activities:

- **Refactoring**: The best place to start refactoring the old code is where the new features are expected. Starting this way, we are prepared for the new feature requests to come.
- **Rewrite**: If we plan to rewrite parts of the old code, we should start from the code that is the most difficult to test. This way, we constantly increase the code coverage in our project.
- **Introducing new features**: During the new feature implementation, it's worth using the **feature toggle** pattern. Then, in case anything bad happens, we can quickly turn off the new feature. Actually, the same pattern should be used during refactoring.

 For this phase, it's worth reading an excellent book by *Martin Fowler, Refactoring: Improving the Design of Existing Code*.

While touching the old code, it's good to follow the rule to always add a passing unit test first, and only then, change the code. With this approach, we can depend on automation to check that we don't change the business logic by accident.

Understanding the human element

While introducing the automated delivery process to a legacy system, it's possible you will feel, more than anywhere else, the human factor. In order to automate the build process, we need to communicate well with the operations team, and they must be willing to share their knowledge. The same story applies to the manual QA team; they need to be involved in writing automated tests because only they know how to test the software. If you think about it, both the operations and QA teams need to contribute to the project that will later automate their work. At some point, they may realize that their future in the company is not stable and become less helpful. Many companies struggle with introducing the Continuous Delivery process because teams do not want to get involved enough.

In this section, we discussed how to approach legacy systems and the challenges they pose. If you are in progress of converting your project and organization into the Continuous Delivery approach, then you may want to have a look at the Continuous Delivery Maturity Model, which aims to give structure to the process of adopting the automated delivery.

A good description of the Continuous Delivery Maturity Model can be found at `https://developer.ibm.com/urbancode/docs/continuous-delivery-maturity-model/`.

Exercises

In this chapter, we have covered various aspects of the Continuous Delivery process. Since practice makes perfect, we recommend the following exercises:

1. Use Flyway to create a non-backwards-compatible change in the MySQL database:

    - Use the official Docker image, `mysql`, to start the database
    - Configure Flyway with proper database address, username, and password
    - Create an initial migration that creates a `users` table with three columns: `id`, `email`, and `password`
    - Add a sample data to the table
    - Change the `password` column to `hashed_password`, which will store the hashed passwords
    - Split the non-backwards-compatible change into three migrations as described in this chapter
    - You can use MD5 or SHA for hashing
    - Check that, as a result, the database stores no passwords in plain text

2. Create a Jenkins shared library with steps to build and unit test Gradle projects:
    - Create a separate repository for the library
    - Create two files in the library: `gradleBuild.groovy` and `gradleTest.groovy`
    - Write the appropriate `call` methods
    - Add the library to Jenkins
    - Use the steps from the library in a pipeline

Summary

This chapter was a mixture of various Continuous Delivery aspects that were not covered before. The key takeaways from the chapter are as follows:

- Databases are an essential part of most applications and should, therefore, be included in the Continuous Delivery process.
- Database schema changes are stored in the version control system and managed by database migration tools.
- There are two types of database schema change: backwards-compatible and backwards-incompatible. While the first type is simple, the second requires a bit of overhead (split to multiple migrations spread over time).
- A database should not be the central point of the whole system. The preferred solution is to provide each service with its own database.
- The delivery process should always be prepared for the rollback scenario.
- Three release patterns should always be considered: rolling updates, blue-green deployment, and canary releasing
- Legacy systems can be converted into the Continuous Delivery process in small steps rather than all at once.

Best practices

Thank you for reading this book. I hope you are ready to introduce the Continuous Delivery approach to your IT projects. As the last section of this book, I propose a list of the top 10 Continuous Delivery practices. Enjoy!

Practice 1 – own process within the team!

Own the entire process within the team, from receiving requirements to monitoring the production. As once said: *A program running on the developer's machine makes no money.* This is why it's important to have a small DevOps team that takes complete ownership of a product. Actually, that is the true meaning of DevOps - Development and Operations from the beginning to the end:

- Own every stage of the Continuous Delivery pipeline: how to build the software, what the requirements are in acceptance tests, and how to release the product.
- Avoid having a pipeline expert! Every member of the team should be involved in creating the pipeline.

- Find a good way to share the current pipeline state (and the production monitoring) among team members. The most effective solution is big screens in the team space.
- If a developer, QA, and IT Operations engineer are separate experts, then make sure they work together in one agile team. Separate teams based on expertise result in taking no responsibility for the product.
- Remember that autonomy given to the team results in high job satisfaction and exceptional engagement. This leads to great products!

Practice 2 – automate everything!

Automate everything from business requirements (in the form of acceptance tests) to the deployment process. Manual descriptions, wiki pages with instruction steps, they all quickly become out of date and lead to tribal knowledge that makes the process slow, tedious, and unreliable. This, in turn, leads to a need for release rehearsals and makes every deployment unique. Don't go down this path! As a rule, if you do anything for the second time, automate it:

- Eliminate all manual steps; they are a source of errors! The whole process must be repeatable and reliable.
- Don't ever make any changes directly in production! Use configuration management tools instead.
- Use precisely the same mechanism to deploy to every environment.
- Always include an automated smoke test to check if the release completed successfully.
- Use database schema migrations to automate database changes.
- Use automatic maintenance scripts for backup and cleanup. Don't forget to remove unused Docker images!

Practice 3 – version everything!

Version everything: software source code, build scripts, automated tests, configuration management files, Continuous Delivery pipelines, monitoring scripts, binaries, and documentation. Simply everything. Make your work task-based, where each task results in a commit to the repository, no matter whether it's related to requirement gathering, architecture design, configuration, or the software development. A task starts on the agile board and ends up in the repository. This way, you maintain a single point of truth with the history and reasons for the changes:

- Be strict about the version control. Everything means everything!
- Keep source code and configuration in the code repository, binaries in the artifact repository, and tasks in the agile issue tracking tool.
- Develop the Continuous Delivery pipeline as a code.
- Use database migrations and store them in a repository.
- Store documentation in the form of markdown files that can be version-controlled.

Practice 4 – use business language for acceptance tests!

Use business-facing language for acceptance tests to improve the mutual communication and the common understanding of the requirements. Work closely with the product owner to create what Eric Evan called the *ubiquitous language*, a common dialect between the business and technology. Misunderstandings are the root cause of most project failures:

- Create a common language and use it inside the project.
- Use an acceptance testing framework such as Cucumber or FitNesse to help the business team understand and get them involved.
- Express business values inside acceptance tests and don't forget about them during development. It's easy to spend too much time on unrelated topics!
- Improve and maintain acceptance tests so that they always act as regression tests.
- Make sure everyone is aware that a passing acceptance test suite means a green light from the business to release the software.

Practice 5 – be ready to roll back!

Be ready to roll back; sooner or later you will need to do it. Remember, You don't need more QAs, you need a faster rollback. If anything goes wrong in production, the first thing you want to do is to play safe and come back to the last working version:

- Develop a rollback strategy and the process of what to do when the system is down
- Split non-backwards-compatible database changes into compatible ones
- Always use the same process of delivery for rollbacks and for standard releases
- Consider introducing blue-green deployments or canary releases
- Don't be afraid of bugs, the user won't leave you if you react quickly!

Practice 6 – don't underestimate the impact of people

Don't underestimate the impact of people. They are usually way more important than tools. You won't automate the delivery if the IT Operations team won't help you. After all, they have the knowledge about the current process. The same applies to QAs, business, and everyone involved. Make them important and involved:

- Let QAs and IT operations be a part of the DevOps team. You need their knowledge and skills!
- Provide training to members that are currently doing manual activities so that they can move to automation.
- Favor informal communication and a flat structure of organization over hierarchy and orders. You won't do anything without goodwill!

Practice 7 – build in traceability!

Build in traceability for the delivery process and working system. There is nothing worse than a failure without any log messages. Monitor the number of requests, the latency, the load of production servers, the state of the Continuous Delivery pipeline, and everything you can think of that could help you to analyze your current software. Be proactive! At some point, you will need to check the stats and logs:

- Log pipeline activities! In the case of failure, notify the team with an informative message.
- Implement proper logging and monitoring of the running system.
- Use specialized tools for system monitoring such as Kibana, Grafana, or Logmatic.io.
- Integrate production monitoring into your development ecosystem. Consider having big screens with the current production stats in the common team space.

Practice 8 – integrate often!

Integrate often, actually, all the time! As someone said: *Continuous is more often than you think*. There is nothing more frustrating than resolving merge conflicts. Continuous Integration is less about the tool and more about the team practice. Integrate the code into one codebase at least a few times a day. Forget about long-lasting feature branches and a huge number of local changes. Trunk-base development and feature toggles for the win!

- Use trunk-based development and feature toggles instead of feature branches.
- If you need a branch or local changes, make sure that you integrate with the rest of the team at least once a day.
- Always keep the trunk healthy; make sure you run tests before you merge into the baseline.
- Run the pipeline after every commit to the repository for a fast feedback cycle.

Practice 9 – build binaries only once!

Build binaries only once and run the same one on each of the environments. No matter if they are in a form of Docker images or JAR packages, building only once eliminates the risk of differences introduced by various environments. It also saves time and resources:

- Build once and pass the same binary between environments.
- Use artifact repository to store and version binaries. Don't ever use the source code repository for that purpose.
- Externalize configurations and use a configuration management tool to introduce differences between environments.

Practice 10 – release often!

Release often, preferably after each commit to the repository. As the saying goes, *If it hurts, do it more often.* Releasing as a daily routine makes the process predictable and calm. Stay away from being trapped in the rare release habit. That will only get worse and you will end up with releasing once a year having a three months' preparation period!

- Rephrase your definition of done to *Done means released*. Take ownership of the whole process!
- Use feature toggles to hide (from users) features that are still in progress.
- Use canary releases and quick rollback to reduce the risk of bugs in the production.
- Adopt a zero-downtime deployment strategy to enable frequent releases.

Index

C

Made in the USA
San Bernardino, CA
25 January 2020